The Sources of Hope

THE SOURCES OF HOPE

edited by
Ross Fitzgerald

PERGAMON PRESS

Pergamon Press (Australia) Pty Ltd,
19a Boundary Street, Rushcutters Bay, N.S.W. 2011, Australia
Pergamon Press Ltd,
Headington Hill Hall, Oxford OX3 0BW, England
Pergamon Press Inc.,
Maxwell House, Fairview Park, Elmsford, N.Y. 10523, U.S.A.
Pergamon of Canada Ltd,
75 The East Mall, Toronto, Ontario M8Z 2L9, Canada
Pergamon Press GmbH,
6242 Kronberg/Taunus, Pferdstrasse 1,
Federal Republic of Germany
Pergamon Press SARL,
24 rue des Ecoles, 75240 Paris, Cedex 05, France

First published 1979

© 1979 Ross Fitzgerald

Cover design by Allan Hondow
Typeset in Hong Kong by Filmset Ltd
Printed in Hong Kong by Dai Nippon Printing Co. (H.K.) Ltd

National Library of Australia Cataloguing in Publication Data
The sources of hope.

Bibliography
ISBN 0 08 023104 7 Paperback
ISBN 0 08 023105 5

1. Hope.   I. Fitzgerald, Ross, 1944-, ed.

~~128.3~~

We are saved by hope,
but hope that is seen is not hope:
for what a man seeth, why doth he yet hope for?

Romans 8:24

Expectancy, Hope, intention toward the as yet unrealized possibility: such is not only a fundamental principle of human consciousness, but concretely grasped, is a basic ingredient within the whole of objective reality.

ERNST BLOCH

Acknowledgements

The extracts by Jürgen Moltmann on pp. 159–61 and 162–6 have been translated from *Im Gespräch mit Ernst Bloch* (Kaiser Traktate, 18, 1970) with the kind permission of Chr. Kaiser Verlag, Munich. Extracts from *Twelve Steps and Twelve Traditions* on pp. 86–7 (copyright © 1952 by Alcoholics Anonymous World Services Inc.) have been reprinted by permission of Alcoholics Anonymous World Services Inc.

In the course of preparing this collection I have incurred many debts. I would like to thank all contributors for their co-operation in meeting what, for many, was a difficult deadline. I am very grateful to Jerry Mayer and his staff at Pergamon Press Australia; in particular, I would like to thank Rosemary Peitso, Ngaire Laundy and Beverley Barnes. Among the friends who have encouraged and assisted me, I would especially like to acknowledge Margaret Simpson, Leon Cantrell, Ken Spillman and, most of all, my wife Lyndal Moor.

ROSS FITZGERALD

Contents

For Lee Parry, in Melbourne,
where it all began.

Introduction

Hope is fundamental to human life. Indeed if we are to continue as individuals and as a species it is something we require as much as bread and water. Yet in the main hope is a neglected topic, especially among scholars. This book is an attempt to help redress the situation: to subject the origins and justifications of hope to detailed scrutiny.

The Sources of Hope is a collection of essays written especially for this volume by scholars from a number of disciplines. The disciplines represented range from psychoanalysis, political science, philosophy and theology, to psychology, history, education and literature. Contributors were asked to elaborate upon what they regarded as the prime source(s) of hope in the modern world: for example, it may be an idea or ideas-system, an attitude, a movement, a form of therapy, etc. The question posed was deliberately ambiguous. It left room both for those contributors who wanted to write about hope in an 'objective' sense (hope for the world, hope for humanity), and for those who wanted to deal with the genesis of hopeful feelings in individuals, for example, to explore the mechanisms by which persons who feel hopeless come to experience hope. A number of contributors endeavour to link personal feelings of hope with hope for the world.

As with my previous collection, *What It Means to be Human**, the theme of which leads on to the present volume, editorial intervention has been kept to a minimum. Some explanation is required however with regard to the essay by Ernst Bloch, whose philosophical masterpiece *Das Prinzip Hoffnung* (*The Principle of Hope**) is as yet untranslated into English. Bloch's manuscript was received a week before his death. With the agreement of Karola Bloch it is published here with an introduction by Wayne Hudson, whose book *The Utopian Marxism of Ernst Bloch* is being published by Macmillan. Jürgen Moltmann, the outstanding German Protestant theologian of hope, has written a postscript to Bloch's essay.

No attempt is made here to summarize the contents of each essay in the collection. Suffice to say that at the very least hope, however conceived, means *possibility*—be it social, political, spiritual, ecological, or individual.

Our age is not exactly brimming over with positive affirmation and joyful anticipation: on the contrary, so many today, especially intellectuals, have fallen into a state of hopelessness and despair. As with its ambiguity, the metaphor contained in the volume's title is not accidental. Unless we can tap the sources of hope, there can be no human future. Hence the critical importance of a collection such as this.

Ross Fitzgerald
Brisbane, Australia

*For details, see Selected Bibliography pp. 260–4.

Steps to an Ecology of Hope

Charles Rycroft

The title of this collection of essays makes two assumptions, neither of which is, to my mind, so self-evident as to be allowed to pass without comment. It assumes, first, that there is such a thing as hope, that it is possible to locate and define some specific mental state called hope; and, secondly, that this mental state is of a kind that can be conceived to have sources—that is, that it has, as rivers do, some place or places of origin from which it begins and from which it takes its being and sustenance. The implication is clearly that hope is something that only exists contingently, since one can imagine its sources drying up or becoming exhausted—in which event hope would cease and be replaced by a negative condition of hopelessness, which may or may not be the same as despair.

There is, in fact, a metaphor lurking concealed within the title of this book, a metaphor based on the perception or presumption of some similarity between the mental state called hope and those natural objects and artifacts that depend for their existence and functioning on a supply of something coming into them from outside themselves. Rivers are only rivers because they receive water from springs and from the rain that falls on their catchment areas, and if springs dry up and the rains fail, rivers cease to be rivers: a state of riverlessness supervenes. Automobiles function as automobiles only if they are supplied with their appropriate source of energy, petrol; and historians and literary critics would soon cease to exist as such if they were cut off from their sources.

The idea that hope has sources implies, then, that it is an attribute of some 'open system', which depends upon input, which consumes what it takes in and which generates activity while doing so. Rivers receive water from springs and rain, and give it to seas, and their energy can be harnessed to mills and hydro-electric stations; cars can be driven places; and historians and literary critics write books and learned papers which, hopefully, others read and are enriched by doing so. Therefore, if the metaphor implicit in the phrase 'sources of hope' is valid, hope is a mental state that has something to do with the maintenance of cyclical processes involving intake and feedback; and, since it is something that can be attributed literally only to living creatures, hope must be a mental state related to the contingencies of life processes. It must refer to some general property of living organisms, which they continue to possess or display as long as they live and without which they cease to do so, but which can be conceived to originate, to have its sources, somewhere other than in the living organism itself. 'While there is life, there is hope' says the proverb, but, as is the wont of proverbs, this one leaves one in doubt. Do we hope so long as we live, in which case hope is nothing more than an epiphenomenon of continued life; or do we live so long as we hope, in which case an inquiry into the sources of hope is an inquiry into what it is that makes living creatures go on living? This is, indeed, the precise sixty-four dollar question. Is hope simply a word we use to affirm that we are still alive and wish to continue to be so, in which case its immediate source is our biological energy and its remoter sources are in the environment from which we derive our nutriment; or is it something we need in order to want to continue to live, in which case its sources are whatever circumstances, expectations, ideas and beliefs are necessary to sustain our wish to continue to live? Before even beginning to discuss which of these two possible general answers is the correct one—or whether, perhaps, they are not as antithetical as they seem—it is necessary to consider briefly what the word 'hope' means.

According to *The Shorter Oxford English Dictionary*, hope is the 'expectation of something desired; desire combined with expectation', and it is therefore an emotion compounded of two elements. To hope for something in particular we must both desire it and have the expectation that our desire may or will be realized; and to have hope in general we must both have desires and have expectations that they can or could be realized. And contrariwise, if we desire nothing or expect that any desire we may have will not be realized, we will be without hope; in the first instance— that of being without desire—because we are beyond or outside hope, in some state of mind in which the question of hope no longer arises; and in the second instance—that of being without expectation that any of our desires could ever be realized—we are hopeless, in the sense of being in despair.

Since hope is compounded of desire and expectation, it is what *Roget's Thesaurus* calls a prospective affection, an emotion or emotional attitude directed towards the future, and its presence or absence depends on an assessment, which may of course be incorrect, of what will happen. In this respect it resembles fearfulness and anxiety, both of which depend on an assessment of what will happen, and is the opposite of satisfaction, sorrow, regret, remorse and nostalgia, all of which depend on evaluations of what has happened, of what we have or have not done.

According to McDougall[1] hope is one of a whole class of 'prospective emotions of desire', which also includes confidence, disappointment, anxiety, despondency and despair, such emotions differing in the assessment that is being made of the likelihood of desire being realized. We are confident, if we assume blithely that desire will be realized; we are hopeful if we anticipate that it will be realized but appreciate that contingencies could arise to prevent them being; we are despondent if we think it unlikely to be realized; we are in despair if we come to believe that our desire never will be realized. And we experience disappointment if we lose all expectation of our desire being realized while still continuing to desire.

It seems to be characteristic of all these prospective emotions that they can exist in both particular and general forms—that is, that we can feel them either in respect of some particular desire, which we may believe will, may, may not, probably will not, cannot possibly, be realized, or about our desires in general, tending to assume that they will, may, may not, will not, be realized. In other words, the assessment we make of the future, which determines whether we feel hopeful or not, seems to depend not only on the information available to us about it but also on how we interpret

---

[1] William McDougall, *An Introduction to Social Psychology*, 22nd edition, Methuen, 1931.

that information, our interpretation being influenced by both our past experience and by what used to be called our temperament. If Eysenck[2] is right, stable extraverts with a choleric temperament tend to assess the future optimistically; unstable introverts with a melancholic temperament tend to assess it pessimistically; stable introverts with a phlegmatic temperament view it philosophically; and unstable extraverts with a sanguine temperament give it little heed.

Hope, then, is an attitude towards the future—a feeling or emotion about it that includes two features: we desire something we do not yet have; and we desire something we believe we could or may gain. Hope, therefore, occupies a key position between the present and the future. If we had already fulfilled all our desires, we would neither have nor need hope, because the future would no longer have anything to offer us; we would be without hope but not hopeless. But if we still have desires, these desires, unless we have hope, will produce despair—unless we are certain that our desires will be fulfilled, in which case again we will not need hope. As Spinoza said, 'Fear cannot be without hope, nor hope without fear.'[3] Hope is therefore a present attitude towards a future known to be intrinsically contingent and uncertain, and it cannot be attributed to creatures with no sense of futurity or to anyone too unaware to appreciate that the future can never be certain.

Religious Christians, who believe that God is both the source and the end of hope, understand this well. There is no hope in Heaven, since its object, the Beatific Vision, has already been attained; there is no hope in Hell, since the possibility of attaining its object has been finally lost; and until the Gates of Heaven or Hell have been reached, hope, 'confidence in God's goodness, tempered by fear of His justice' (as *The Oxford Dictionary of the Christian Church* defines it), with faith and charity, constitute the three heavenly graces or theological virtues—as opposed to the more secular, worldly cardinal virtues of prudence, temperance, fortitude and justice.

It would appear then that hope, in its general sense, is an attitude of mind towards the future, one that admits it is uncertain—as, indeed, it always is—but nonetheless envisages the possibility or likelihood that it will include opportunities for the realization of

[2] H.J. Eysenck, *Fact and Fiction in Psychology*, Penguin, 1965.
[3] Benedict Spinoza, 'The Origin and Nature of the Emotions', in *Spinoza's Ethics*. Dent, Everyman, 1960.

desires. If we are religious, this future about which we may have hope is not in this world or in this life but in heaven and in the after-life, and the source of our hope resides in our faith and charity. But if we are not religious, in the traditional Christian sense, the future for which we may have hope can only be in this world, and our sources of hope can only reside in our assessment of what the future will hold—for both ourselves individually and those to whom we are attached and who will, we hope, survive us—and in our temperament and personality; or, more precisely, in the dialectical interaction between these two facets of our being, between the prospective vision we have of the (or our) future and the retrospective vision of our past, which constitutes the source of our present conception of ourselves and of our likely future.

It is, I suppose, just necessary to add that both these interacting visions may be untrue. The future may turn out to be very different from what we had expected and may therefore surprise us, pleasantly or unpleasantly; and future events may compel us to reassess our conception of our past, to rewrite our biographies to take fuller account of events we had previously thought trivial or to attach greater importance to aspects of our personality we had previously disregarded. For instance, some success may force us to admit that we had hoped more for recognition that we had realized, and some failure may leave us feeling more disappointed than we had expected. But the point I am making here is that hope is generated at the interface between the past and the future, and is a quality possessed by that Janus-faced entity, our present self.

Our conception of the future into which we expect to move is, rather obviously, a function of the time, place, society and class into which we happen to have been born. In static, rigidly hierarchical societies this conception may seem to be preordained, life being envisaged as a passage through a series of familiar stages down which our ancestors have trodden from time immemorial, and time being envisaged as a circular process in which events recur. Under such circumstances, hope will only arise in connection with those aspects of life in which uncertainty inevitably reigns— we may hope to survive long enough to experience all the preordained stages of life and to avoid such natural disasters as famines, floods and failure of the crops. But hopes contingent on progress and individual freedom will never arise.

In open societies, on the other hand, in which social mobility exists and ideas of individual and social progress are in the air, more complicated and sophisticated hopes will arise, because it will be possible to hope to achieve positions very different from where one started and to attain greater self-awareness, culture and wisdom than one's point of origin automatically granted one. In other words, hope can manifest itself as ambition and aspiration, and fulfilment and disappointment can be experienced in respect of such desires as those for wealth, power, social advancement and professional recognition on one hand, and those for self-realization, self-knowledge, wisdom and righteousness on the other.

In the liberal democracies, indeed, ambition and aspiration are so inculcated by education that hopes doomed to disappointment are engendered in every child. If success is the ideal to be aimed at, realization of the hopes of the few is, of necessity, purchased at the cost of the failure and disappointment of the many, because the top would not be worth getting to if there were room on it for everyone. This state of affairs is only made tolerable, to the extent that it is tolerable, by two things: first, by the fact that some hopes seem to fade away or be replaced by others without leaving behind them scars of bitterness and disappointment; and, secondly, by the fact that society is complex enough to grant failures in one sphere of life success in another. I doubt whether many of the thousands of girls who hope to become ballerinas, or boys who hope to play in a Test Match, or Americans who hope to become President of the United States, are permanently traumatized by their failure to achieve these ambitions, and, as Geoffrey Gorer[4] has pointed out, one of the advantages of complex societies containing several élites is that they provide a variety of socially recognized hierarchical ladders, so that ambitious people who aspire to success can achieve it in one area even though they may fail in others.

However, I believe it remains true that where hope manifests itself as ambition and the desire for fame, the success of the few is purchased at the price of creating envy and disappointment in many. Hence, of course, the pleasure many people take in the misfortunes, scandals and downfalls of the famous; and hence, too, Andy Warhol's presumably ironical prediction that society will eventually be organized to ensure that each of its members enjoys half an hour's fame.

---

[4] Geoffrey Gorer, *The Danger of Equality*, Cresset, 1966.

Religious people are perhaps fortunate in being able to detach hope from the contingencies of the material future and from the possibility of disappointment in this world by the hope of salvation in the next. Although there is no room at the top for everyone here, there is room for everyone in Heaven, and if people really are religious, their source of hope is not their position in the rat-race but their inner state of mind. The same holds for everyone who has a 'philosophy of life', regardless of how they formulate it; so long as they have some ideal, be it for wisdom, self-realization, understanding, acceptance or truth, they will be able to transcend and survive adversities and disappointments. Unfortunately too little is known about the psychology of those who have indes-tructible ideals and are immune to demoralization by disappoint-ments, bereavements, persecution and torture. They do not seek psychotherapeutic help, are not Suitable Cases for Treatment, and as a result the origins of their hope, or rather faith, have yet to be located by the psychiatrists and psychoanalysts. But ordinary language asserts that they possess 'inner resources'.

At this point it has become clear to me and will, I suspect, have become clear to some of my readers that there really is some substance in the distinction made by theologians between hope and faith. Hope is for something, be it success, love or the Beatific Vision, and is a contingent emotion, which depends on the in-dividual's expectations, on his assessment of his future seen from the perspective of the experience he has acquired during his past; whereas faith is an absolute, timeless emotion, which one either has or has not independently of whether one has grounds for hope. Theologians, I gather, distinguish between objective faith, 'the Faith believed in' by believers and formulated in creeds, and subjective faith, 'the Faith whereby belief is reached', the former being whatever set of beliefs the religious person holds, the latter being that act or attitude which enables him to hold beliefs.

According to Erik Erikson[5], who is, so far as I can discover, the only psychoanalyst to mention faith, even in passing, faith is identical with what he calls Trust, which is something that infants acquire in their mothers' arms or not at all. 'Mothers, I think, create a sense of trust in their children by that kind of administra-tion which in its quality combines sensitive care of the baby's

[5] Erik Erikson, *Young Man Luther*, Faber, 1959.

individual needs and a firm sense of personal trustworthiness within the trusted framework of their culture's style.'[6] In Erikson's view, then, trust is transmitted from mother to infant in a context and at an age when faith, hope and charity cannot yet be differentiated. When a mother cares for her infant's individual needs in a trustworthy way within a trusted framework, she is both displaying and transmitting the three theological virtues in their most elemental forms.

The neglect of faith by psychoanalysts and psychologists is paralleled by an equally striking neglect of hope. As John Cohen[7] has put it, 'But although life without hope is unthinkable, psychology without hope is not, judging by the conspicuous absence of any study of hope from the literature.' The subject index of Freud's Collected Works contains no entries for Faith, Hope, Despair or Hopelessness, and even McDougall, despite his meticulous phenomenological analysis of hope, is silent about faith.

The reason for this neglect, or rather avoidance, of hope and faith is, I think, twofold. Both psychology and Freudian psychoanalysis claim to be sciences, science is concerned with causes, and causes are always located in the past; there are therefore methodological and, indeed, ideological difficulties about the prospective emotions, which depend upon the individual's subjective sense of himself as a continuous entity passing through time into the future. Furthermore, psychoanalysis began as a branch of medicine and its raw material still derives from people who are in trouble and seeking help; it has therefore more to say about illness than about health and a tendency to describe human nature in a terminology derived from pathology. As a result, it has more to say about depression and the schizoid sense of futility than about the faith and hope of the healthy, and more to say about the divisions in the divided self[8] than about the self that is liable to become divided.

Psychoanalysis and psychology have therefore a retrospective, pathological bias, which makes them apter tools for explaining the present in terms of the past than for elucidating the role played by the envisaged future; and for explaining why people may become depressed or despairing in the absence of rational grounds for doing so than why people may continue to have faith and hope in the

[6] Erik Erikson, *Childhood and Society*, Norton, 1953.
[7] John Cohen, *Humanistic Psychology*, Allen and Unwin, 1958.
[8] R.D. Laing, *The Divided Self*, Tavistock, 1960.

absence of rational grounds for continuing to have them. In his book *The Informed Heart*, Bruno Bettelheim[9] makes it clear that those inmates of concentration camps who remained undemoralizable were not people who would have satisfied psychoanalytical criteria of normality.

Erikson's equation of faith with trust and his assertion that trust is a quality of mind created and transmitted by good mothering in infancy is, in fact, a good example of the way in which the retrospective bias in psychoanalysis works. If this statement is not only true but also the whole truth, the source of hope is quite simply in the past. If we have had good mothering, we will have faith and hope, and their source will be our unconscious recollection of that good mothering, and any lack of faith, hope and charity from which we may suffer will be classifiable as a neurotic symptom resulting from maternal deprivation in infancy. According to this simple view of the matter, hope is the effect of a prior cause, viz. good mothering; hopelessness is the effect of another prior cause, viz. defects in mothering; and both have been explained without any reference to the future and without any breach in the natural-scientific model constructed and bequeathed by Freud.

But, in fact, this is not what Erikson thinks at all. His heroes have been people like Luther and Gandhi, both of whom were far from normal by Freudian standards, and his writings have been concerned not only with causation but also with problems of meaning and value. And he has even introduced the word 'virtue' into psychoanalysis to describe such 'ego-strengths' as fidelity, love, care and wisdom.[10] Furthermore, as has recently become public knowledge, he has spent his life trying to reconcile or integrate Freudian psychology with Christianity[11], an activity that has led him to 'rediscover prescientific truths' and, less admirably, 'to blur the extent of his divergence from the psychoanalytical movement' of which he has always been a prominent member.[12] So when Erikson describes trust as arising when mothers minister to their babies' individual needs with 'a firm sense of personal trustworthiness within the trusted framework of their culture's style', he is not, I think, referring just to adequate child-care consonant

[9] Bruno Bettelheim, *The Informed Heart*, Thames and Hudson, 1961.
[10] Daniel Yankelovich and William Barrett, *Ego and Instinct*, Random House, 1971.
[11] Paul Roazen, *Erik H. Erikson: The Power and Limits of a Vision*, Free Press, New York, 1976.
[12] Yankelovich and Barrett, *op. cit.*

with prevalent pediatric opinion, but also to the transmission of the virtues of faith, hope and charity from one generation to another. If this is right, and personally I think it is, the sources of hope in any single individual reside in his past, present and imagined future relationships with others, from whom he acquires hope and to whom he may give hope; and hope is not simply an individual quality, which some people have and others lack, but a social, cultural quality, which is engendered within a social, historical matrix and transmitted from one generation to another— in the simplest instance from parents to their children, but also from teachers to their pupils, from political leaders to their followers, from priests to their congregations, and from psychotherapists to their patients.

It was this social matrix of hope that I had in mind, when at the beginning of this essay I drew attention to the metaphor implicit in this volume's title, which suggests that hope is like a river which continues to be a river only if springs and rain feed it—and that it is an aspect of an open system which depends for its maintenance on an input from outside and in its turn returns feedback to the outside. To take this metaphor a step further, just as rivers, rain and springs are part of the water cycle that also includes seas and clouds, so too children, pupils, followers, congregations and patients return hope to their parents, teachers, leaders, priests and therapists. Hope is, in fact, something that circulates within that total, wider, system of relationships we call society.

If then, as I am suggesting, hope is a social quality that is transmitted from individual to individual, from generation to generation, the sources of hope in any particular person are all those relationships which he has had in the past, which he is having in the present, which he envisages having in the future, and which endow his life with meaning and value. At the risk of being over-schematic, I am tempted to say that these past, present and future relationships constitute the sources of some general quality, strength or virtue*, of which hope is the prospective facet; past relationships being the source of faith, present relationships being the source of charity, and future relationships being the source of hope. It would seem to me too that faith, hope and charity can to a measure

---

*Readers who find this usage of the word 'virtue' puzzling are reminded that it once meant manliness and valour and is still occasionally used to mean strength and efficacy.

substitute for one another, so that if someone has in the past had relationships which have given him faith, have provided him with what psychoanalytical jargon calls 'good internal objects,' he will be able to survive and endure without loss of virtue circumstances in which both charity and hope are in short supply; but that if, on the contrary, someone lacked good relationships in the past and has no 'good internal objects', he will require and demand enormous quantities of charity now and hope for the future.

The latter is the state of affairs with which psychotherapists are professionally most familiar. For instance, a woman, whose mother certainly had not ministered sensitively to her individual needs with a firm sense of personal trustworthiness but had on the contrary palmed her off with a succession of nurses, became depressed when she realized that her marriage had become a desert, but recovered, after a fashion, when she heard the late D.W. Winnicott speaking anonymously on the radio about mothering. She could, she suddenly thought, ring the B.B.C., ask for his name and address and become his patient, if she ever became desperate. She cherished this thought for several years, until she eventually did become desperate. She then rang the B.B.C., who refused to give her Winnicott's name, and she was later referred to me as a patient through the conventional medical channels. In treatment with me she rapidly developed what the jargon calls an idealized positive transference, following me at a discreet distance wherever I went, and at times developing hysterical loss of voice when I was out of reach at weekends or on holiday—that is, she would not, could not, talk to anyone other than me. In this patient, and in others too, the absence of faith, of 'good internal objects' led to both an importunate need for a present relationship with me and an absurd over-exploitation of hope to compensate for her lack of faith and inner resources. Even if her mother never had loved her, and her husband no longer did love her, she had received a sign, in the form of a voice on the radio, that there existed somewhere a man who could mother her and whose patient she could, at some unspecified time in the future, become.

This clinical anecdote, which I have told in order to illustrate the way in which hope can be mobilized to compensate for deficiencies in faith and charity, will have additional point for those readers who are familiar with Winnicott's writings[13], because they will ap-

---

[13] D.W. Winnicott, *Collected Papers*, Tavistock, 1958.

preciate that he really did understand about mothers and infants and that my patient was right in supposing he would have understood her immediately. He also belonged to that school of psychoanalysts which holds that health is dependent on relationships with others ('objects'), not on satisfactory discharges of instinctual tension, and he is one of the few analysts to have discussed hope, even if only briefly.

The use, or rather over-use, of hope to compensate for deficiencies in faith is a phenomenon well known to psychoanalysis, which categorizes it as the defence mechanism of idealization. This defence consists in the construction of ideal images which are projected either on to real persons, whose imperfections are denied, or on to ideals and religious or political movements, and is motivated by the need to deny the anger and resentment that has been engendered by past and present frustrations. The hazards associated with idealization are disillusion, which occurs if the idealized object fails too conspicuously to live up to expectations, and transformation into denigration, which occurs if the repression of anger and resentment breaks down. Another patient of mine depicted the conversion of idealization into disillusion and denigration by a dream in which the moon fell out of the sky into a dustbin. I have discussed idealization and disillusion in detail in Chapter 3 of my book *Imagination and Reality*[14], where I offer an interpretation of a dream dreamt by the Italian poet Giacomo Leopardi, fairly soon after he lost his faith. This dream is also about the moon falling out of the sky.

Idealization, disillusion and denigration play an important part in what might be called the social pathology of hope. It would seem that revered rulers and leaders are always at risk of being overthrown by their erstwhile followers, and that religious institutions are recurrently threatened by iconoclastic revolts.

If hope is the prospective aspect of virtue, of the sense of identity, of health, of integrity, of ego-strength—it is difficult to know which term to use—it must bear a functional relationship to age. At the beginning of life there is little past to look back on and a long future to look forward to, at the end of life there is little future to look forward to and a long past to look back on. As a result the health of the young must include hope for the future, both for themselves individually and for the world they envisage themselves entering

[14] Charles Rycroft, *Imagination and Reality*, Hogarth. 1968.

and becoming members of, while the health of the old must depend, not on hope for their individual future, but on the wisdom they have acquired during their past and on vicarious hope for those to whom they remain attached—their children, their pupils, and whatever groups of which they feel themselves to be truly members. According to Erikson[15] wisdom is 'the detached and yet active concern with life as with death' and is the reward of 'successful' old age, the punishment of unsuccessful old age being despair, bitterness and disgust. In youth, then, hope predominates, since desires are psychosomatically active and expectations of a future are 'normally' justified, whereas in age hope retreats to a lesser or vicarious position and is replaced by wisdom and serenity.

Having committed myself to the view that hope is a social quality and that each individual's store of it is a function of his relationships with others, it behoves me to say something about the sociology and history of hope, even though I could plead that this is outside my professional competence, which derives from listening to single individuals talking to me about their private hopes and fears, satisfactions and disappointments. But no man is an island, even when he is lying on an analyst's couch, and the stories my patients tell me and the ways they interact with me are, in fact, parts of a social network that has ramifications embracing all the persons they have known, loved and hated—and indeed embracing all the persons whom I have known and who have contributed to my competence to be their analyst. A curious effect of Freud's attempt to construct psychoanalysis on a scientific model has been to obscure an obvious and yet important fact, viz. that nothing can happen between an analyst and his patient unless they share a language in common, and to share a language in common means to share much more than a collection of words and grammatical conventions; it involves sharing numberless implicit assumptions, allusions and iconographic connections and mutual participation in a common cultural heritage—a mutual participation which may be intensive if analyst and patient come from similar backgrounds and have had similar educations, but will be more tenuous if either has to use a language that is not his mother tongue.

As a result the relationship between analyst and patient is not, in fact, that of a pure scientist detachedly observing an isolated specimen of the species *Homo sapiens*, even though analysts often

[15] Yankelovich and Barrett, *op. cit.*

write as though it were, but a social encounter between two members of the same culture, one of whom has, or claims to have, symptoms, the other of whom has, or claims to have, expertise which will, hopefully, enable him to elucidate the meaning of those symptoms—this expertise consisting of some understanding of symbolism, defence and transference; in other words of how people, when they talk, can mean more than they know they mean, of how people can conceal their true thoughts and feelings from even themselves, and of how people can react to one person as though he were someone else.

The two parties to this microcosmic social unit, in which the multitudinous others of the macrocosm appear only as images or phantoms, differ from one another not only in the fact that one has symptoms and other, perhaps, has not and that the other has expertise which the former, perhaps, lacks, but also in the fact that their sources of hope differ in both quantity and quality. Although the patient must have some hope, since if he did not he would not stir himself to come for treatment, his sources of hope must be in some way depleted or contaminated, since if they were not he would not need to come for treatment. The analyst, unless he is a hypocrite or charlatan, must have faith and hope deriving, in the first instance, from his belief in the efficacy or virtue of his professional skills but more fundamentally from the 'sensitive care' and 'personal trustworthiness' he has received from his own analysts and his own parents.

Curiously enough, analysts are well aware of and entirely open about the value of what they have received from their training analysts—a mystique has, indeed, developed within the analytical fraternity analogous to that of the apostolic succession in the Christian Church, according to which virtue is acquired by the lying on of couches instead of by the laying on of hands—but tend to be mute about the value of what they have received from their parents. This is presumably because until recently no one ever became an analyst unless he needed to make a radical break with his past.

What I am suggesting here is that the relationship between an analyst and his patient is a social encounter between two persons, one of whom has already acquired virtue and hope from somewhere, and the other of whom hopes to acquire it from him, that the symbolic interaction they engage in evokes imagery derived from the culture they both share, and that what goes on between them is a microcosmic version of processes that occur in society at large. If I am right about this, the secluded, isolated, apparently individualistic occupation of psychoanalysis does not debar its practitioners from having insights into the social sources of hope.

Acting on this presumption, the first point I want to make is that all societies of any complexity seem to have a tendency to divide themselves into purveyors and recipients of hope, the purveyors being special people—shamans, gurus, priests, psychoanalysts—who receive an esoteric training and are endowed with some sort of 'mana' or charisma by the others and who may or may not themselves privately believe in the superior qualities attributed to them. In Europe the traditional purveyors of hope were the Church and the Aristocracy. The former were entrusted with the 'cure of souls' and were trained in special knowledge of the road to salvation. The latter were entrusted with defence of the realm and, as Peter Laslett[16] has pointed out, acted as symbols of continuity in a world in which life was for most people nasty, brutish and short. Royalty, in particular, was endowed with, and believed itself to have, therapeutic powers. Charles II is believed to have touched 100,000 persons for the King's Evil (scrofula) during his reign, and a form of service for touching was included in the Book of Common Prayer until 1719. And both the Church and the Aristocracy demanded of their members privations during their training, which modern man would consider inhuman, in return for which they were rewarded by privilege and deference. And both officiated at ceremonials which affirmed the reality and meaning of the realm, of its past and of its future.

Although traces of this theocratic, aristocratic system of supplying hope and a sense of social cohesion still survive, particularly perhaps in Great Britain, they are anachronistic anomalies, since the idea that society should be divided officially and visibly into two groups, one special, privileged and deserving of deference, the other ordinary and deferential, is deeply offensive to the democratic ideal, which asserts that all men are born equal and regards as mere mythology the ideologies that once sustained the Church and Crown. I doubt, for instance, whether many readers of this book can accept as a sober fact, rather than as an absurd or perhaps endearing fiction, the idea that our Queen is a fountainhead of honour (and is the source of another virtue) and derives her

---

[16] Peter Laslett, *The World We Have Lost*, Methuen, 1965.

capacity to be so from her anointment with oil at her coronation, as a result of which she has been infused with Divine Grace. And yet this is what almost all men did believe until the Enlightenment and the Age of Reason. Nor do many people nowadays believe that genealogies can be invoked as evidence of personal superiority, as aristocrats once openly did.

However, despite the fact that these traditional means by which European societies used to maintain their sense of social cohesion and affirmed their belief in their past and their hopes for the future have become obsolescent if not obsolete, the need for purveyors of hope still remains, and a tendency to create inspiring élites can still be discerned in the modern world. In communist countries the Party performs this role quite openly, but in the liberal democracies the impulse to hive off a section of the population into a special élite of purveyors of hope manifests itself clandestinely and hypo-critically by the creation of two classes of people, one of which satisfies that aspect of hope that can be appeased by idealization, hero worship and identification, the other of which is paid to provide hope.

The former class consists of those people who are correctly styled stars—pop stars, film stars, football stars, even, in England at least, hairdressers and newscasters—whose lives are followed as avidly as those of royalty ever were and whose deaths, which are often premature and tragic (Marilyn Monroe, James Dean and Elvis Presley, for example), lead to mass demonstrations of grief—assuaged only when a new star appears in the firmament. Such people purvey pseudo-hope, since their appeal is, as Erik Erikson[17] again has shown, primarily to people who have yet to discover their own identity and therefore 'over-identify, to the point of apparent complete loss of identity, with the heroes of cliques and crowds'. The stars themselves are, I think, better regarded as victims than as exploiters of society, since they pay a heavy price emotionally for the adulation they receive and the money they and their promoters earn. And they may at any time, if they make a false move, be thrown off their pedestals and into the dustbin.

The second class, those who are paid to provide care and hope, comprise the counselling professions—the psychiatrists, psycho-therapists, social workers and probation officers. As Paul Halmos[18]

[17] Erikson, *Childhood and Society*, op. cit.
[18] Paul Halmos, *The Faith of the Counsellors*, Constable, 1965.

has shown in his book *The Faith of the Counsellors*, these professions practise a benign form of double-think. They purport to provide professional services and skills based firmly on scientific principles derived from psychology and sociology, which they apply 'non-directively' and 'non-judgmentally', when in fact they provide concern, love and hope and are actuated by faith—though what the faith is in is never articulated. Society colludes, and indeed encourages, this double-think, by treating the counsellors as ordinary professional people, paying them salaries and fees for their technical skills and providing them with career structures, but at the same time covertly endowing them with extraordinary miraculous powers, particularly that of being able to give hope to hopeless cases, and delegating to them the responsibility for making decisions about matters that are moral not scientific. In England at least, the onus for deciding whether a pregnant woman *should* have an abortion falls on psychiatrists; and drug-addiction, which is surely a symptom of social malaise and not of physical illness, is treated by psychiatrists, none of whom receive any training in ethics or sociology and only a minority of whom receive any training in psychotherapy. In other words, they are expected to make moral decisions and to provide hope for the despairing, while pretending that they are exercising professional skills derived from their scientific knowledge, a state of affairs only relished by those psychiatrists who enjoy playing God. Social workers are similarly expected to deal with the consequences of poverty and bad housing as though they were illnesses amenable to treatment; and not surprisingly many of them fortify themselves by becoming believers in psychoanalysis or Marxism. In his book *The Triumph of the Therapeutic*, Philip Rieff[19] has described a similar tendency in the United States to regard all human problems as illnesses amenable to treatment by scientific experts. The elevation of psychoanalysts to guru status is another example of the same collusive process.

The assumption underlying this development is that faith, hope and charity are commodities that can be bought and sold in the market or provided by the State, and that it is possible to train people in techniques that will make them competent purveyors of them. As Halmos has pointed out, this emergence of a special class of counsellors implies that society is throwing up people who have hope in the future, who believe that science is the only ideology that

---

[19] Philip Rieff, *The Triumph of the Therapeutic*, Chatto, 1966.

can be invoked to justify action, and who are disillusioned in politics. It also implies a widespread assumption that it is not the responsibility of each individual to develop his own virtues—as it would be if the liberal democracies really were democracies in which all men are equals and opportunities to achieve the good life really were open to all.

The second point I wish to make is that the traditional symbols of hope seem to have lost their virtue, without having as yet been replaced by any new set of efficacious ones. If science really had proved, as many people nowadays believe, that religion is an illusion, that all rituals and ceremonials are obsessional symptoms, that love is nothing more than a technique for relieving instinctual tension, that all behaviour is motivated by infantile causes, that all virtues and achievements can be interpreted reductively, that all human relationships are games people play, that social activity is role-playing and play-acting, then life really would be a racket and the world really would be a wasteland, in which all that one could do would be to wait for Godot or search for exotic sources of hope in Eastern philosophies or psychedelic drugs.

But, in fact, as anyone who actually bothers to read Freud, or Eric Berne, or even Erving Goffman[20] will discover, all these disillusioning, corrosive ideas are either misunderstandings and over-simplifications of what they said—or are examples of people foisting their personal attitudes to life on to the world as though they were conclusions to which their scientific researches had led them. For instance, Eric Berne believed that people can achieve awareness, spontaneity and intimacy and that, if they do so, they stop playing games, but one has to persevere to the last chapter of his *Games People Play*[21] to discover that he did so. And Freud believed that religion is an illusion long before even a glimmering of psychoanalysis entered his mind, having been brought up by free-thinking parents against whom he did not rebel.[22]

What seems to have happened is that the psychological and social sciences, flying the flags of Reason and Science, explored territory where angels fear to tread without appreciating the symbolic havoc they were creating. The main victims of this havoc have been, I think, the children of people who in the 1920s to 1940s were

[20] Erving Goffman, *The Presentation of Self in Everyday Life*, Allen Lane, 1969.
[21] Eric Berne, *Games People Play*, Penguin, 1968.
[22] Philip Rieff, *Freud: The Mind of the Moralist*, Gollancz, 1959.

marginally influenced by progressive, enlightened, rationalist ideas; they have had transmitted to them symbols of hope and virtue, which, if modern, are half-baked, and, if traditional, are half-decayed. As many observers have pointed out, young people who drop out, take off, make the pilgrimage to Katmandu, become flower children or disciples of Hare Krishna, are usually children of middle-class parents whose lives have been moral compromises. And in Great Britain they are grandchildren of people whose belief in progress or the natural order of things was shattered by World War I.

Finally, I must say something about the effects on modern man of living in an epoch overshadowed by the possibility that the human race may be about to annihilate itself, either directly and in one move by nuclear warfare, or more insidiously and yet inexorably by exhausting its sources of energy and disturbing the ecological balance between man and nature. If it were certain that such a man-made end of the human race was nigh, hope for humanity as a whole would indeed dry up, because there would cease to be any expectation of any future in which desires could be satisfied; and the best any single individual could hope for would be that the cataclysm might be postponed until after his own natural death. This is a position that some people do adopt; it leads to a curious coalescence of hope and despair, which entitles them to fiddle while Rome burns and make hay while the sun shines, 'for tomorrow we die'. It is a stance which people, particularly older people, who do not share it, are apt to consider cynical or decadent, but is, I think, better regarded as courageous, as the re-emergence of an epic virtue in a world that is apparently affluent and secure. (The epic virtues of courage, heroism and endurance seem to flourish under conditions of scarcity, in which life is, and is known to be, nasty, brutish and short, while the religious and romantic virtues can only flourish under conditions of prosperity and security, in which there is time and leisure for meditation, self-exploration and dalliance.[23] The present state of affairs is anomalous, in that security and affluence co-exist with widespread awareness that life could come to an end at any moment. What kinds of virtue flourish under such conditions?)

But, in fact, it is not certain that the world is coming to an end, with either a bang or a whimper, since the reasons why it is at risk

[23] R.W. Southern, *The Making of the Middle Ages*, Hutchinson, 1953.

are all man-made and counter-measures are therefore, in principle, possible. Whether they will in fact be taken, and whether the risks really are as great as they are often presented as being, are matters for prediction; and predictions depend upon extrapolations from present facts: in this case, from political facts about the policies and intentions of governments possessing nuclear weapons, from technological facts about resources and their utilization, and from demographic facts about population trends. Discussion of these facts, and of the predictions being made on their basis, certainly is outside my professional competence and in any case belong to an essay on the grounds not sources of hope, so I shall confine myself to a few general comments.

First, predictions are not always accurate and actions based on them are acts of faith not reason, since it is possible to collect examples of predictions based on all the available evidence which have proved wildly wrong. In the 1930s all the evidence suggested that the population of the United Kingdom would fall to 35 million by 1970, but in fact it rose to more than 55 million, an increase of 9 million as opposed to the estimated decrease of 11 million. In any case, human behaviour is influenced by the predictions that are made about it, since they alter the assessments that are made of the likely future and evoke reactions based on suggestibility and counter-suggestibility.

Secondly, predictions are inevitably based on those facts that are known and cannot take account of facts that are not yet known. For instances, estimates of energy resources can only be based on sources that have already been located and cannot take account of those that have yet to be located. And as there are, of necessity, more not fewer things in this world than have yet been observed, predictions of resources have an inherent tendency to be underestimates. British nuclear energy policy after the last war, for instance, was based on an underestimate of how much coal there was under Britain and complete ignorance that there was any natural gas under its waters.

Thirdly, gloomy predictions circulate more thoroughly than cheerful ones do, just as bad news travels faster than good news and disasters make better headlines than continuing felicities. As a result the information on which we base our expectations of the future is contaminated by a factor that derives, not from the future as it can be rationally assessed, but from that present boredom, discontent and malice which make prospects of disaster exciting and fascinating. Just as people can maliciously enjoy other people's misfortunes and take a delight in spreading alarm and despondency, so the prospect of universal cataclysm can have its charms. And just as faith, hope and charity generate millennial, utopian and progressive ideals, so envy, hatred and malice generate catastrophic hopes.

Finally, as I have no wish to end this essay on an unduly optimistic note, I must say something about the effects of disseminating the idea that the world is over-populated. Although this may well be true and it may be necessary to discourage births, it has, I think, to be recognized that it is an intrinsically demoralizing idea, which strikes at one of the basic biological sources of hopes, the belief that fecundity is virtuous: that one's own birth added an asset to the world and procreation increases the store of goodness. 'Be fruitful, and multiply, and replenish the earth, and subdue it'[24] is one of the oldest and most elemental injunctions; and the present must be the first time that humanity has had to consider the possibility that its success in subduing the earth, combined with its failure to replenish it, may compel it to enjoin its members to be sterile and avoid multiplication. I find it hard to see how we could elevate contraceptive competence to one of the cardinal virtues and turn births into occasions for reproach and condolence, without threatening the self-assurance of both men and women and contaminating the river of hope at its physical sources. A world in which we had not only learned to live with the Pill but also to love it would form a suitable subject for an Erewhonian novel.

[24] Genesis, ch. 1, v. 28.

Varieties of Hope

A.F. Davies

It is striking how split in popular understanding is hope's image. Proverbs, we know, are apt to troop up in self-cancelling pairs, but the sayings that have come down to us as perceptive about hope seem grossly and obsessively at odds.

> Hope never comes—Hope never leaves us wretched
> Hope is worth any money—Hope is as cheap as despair
> Great hopes make great men—He who lives in hope will die fasting
> No hope, no endeavour—It is not necessary to hope in order to undertake
> He that lives in hope dances without music—Hope well, have well
> To hope is to enjoy—Less hope, hotter love
> Hope will make thee young—Every man knows better than he hopes

For the idealists who subscribe to Luther's 'Everything that is done in the world is done by hope' (and who are, perhaps, self-defined in this very agreement), hope is the precious affect of construction, social and personal, which must therefore be secured by any means and safeguarded at all cost. On the contrary, for stoics and cynics, hope is above all what must be seen through and given up, since it habitually deludes, betrays, makes fools of us—or worse. The historic root of the first perspective is in Judeo-Christian thought, of the second in Classical thought; but in terms of their contemporary appeal the two perspectives are at once temperamental, experiential and political.

Robert Bales, in his path-breaking study of the relation between outlook and character[1], has taught us to see optimistic-idealism and pessimistic-cynicism as the corner-stones of pivotal world views, reflecting contrasting personality types forged in distinctive early family settings and styles of upbringing. Whenever action is debated in society at large or in the microcosmic small groups that have been Bales' laboratory, proponents of each 'position' will predictably crowd to opposing sides of each choice. He brings out well the mutual fascination such polar positions exert, and suggests, indeed, that each may be read as in part a defence against the unconscious temptations of the other.

That actual experience with hoping can confirm people in either an elevated or a jaundiced view of it, is also clear from the collective testimony. Indeed, one exceptional proverb, straddling the warring perspectives, gives us this directly: *Hope is a good breakfast, but a bad supper.* The idealists can report truthfully on energizing encounters with charismatic personalities, the excitement of the incorporation of high ideals and worthy purposes, the comradeship of fellow enthusiasts. Equally, the disillusioned, now bitter or sour, legitimately dwell upon their sense of having been driven right off course, of having wasted energy and spirit, of having been used . . . they want their innocence back.* Our perspectives give us then, hope on the way up, and on the way down.

Politically, this translates all too readily into 'We/They' testimony. The leaders, the 'movers and shakers' of history, are the great exponents of hope, that is what puts the wind in their sails, and they would have it a duty, compulsory even, in their cause. Yet such men have not seldom put before their followers programmes of remarkable vulgarity and ineptitude. After the letdown, the rank and file, owning sheepishly that it was precisely their having cherished these hopes that opened them to manipulation, vow never to be caught again, and greet later promises of even minor improvement with the implacable slogan, 'That'll be the day!' The figure may most quickly be illustrated with the phenomenon of the Papua-New Guinea cargo cult:

---

[1] Robert F. Bales, *Personality and Interpersonal Relations*, Holt Rinehart and Winston, New York, 1970, especially chapters on 'PF' and 'NB'.

* Indeed, the metaphors of disillusionment are often lurid: hope 'makes the heart sick', 'corrupts', 'lays putrid eggs' and 'cold' hopes 'swarm like worms within our living clay' (Shelley). We shall return to this.

A prophet announces the coming of the millenium and the end of the present time of troubles. The ancestors will return to join the living, bringing with them in ships or aeroplanes abundant 'cargo' (the sorts of goods found in a trading store, plus telephones and jeeps) so that material well-being will be enjoyed by all and the community will be respected and self-respecting. Present wrongs will be righted, for example, brown skins will become white, and white will become brown, and/or the whites will be driven away.

The prophet commands zealous preparations: maybe re-settlement (with suitable new accommodation for the returning spirits—and the prophet), or the disposal, as proof of faith, of produce and wealth, e.g. the destruction of pigs and crops, sometimes new religious rites or economic arrangements ... above all, the construction of the jetties or airstrips to receive the dead and the cargo. The faithful must adhere strictly to the regimen, otherwise they will not be saved, and perhaps, even, the millenium will not come.[2]

We would do better, I fancy, to see this cult less as exotic or primitive than as a 'late echo of the most exalted hopes of the West— the coming of the Kingdom, and of a just society after the Revolution. Visions of an end of yearning, waste and grief, all start from an interpretation of the present life under an aspect of deprivation.'[3] And the inevitable disillusion of the cultists seems, in the end, not so very different from that of the descendants of nineteenth-century political nationalism, the noisily plaintive ex-Communists of the West, or the mute reproach of our very cemeteries to the promise of physical resurrection, that central element of the Christian hope.

So set on sheer affirmation or denial of value, the proverbs on hope seem flat, second-rate, pre-psychological—with one exception, which may very suitably serve as an epigraph to our own first moves to catch hoping at work in contemporary settings of public and personal construction: La Rochefoucauld's 'Hope and fear are inseparable.'

* * * *

Thinking about hope in relation to contemporary politics, what first impresses one is its tacitness and modesty. There seems less expectation today than ever in the century that politics can marked-

---

[2] I.C. Jarvie, Cargo Cults, in *Encyclopaedia of Papua and New Guinea*, Melbourne University Press, 1972.

[3] Bert Kaplan, in *Our Own Metaphor*, ed. Mary C. Bateson, Knopf, New York, 1972, p. 98.

ly improve the collective life. Partisanship is still the rule in domestic politics, but it becomes increasingly tepid: both less in toto being hoped from its standard-bearers, and less in detail.[4] In 1973, seventy volunteers from the political sociology class at Melbourne University kept a diary of their political affects for a month. When the entries were brought together, what immediately stood out was their solidly negative cast: subjects recorded two adverse reactions to events for each positive one; there was no single day on which positive affects predominated. Much of the disappointment and grievance was, of course, minor, a routine response to stereotyped happenings relayed in the media, but sometimes it was very strong indeed. Anger, hatred, contempt and moral indignation accounted in all for one-third of the total; cynicism, powerlessness, depression and boredom made up a further fifth ... and fear (in an evidently secure sample) at 6%, still managed to score double hope's 3%. In fact, the hope entries regularly fed simultaneously into fear, for example 'I do hope the Labor Government proves it can manage the economy, but I'm becoming afraid that they just haven't got what it takes.' (It was less often possible to infer from named fears what latent hopes might somehow be associated with them.) But the most striking thing about the sample's hopes was their perfunctoriness: they were usually neither spelt out enough to be seriously at risk, nor apparently taken far enough into the self to be distinguishable from those of any standard well-meaning partisan. As I read them, these hopes seemed essentially a wing of a loyalty system; subjects, having consciously set up a loyal relation with one or more political groups or movements, felt in consequence larger for any triumphs, threatened or diminished by any reverse: they simply applauded, hated, feared—and hoped, as loyal supporters should.

[4] cf. 'From, say, 1850 to 1950, the movements of the left—whether they called themselves socialist, communist or syndicalist—like everybody else who believed in progress, knew just where they wanted to go, and just what, with the help of history, strategy and effort, they ought or needed to do to get there. Now they no longer do ... [Nor do any other established political groupings.] Old landmarks have disappeared, new ones are not yet recognized as such, and intellectual navigation across the suddenly estranged landscapes of human society becomes unusually puzzling for everybody.'
E.J. Hobsbawm, *New York Review of Books*, 23 March 1977, p. 44.

In the light (or, as I would now see it, the shadow[5]) of this finding—and the accompanying thought that people who declined to spell out their hopes stood little chance of converting them into energy—I proceeded in writing *Political Passions* to ignore hope altogether, consigning it formally to that class of affects that relates principally to the individual's primary, rather than to his secondary, environment.[6] It is now clear to me that I then had altogether too narrow and rationalistic a conception of hope (a conception my main mentor in the analysis of affects, Alexander Shand,[7] did nothing to undermine)—seeing it pretty much as a kind of contract with oneself to wish, at a certain strength for a certain time, for a given outcome. But explicitly formulated hopes, about which people can be expected to testify easily and without embarrassment, may well be both the least common, and the least important, kind. If, as with feelings of envy, there are often powerful reasons for the individual to hide from himself the knowledge that hopes are beginning to stir, if *unconscious* hopes, in short, are a major part of the picture, then our model of how politics engages them needs to be radically changed. The New Guinea villager, for example, *till the prophet appeared*, may hardly have known that he longed for the return of the ancestors. Such hopes are not pinned on to

---

[5] The mistake was a double one: first in giving general significance to a detail from a somewhat blasé sample in an unusually low-pressure political system; second, in getting it wrong even within the Australian context—as the remarkable 1977 election result soon showed.

When at the end of the year the Liberal-Country Party Government went to the polls after only two years in office, it had, by general journalistic consent, not done well enough to be returned by more than the narrowest of margins, but in the event it increased its already record majority! The explanation lay, not in the voters' feelings about the Government, which took a back place, but in their unfinished emotional figure with the Opposition. What I had seen as 'modest' and 'routine' enthusiasm for the Labor Government in 1972, was in fact Australian political hope at a high peak.

The Labor Party, and particularly its leader, Mr Whitlam, who had managed to coax from the electorate this rare and uncharacteristic emotional investment in the prospect of political change ... and then signally failed to produce solid gains, had in the public's view, *still to be punished* for this hubris. Even in small quantities, hope is evidently a dangerous commodity to deal in—as the lurid metaphors at the foot of p. 25 remind us. They deal with the subjective sensations of disillusionment. Just occasionally, the political forms give people a chance to get back at a person who 'cheated' them in this trade and show their fury with a leader who dashed the very hopes he dared to raise.

[6] *Political Passions*, Melbourne Politics Monographs, 1976, p. 21.

[7] Alexander Shand, *The Foundations of Character*, Macmillan, London, 1914. His remarks on hope are on pp. 462–6, 470–1, 477–80.

people like campaign buttons, but drawn out of their very bowels. Political hopes are, indeed, organized in loyalty systems, but the contracting loyalist may barely surmise the penumbra of hopes his allegiance carries along with it. One may talk, for example, amicably and at length to a Québecois about his life and problems, and find him altogether as straightforward and sane as a man from Geelong, but one is, as a tourist, unlikely to pick up—indeed, the Québecois, himself, hardly knows how to assess—those parts of his identity that give him the full political potential of a cargo cultist. For he is likely to believe at a middle to deep level that some drastic ritual gesture is necessary to right intolerable deprivation and restore communal self-respect among French-Canadians, something that will symbolically call up and re-unite the group with the ancestors, some forcible separation out of the 'nation' from its exploiters and some resounding declaration of *their* inferiority ... All of which done, the cargo is in the bag.

But why should one wish not (fully) to know one's hopes? It happens that one of the few psychoanalytic essays on the affect, Thomas French's 'The therapeutic value of hopes'[8], addresses itself to this very question. What, asks French, are the sources of the patient's therapeutic incentive and of the integrative capacity that makes learning possible? In both cases, he answers, 'his hopes, successively emerging, for a solution to his conflicts ... his specific hopes, focussed on just what is to be achieved by analysis (not just vague anticipations of help from treatment or confidence in the analyst), *plus* an emotional commitment to the possibility of realising them.'

> Our thesis is that such specific hopes, repeatedly emerging and continually undergoing modification in adaptation to the therapeutic situation, are essential for the maintenance of the gradually increasing integrative capacity on which success in therapy depends ... Unfortunately these therapeutically significant hopes are closely tied in with other hopes from the past, which once ended in disastrous consequences. For this reason the newly emerging hopes must first be repudiated—and promptly, before they begin to reactivate the associated traumatic memory patterns.
>
> Repudiation of his seductive hopes may occur either before or after the patient has become (more or less) committed to them. In either case, the

---

[8] Thomas French, *The Integration of Behavior*, Vol. 2, University of Chicago Press, 1958, chapter 10. His book-length report on the asthmatic railwayman, 'John', amply bears out this sequence. But for a succinct case-summary that could have been written precisely to illustrate French's thesis, see Charles Berg, *War in the Mind*, second edition, Macaulay, London, 1944, pp. 69–76.

analyst can come to the rescue by explicitly formulating for the patient the realities in the present towards which his emerging hopes are oriented. He should also explain that the need to repudiate his new hope is a consequence of disturbing events of the past.

One should not expect such an interpretation to have a quickly bene- ficial effect—that will be weak indeed, in comparison to the patient's need to repudiate. (Or, if the associated traumatic memory pattern has begun to be activated, he may be preoccupied for weeks or months with defences against it.) The interpretation is designed for future effect, when in time the disturbing affects will have been dissipated or discharged. Then hopes similar to the first will again begin to emerge and one's earlier inter- pretations and explicit recognitions, though they have remained latent, will have increased his integrative capacity. Then these hopes will emerge more boldly and persist longer.[9]

The parallels with the mobilization of hopes in political movements cannot be close, but there are several points to compare. The political protagonist, like the patient, not uncommonly sets out from an initial state of acute self-dissatisfaction. However, his project is fundamentally allo- not auto-plastic: he seeks in no way to re-make himself or to gain insight into his condition, but to amend social practice, particularly those arrangements according less than full value or consideration to the social type he represents (or identifies with). Nor is the political leader, unlike the therapist, intent on presiding over a learning experience; he may, for strategic purposes, have to subdue recklessness, panic or wild impatience, but essentially he confirms the supporter in congenital 'understand- ings', accustomed fears, prejudices and enmities. Indeed, in militant groups his central message is that hate is now possible without guilt; is in fact a virtue.

The resuscitation of old and painful hopes *is*, however, part of the political experience; though the hopes are less those of infancy and early childhood, centred on relations with the parents and all their portentous derivatives, than of late childhood, concerned with ambitions, ideals and the social self-image. To be rid of a sense of spoilt self or inferior identity is the protagonist's basic plea, and this

---

[9] *Ibid.*, pp. 43–4. It is interesting that from the other side, psychiatrists faced with the choice of patients most likely to benefit from therapy have worked to devise an instrument to measure personal levels of hope. See Louis A. Gottschalk, *The Measurement of Psychological States Through The Content Analysis of Verbal Material*, University of California Press, 1969. In *Political Passions* I speculated on the prospect of adapting certain other scales of Gottschalk's, especially one on anger, for political use (*op. cit.*, pp. 203–6). It seems a daunting enterprise in this case.

does carry him back in memory and desire to earlier days of promise behind the 'fault'. Finally, while analysis enables one's accounts with the parents at last to be realistically settled, political recruitment simply interposes a new, higher authority, the leader who cannot be hated and must be loved, thus 'solving' the long-carried strains of ambivalence towards parental authority by splitting and idealisation, to produce an illusion of peace, oneness and even re-birth.

*   *   *   *

If reflecting on French's finding, that much of the energy of 'new' hopes in adults comes from a reactivation of childhood hopes defeated, led us to seek in private pains and disappointments suffered between the ages of, say, six to twelve the *matériel* of much later to be displaced on to political hopes, a second psychoanalytic essay, which fixes on the style rather than the content of hoping, suggests the prevalence of an even deeper regression. Ernest Schachtel invites us to consider a continuum with the end-points, magical hope and realistic hope.[10]

The first style involves the mere wistful expectation that somehow things will change for the better through the action of some external agency.

> God, fate, some event such as marriage, the birth of a child, moving to another city, a trip, or—quite often—the mere flow of time, the beginning of a new year, the eternal tomorrow, will magically bring fulfilment without one's having to do anything about it. Such hopes may go either with a resigned, passive waiting (as for Godot), or with insistent and often angry demands, but what is wished for is characteristically vague: to 'be happier ... more satisfied', i.e. to be comforted, relieved of distress as the infant is, without knowing quite how mother does it or what she does. (In therapy such patients hope that 'analysis' or 'the analyst' will do all the work.)

Since at its heart is a wish for a complete change in one's state of being, a sudden turn for the better in the whole character of life and the world, this style of hoping in its stress on the future, empties the present, 'which may be felt as an unwanted obstacle, a span merely to be waited out, without meaning, fullness, weight, stretching on endlessly in boredom, restlessness and futility, or as a time to be kept free for the hoped-for event, but actually empty,

---

[10] Ernest G. Schachtel, *Metamorphosis: on the development of affect, perception, attention and memory*, Basic Books, New York, 1959, pp. 37–44.

and in retrospect, shrunk, wasted, evaporated'. Further, the golden outcome is not earned, but bestowed, by some outer event like 'the possession of the desired or beloved woman, the passing of an exam, acquisition of a desired object, being of a certain age (like being grown up, or remaining young), achieving success or fame'. Magic hope then, is an expectation of future embeddedness, a return to a quasiuterine existence. Finally, Schachtel observes, magic hope isolates: the lucky one, in his putative triumph, has the sense of being singled-out, favoured above others, in having found the way back to his own good mother; there is a sense of precariousness about it all and in his imagination he fears envy.

By contrast, realistic hope is the affect of one living—and acting— in an adult real world. It is based on an attempt to understand the concrete conditions of life, to see one's role in it truly and to try appropriate, thoughtful action. The contemplation of realistically hoped-for changes helps mobilize the energies necessary to promote them and may well go with an attitude of loving concern for another or others. To the realistic hoper the present is highly significant, deriving its meaning, indeed, from the chance it gives to perform purposeful, hope-related acts. Finally, realistic hope connects: calling out feelings of brotherliness and 'being related to all things living'.

The styles are drastically polar: one empty grandiose fantasy, viciously enervating and selfish, the other measured, practical and caring (and a mite dull?); so that it is tempting for an instant to suppose that the proverbs' discordant testimony about the value of hope may simply have been the result of the 'cynics' looking only at magical, and the 'idealists' only at realistic, hopes. But, of course, they largely report on identical matters. Political activists themselves, in turn, dispute with heat and endlessly over what is, and is not, realistic (*Soyons réalistes, demandons l'impossible!*); and the analyst of political hopes in most systems must expect to work mainly at the populous centre of Schachtel's continuum.†

We should also expect dedicated political actors to report wide

---

†Certainly the New Guinea cultists stand as near as may be to the magic pole, despite their labours on jetties and airstrips; but the French separatists put a weight on symbolic readjustments and reassurances which they alone can finally be the judges of the nutriment in.

fluctuations in the scope and texture of their hopes over the years. ‡
The recent autobiography, for example, of the high-minded English
communist Edward Upward, which is notable for its meticulous
cataloguing of explicit political hopes at different dates, (lending
the narrative, it must be said, a somewhat mawkish tone) fixes as
a high point a notable experience of magic hoping:

> Walking through these woods high above the sea fifteen years ago during
> one of my holidays before I retired from teaching, I turned from this path
> to go down towards three white poplar trees at the edge of the cliff with
> the sea beyond them and with the pale undersides of their wind-lifted
> leaves showing, and suddenly I entered into a different existence—on
> earth, not in heaven, but incomparably better than I had experienced
> before—an existence in a world where monopoly capitalism with all its
> anti-human crimes had been ended for ever, and though I knew this was
> an illusion, I felt utterly justified in trying to keep it alive in me for as
> many minutes as I could, because I believed it prefigured the reality of
> the future and could strengthen me in supporting the fight to bring that
> reality nearer.[11]

It is the juxtaposition of two subsidiary terms in Schachtel's
scheme that will most catch the social psychologist's eye—'privatizing' as contrasted with 'integrative' hoping. Both Phillip Slater
in *The Pursuit of Loneliness*[12] and Richard Sennett in *The Fall of
Public Man*[13] have recently warned that society reaches a certain
kind of crisis point when the first type of hoping becomes in effect
the near-universal mode. The pursuit of privatizing goals does not,
of course, strike the ordinary individual himself as in any way
'unrealistic'—and will not, until the bad consequences in systemic
terms can be clearly demonstrated to him. We urgently need
work now on possible ways (besides preaching) of cultivating
altruism.

---

‡ Such accounts often express a sense of the painful roundaboutness in links between
the unit dutiful act and the long-term political hope. One must operate a very
complex and extended cobweb of causal inference to be certain one's act really
helped. Survey interviewers asking about 'interest in politics' regularly turn up
the response, 'I'm not at all interested—I'm more concerned with doing good
directly'. Vital, too, for politics is the distinction between 'entertaining a hope'
and becoming 'emotionally committed to it' (especially, one might think, for
liberals). And consider the necessity in achieving large-scale mobilisation, for
keeping key objectives vague and somewhat ineffable, if not downright ambiguous.

[11] Edward Upward, *The Spiral Ascent*, Heinemann, London, 1977, p. 693.
[12] Phillip Slater, *The Pursuit of Loneliness*, Brown, Boston, 1970.
[13] Richard Sennett, *The Fall of Public Man*, Cambridge University Press, 1977.

In a third psychoanalytic observation on hope, Wilfred Bion[14] remarks on its propensity, when it becomes the ruling mood, to paralyze the work of the therapeutic small group. It frequently happens, he noted, that two members of a group (of different sexes) become involved in an extended and increasingly intimate dialogue, and that the others, including often the therapist, far from reacting with jealousy or rivalry, not only tolerate this 'pairing' but stimulate it, and fall into a special state of sentimental and passive admiration. In the group members' unconscious, Bion suggests, the pair promise to produce between them the 'saving' idea, or even to give birth to the child, the future leader, who will definitively solve the group's problems. The messianic hope that an idea or person can arise to save the group from its feelings of hatred, destructiveness and despair is, he judges, as potent a cause of group stasis as moods of abject dependency on established leaders or paranoid preoccupation with 'enemies'. And, he wittily suggests, just as the Church in the larger society may represent the dependent 'assumption', and the Army the paranoid, the aristocracy may once have embodied the hoping one.

The most inept item in the *Dictionary of Quotations* must surely be 'Hope and youth are the offspring of each other'—a biological absurdity! Yet there is something important, if not in the idea that hoping makes or keeps us young[15], in the idea—which we may conclude with some remarks upon—that the young are uniquely the carriers of society's hopes. Some may at once wish to put it another way: hope is a key social affect because it is the one principally concerned with servicing ideology. It is aided in this, of course, by several auxiliaries, for example *faith* in leaders and doctrine, and general *idealization* of the cause and membership. We must not forget that ideologies do not stand alone like theorems: they are buttressed by works of art—the world seen through 'faithful' eyes—and the model of exemplary lives fashioned in the new manner, as recruits' sensibilities and ego-ideals are trained to rework staple social themes more conformably to the new ethos. The social springs of hope lie in the urgent conviction of adolescents and young adults that they can creatively re-set society's agenda in a way that sufficiently reproves and efficiently repairs what has been most shameful in the arrangements their parents' generation contrived

---

[14] W.R. Bion, *Experiences in Groups*, Tavistock, London, 1959, chapter 3.
[15] Simone de Beauvoir, *Old Age*, Secker & Warburg, London, 1966, chapter 12, on the importance of keeping before oneself a succession of 'projects' in old age.

or suffered.[16] In so doing, the lucky among them find life-work worth their devotion.

But young people are uniquely a prey to 'totalism' (Erikson[17]) and wild swings of mood from manic elation to despair, and the social plight lit with lurid paranoid anxiety seems to be a staple product of adolescent thinking. Students of the late 1970s will announce that the ecology crisis 'means that we have only 14 or 15 years left' or 'that it's already too late, we're doomed and nothing can now be done'. This same conjuring with a *world spoilt*§ and sense of a whole generation maliciously dealt an unplayable hand lay behind 1950s students' certainty of nuclear holocaust, and 1940s students' conviction that the war would inevitably mince up their generation to the last man. Yet, back to back with this panic, goes the idea that if only *this* generation can stay pure and stick together and exert its full will, then the world can be remade. Either nothing is possible or everything is.

While Erikson may have somewhat romanticized[18] and Lewis Feuer rather savagely debunked[19] the reparative pretensions and resources of young people—crystalized for each of them in the leading student cohort of the time—both, it seems to me, give good reasons for thinking that it is less the dearth of vaulting hopes in young people that we should currently deplore than something as plain as deficient assurance. We need some name—'mundane' consciousness, perhaps—for that tacit, rooted social wisdom in a society *against* which ideologies strain (and must, to test and stretch it), and which is finally proof against both the magic hoping and the plunging despair implicit in whatever contemporary assortment of 'radical' consciousnesses is on offer. Young people confident (if necessary, brashly) that they can and will do things distinctly better but not unrecognizably differently from their parents are themselves in any case the best hope of their elders.

[16] I have found the most illuminating discussions of generational agenda-setting in Kurt Riezler, 'Shame and Awe', chapter 8 in his *Man, Mutable and Immutable*, Regnery, Chicago, 1950; and Harold D. Lasswell, 'Political Constitution and Character', *Psychoanalysis and the Psychoanalytic Review*, 1959, 3–18.

[17] Erik Erikson, 'Identity and Totality, Psychoanalytic Observations on The Problems of Youth', *Human Development Bulletin*, 1954, 50–80.

§The projection outwards, on to the society at large, of the *revived* late childhood anxieties about the 'spoilt self'.

[18] See especially his (ed.) *The Challenge of Youth*, Doubleday, New York, 1965.

[19] His *The Conflict of Generations*, Basic Books, New York, 1969, argues that parricidal drives, deriving from unresolved Oedipus complexes, invariably break through adolescent idealism to give it a demonic quality.

The Absolute Enemy of Hope

William F. Lynch, S.J.

It is easier to describe what we commonly mean by hopelessness than what we mean by hope. Therefore let us first take the adventure of describing the hopeless. If we follow this method, we may find we are doing an essential thing in our search for hope; we may be cutting down much of the undergrowth of intentions and projects that are really hopeless—that have been obstructing the vision of the real thing called hope.

As I began, years ago, to commit myself to a study of and a book on hope, I could not help becoming increasingly aware that I was identifying hopelessness with a part of human instinct or drive to be summed up under the title *the absolutizing instinct*[1]. This instinct wants some form of the absolute in everything it does, and, human though we be, it can never be satisfied with the human. The best thing to do at this early point is to look for examples. Fortunately— or unfortunately—the examples abound and have no limit.

A fundamental principle in the working of the absolutizing instinct is that it is not all right to have human feelings. Those who live by this principle are satisfied only by the perfect and cannot tolerate any form or limit of the human. Whether it be anger or

[1] See William F. Lynch, *Images of Hope*, Helicon Press, Baltimore, Dublin, 1965. (Ed.)

envy or hatred or sexual impulse or domination or pride, the path
to humanity, if absolutized, is not *through* the actuality of these
things; the path, rather, is through denial or repression; what
happens is a taking of scandal at all these human things.

The absolutizing instinct will never accept the usual mixture of
fifty per cent of the ordinary and fifty per cent of the ideal as a
definition of human life. It is not too much to say that the deadly
enemy of this instinct is precisely the human and human feeling.
Its goal is precisely to be free of human limit and to be scandalized
by human feeling. But since it is hopeless, even if desirable, to reach
such a goal, it is precisely this goal as project that is our major
source of hopelessness. The root cause of hopelessness is the quality
of impossibility in any and all the hopeless projects of man. From
a book I have done on the subject of hope, I see the following as
one of a number of definitions of the hopeless.

> The kind of system or ideal I am now talking about does not recognize
> the hopeless; by this very act of non-recognition it destroys hope. It sets
> up a self that cannot be reached. The striving self cannot reach the ideal
> self. The project is hopeless. Thus there can be no taste of the ideal self,
> and no rest. But *this* project is often to be found full blooming in members
> of the most reputable systems.[2]

I see that at this point I have quoted Dr Leslie Farber as, with
understandable and understanding pity, he makes note of his belief
that psychiatrists and priests are especially susceptible to this
demanding disease of absolutizing. The ideal emotional life that is
unconsciously asked of them can be a very great burden. Let me
cite a small part of Farber's analysis, in this area, of the hopeless
projects of the most professional people.

> Unlike any other profession I know, with the possible exception of the
> priesthood, psychoanalysis places a double burden on its candidates: not
> only must they acquire psychoanalytic skills, a difficult enough task in
> itself, but they must in addition undergo a lengthy period of psycho-
> analytic therapy, which at once calls into question what they had
> previously taken for granted—mainly their characters—while promising,
> or stipulating, something variously called growth or maturity as the
> outcome of this experience . . . When man believes in his perfectibility he
> experiences his own real being almost as a disease, a fatal sickness whose
> cure—perfection—seems unattainable for himself, and whose tormenting
> symptoms can only partially be eased by the exchange of seeming for
> being.[3]

[2] *Op. cit.*, p. 45.
[3] *Op. cit.*, pp. 234–35.

So much for the consequences of the absolutizing instinct as burden imponderable, even for psychoanalysts and priests. Now let me present its sorrowful consequences for those in our society whom we call *the well*. Here is a widening instance of a case wherein human beings, in the very attempt to produce hope, produce in the underbrush only another form of the hopeless. I think now of the desperate effort of the well, whether in the name of physical or mental beauty or salvation, to insist to the point of madness that they are not mad, that only the mentally ill are mad. The well, because of their enormous fear of mental illness, proclaim to themselves and the world that they are absolutely well in the face of this monstrous thing called mental illness. They are happy that there is such a world, and such people as the mentally ill, because this is a world to be used as a repository for all their vague fears of so terrible a thing as *this* kind of illness. It is because of *these* fears that they must create an absolute boundary between themselves— the beautiful people—and these others who are not beautiful. If there is such a citizenship of the world as the sick and the mentally ill, then all of this mental pollution is triumphantly dumped upon them by those who think of themselves as well and beautiful. The result is the political creation not of one single 'city of man' but of two: the city of the absolutely beautiful and the city of the absolute and sick untouchables. The great and final form of irony here is that with every success in raising such boundaries the terrible burden not of the sick but of *the well* becomes worse and worse— for the project is absolute health and beauty, and again it is hopeless. Modern health becomes the worst of all diseases; it becomes a great and frightened form not of health but of disease. The hero and the heroine become more and more the product of an absolute demand that we join the city of beauty. To reach this city—and not the other, the true city of man, the human mixture of sanity and madness, the beautiful and the ugly—becomes the ultimate goal of the American city of man. And as the project of this city becomes more and more absolute, the hopelessness has to dig down underneath to hide its impossibility.

The city of man. Shall there be one such city or shall there be two? That is the question. If there shall be two then there is no such thing as hope for either of these two cities. If there are two cities then there is no salvation or hope for either. For consider again: If there is a city for the beautiful and for only the beautiful and the well then its citizens are damned to an impossible search for perfection and sanity; they are condemned to a ridiculous world of no mistakes, no weaknesses, nor the endless degrees of madness our flesh is heir to; worst of all they are forbidden to be human. But if there are not two worlds of man but only one, then all things become possible, including hope. In such a city, the well can be always a little mad, as indeed they are, more, unfortunately, than a little; the inclusion in this one city will save them from the absolute goal of absolute sanity. As for the sick, their various madnesses will fit more easily into one city of the human; no less than the madnesses of the well and the beautiful. This, I suggest, is the hope of all of us: that everything in us be found to be human.

It cannot be stressed too much that this is the central goal of the mentally ill; that whatever be worst in us be found to be human and therefore never take us out of the city of man. It is the crowning achievement in the life and work of Dr Harry Stack Sullivan that he is remembered above all for his dictum, and the medical practice it guided, that nothing in man is inhuman. That dictum—on the surface so simple but offering so much salvation to those we call mad—was *everyone is much more simply human than otherwise.*

We understand the greatness of this phrasing only if we understand, as many of us do, that the most painful and most hopeless diseases of the mind are those that exclude the sick from citizenship in one single humanity. This exclusion is something like the proclamation of a curse, a curse exiling those who are not beautiful.

Here are a few of the sentences of Sullivan:

> ... the differences between any two instances of human personality—from the lowest-grade imbecile to the highest-grade genius—are much less striking than the differences between the least-gifted human being and a member of the nearest other biological genus. Man—however undistinguished biologically—as long as he is entitled to the term, *human personality*, will be much more like every other instance of human personality than he is like anything else in the world. As I have tried to hint before, it is to some extent on this basis that I have become occupied with the science, not of individual differences, but of human identities, or parallels, one might say. In other words, I try to study the degrees and patterns of things which I assume to be ubiquitously human.[4]

I cannot recall who it was who wrote or said that the schizophrenic group among mankind is always in a desperate hurry; but this hurry must be recognized as a great and laudable thing as soon as

[4] H. Stack Sullivan, *The Interpersonal Theory of Psychiatry*, eds H.S. Perry and M.L. Gawel, Norton, New York, 1953, pp. 32–33.

it is recognized as a hurry, on the pleading edges of the human world, to be human. That is the hope of all of us.

Let me review again this part of the problem and the life of hopelessness. From our present perspective it is the well who create or enlarge the life of hopelessness for the sick. This they do by transferring their own illnesses, their aggressions, their angers, their wishes to destroy, over to the mentally ill. The transferral is so complete, and so generally successful, that the consequence is the building not of one but of two cities of man. There are many forms of excommunication and exile brought against the ill. With every unconscious success of the well there must be a decrease of hope and an increase of hopelessness. Even among those who count themselves as pious and religious souls there is an ironic boast that they are more than willing, indeed they are anxious, to forgive any sin, no matter what its scope or malice or inhumanity; there is in fact a kind of game often played, a game of forgiving the sinner in order that the social status of the forgiver be enhanced and beautified. There is love of the sinner but fear of the sick. And the sick may not be admitted to the resplendent, shining city of the well and the beautiful until they are well.

I have always been in admiration of the way in which Dr Martti Sirala has described this process:

> We in our modern society tend to build upon a myth of an ideal society, consisting of selected and approved individuals—of 'normal' human beings, with average intelligence, average bodily health and with a sufficient degree of psychic maturity. These selected and privileged individuals have, it is true, to take care of the others who do not belong to this class of the 'true' society. This kind of care does not, however, acknowledge the sick as belonging to the body, *unless* they recover. One might say that sick people do not belong (according to the dogma we enact in our shared life—without, it is true, ever becoming aware of this doctrine by practice) to the true society. The prevalence of this idea among us is obvious if we think how we speak of the sick man's *return* to society, as if he had not been in his society while sick—especially if he has been in a hospital. Racial discrimination is not in any way an isolated phenomenon among us! It is as if we thought that human defects and illness do not belong to our 'proper life' and that individuals who had by accident succumbed to the fate of being ill (or dying!) were not actual, proper members of society—unless they recovered—unless they could be made healthy again.[5]

I cannot help thinking and repeating that a major problem of all of us—a problem not only for those who need hope but for all of us

---

[5] From an unpublished paper.

—is this terrible search for emotional perfection or emotional simplicity in any human situation. This is so ideal and so simple a human project that it seems difficult to understand that it is not only a hopeless project; we should add again that it is neither good nor human. But as it is the most ordinary form of the absolutizing instinct, we ought to confront it still another time. This time I would like to come at it under the rubric of some comments on the absolute drive behind modern totalitarian systems. As a central focus I will suggest reflection on Robert Jay Lifton's *Thought Reform and the Psychology of Totalism*.[6] Other studies of the absolute forms of human thought behind modern totalitarianism are, of course, of very great number and varying substance. My own study of the totalistic mind is *The Integrating Mind*.[7] Because of the special way in which it brings my own present thoughts to focus, I would suggest a book entitled *Coercive Persuasion* by Edgar Schein and Curtis H. Barker.[8] The Schein-Barker book has as its difficult task a commentary on the successes and failures of the processes of 'brainwashing' during World War II in China.

It made me happy, as I considered the inhumanity but effectiveness of the brainwashing process, to find the following crucial sentence in this book with so ambiguous a title as *Coercive Persuasion*:

'If only *I had been what I thought I was*, I would have been able to resist.'[9] One might turn the idea around: 'If only I had been able to accept what I was, I would have been able to resist [the brainwashing process].'

Because they seem to me to offer an incisive summary of the difference between relative and absolutizing forms of thought I would like to spend a little time, not wasted, on the contrast between these two sentences. I shall do it in terms of my own brief description of brainwashing and just as brief a description of a living through this process by a Jesuit colleague.

As I understand the matter, especially after the help of Robert Jay Lifton's analyses, there are two basic steps (both of them absolute) in the process of brainwashing:

[6] Robert Jay Lifton, *Thought Reform and the Psychology of Totalism*, Norton, New York, 1961.

[7] William F. Lynch, *The Integrating Mind*, Sheed and Ware, New York, 1962.

[8] Edgar Schein and Curtis H. Barter, *Coercive Persuasion*, Norton, New York, 1961.

[9] *Op. cit.*, p. 149

1. 'Brainwashing' is the scientific elaboration of a process that goes on to some degree in all of us. Its central technique is to explore every element of what might be called 'negative identity' in a human being and to bring this negative identity to a point of complete pre-occupation and guilt in the consciousness. By negative identity, we mean all those elements in our character that fall short of the positive ideal we have set for ourselves, all those things in ourselves we neither approve nor like. What happens is that a hypothetical ten per cent of a total self is deliberately and diabolically made to invade consciousness, not to heal by revealing the proper proportions of the negative, but to destroy by projecting the self as totally and absolutely negative, bad, false to itself. The part is made the whole. The ten per cent becomes an absolute. This is the method. It is deliberate, calculated, spiritual murder. The only way out of it is a new birth under new leaders who will give these washed and now submissive victims a new self in a bright new world. If you give them your soul, they will make it rise again.

2. The new radiant self places itself totally on the outside of itself, without reservations. For it cannot stand the human. It is ready for complete exploitation and for the kind of submission that is rooted in a complete inability to live with oneself. The victim, unable to endure this hell of the self, has rushed to the state for forgiveness. He confesses all his sins, leaving nothing out, and he dedicates his whole self, nothing held back, to a new life.

The displacement of the self that is created by such techniques is now complete and is called rebirth, resurrection. It gives a new hope, but this new hope is profoundly ambivalent for it does not exclude its opposite, hopelessness, and is in fact a crooked name for the absolute helplessness which the whole technique is intended to create.

A Jesuit colleague of mine told me how he had been submitted, in China, to this process. As well as I can remember now, he told me that somehow he had not come out the victim; but he thought that were he a more holy and perfect priest, as another Jesuit had been, he would have emerged a far better victor. But, I told him, I did not agree. He was a good man, with a sense of the ordinary, and a sense of humour about himself. He could not imagine that he had only ten per cent wrong with him (though his 'perfect' colleague could!). He was the victor over his tormentors because it had never occurred to him that he did not have the vices, the imperfections, the weaknesses, the self-contradictions, that the absolutizing torturers thought so terrible. But those who are already maddened by the search for perfection and by the failure to reach it will be easy marks for the brainwasher.

I have tried to push my own description of the process of brainwashing beyond the manner in which, at certain historical moments, external forces can overwhelm us by their absolutizing tricks; I have tried to clarify the internal way in which the self, in the name of pretended virtue and perfection, plays this awful game with itself: '. . . the absolutizing imagination cannot endure the taste and the smell of the ten per cent. It is really an interiorized critic that becomes part of the sick man and demands a perfection that is inhuman, without boundaries. It expects everything, criticizes everything, and *counterfeits true hope because it insists that no task is hopeless.* The more it is allowed to grow, the less it is pleased with anything. Thus it gives the constant feeling of being check-mated, no matter what move he makes. It takes away the hope that any action will satisfy it. It is demanding, it is a dictator and a bully. And it thrives on keeping itself hidden. It tries to reduce the self to a hopeless and submissive state. In other words, what we are up against here is an internalized form of brainwashing. We brainwash ourselves.'[10] The only antidote to the above is a human imagination that can circle around the mountain of the human until it sees all that is there. Such an imagination is not easily taken in by the fascination of the hopeless. It will not condemn itself too quickly.

What I have been trying to do in these few pages is to put the finger on one of the greatest enemies of hope: the absolutizing instinct. And I have tried to say that most of the forms of this instinct are within: the enemy is within. A final summary might be: the greatest victory we could win in these generations is to stop being our own executioners.

---

[10] *Images of Hope*, p. 220.

Despair and the Object of Hope

Joan Nowotny

The theme that unifies Gabriel Marcel's reflections on existence and being is that of man as *Homo viator*. What constitutes the human being as wayfarer is hope.[1] In an article written in 1951 'Structure de l'espérance', Marcel stated:

> I believe that it is only beginning from a reflection on despair and perhaps only from there that we can rise to a positive conception of hope … hope can only be an active struggle against despair.[2]

Marcel stressed that the tragic aspect of life, with its possibility of despair, cannot be taken lightly, as a superficial optimism would have us do. The passage of the years did not cause him to change his opinion, as an article published in 1968 makes clear:

> We must declare very strongly that a philosophy which, yielding to the complacency of optimism, refuses to give a place to the temptation to despair, misunderstands in a very dangerous way a fundamental datum of our situation. In some way this temptation resides at the very centre of our condition.[3]

---

[1] This unifying theme is demonstrated in the author's unpublished Ph.D. dissertation, 'Gabriel Marcel's Philosophy of Hope', University of Toronto, 1974.

[2] Gabriel Marcel, 'Structure de l'espérance' in *Espoir Humain et Espérance Chretienne*, Pierre Horay, Editions de Flore, Paris, 1951, p. 48.

[3] See *Pour une Sagesse Tragique*, Plon, Paris, 1968, p. 208; *cf. Being and Having*, transl. Katherine Farrer, Harper and Row, New York, 1965, p. 93. The conditions that make it possible to hope are strictly the same as those that make it possible to despair.

It is not despair *per se* that lies at the centre of our condition; rather it is the temptation to despair. This temptation to despair can arise in my own personal situation, as a result of my own particular tragedy; the fundamental datum here is that 'I can take a stand before my life considered as a whole, that I can refuse it, I can despair.'[4] On the other hand, when confronted with the evil, suffering and betrayal that surround me on all sides, I can despair of reality as a whole, I can make the negative judgment that 'there is nothing in the realm of reality to which I can give credit—no security, no guarantee.'[5] This is a statement of complete insolvency. For each of us, at every moment of our lives, the worst is possible, or what we consider to be the worst. There seems to be no objective guarantee. What, then, is the nature of the despairing act, what is the situation of the person who despairs?

The essence of the act of despair seems to be 'capitulation before a certain *fatum* laid down by our judgment.'[6] Therefore it is *my* act, *my* decision, to adopt the perspective of the worst. But there is more to it than a fatalistic judgment regarding, for example, an ordeal or illness of some kind. To capitulate is not just the attitude of recognizing the inevitable; the hoping man can recognize the inevitable too. Despair is to '*se défaire en présence de ...*'[7], to unmake myself, to go to pieces under this sentence, to 'renounce the idea of remaining my self'[8], to lose my inner cohesion and consistence[9], to bring about my own destruction.[10] Such a 'going to pieces' constitutes a fundamental despair, one that like its counterpart in hope transcends the particular context in which it has arisen. Despair, Marcel says, is not fear at all. It consists in establishing oneself in the irremediable in such a way as to let oneself be interiorly dissolved by it.[11] Such a despair has its logical outcome in suicide. If to despair is to 'refuse that perpetual act of *redressement* without which a man ceases to be a man'[12], hope is to 'keep a firm

[4] *Being and Having, op. cit.*, p. 95.
[5] Gabriel Marcel, *The Philosophy of Existentialism*, transl. Manya Harar, Citadel, New York, 1966, p. 27.
[6] Gabriel Marcel, *Homo Viator*, transl. Emma Craufurd, Harper, New York, 1962, p. 37.
[7] 'Structure de l'espérance', p. 48.
[8] *Homo Viator*, p. 37.
[9] See 'Structure de l'espérance', p. 49.
[10] See *Homo Viator*, p. 38.
[11] See *Pour une Sagesse Tragique*, p. 51.
[12] 'Structure de l'espérance', p. 49.

hold on oneself, to safeguard one's integrity.'[13] Hope, in so far as it is an active battle against despair, is a refusal of fatalism, an active non-capitulation.

A further aspect of despair is its immobilizing character. Despair anticipates the ceaseless repetition of a life frozen in an inner determinism:

> The despairing man not only contemplates and sets before himself the dismal repetition, the eternalization of a situation in which he is caught like a sea of ice. By a paradox which it is difficult to conceive, he anticipates this repetition ... Despair here appears an enchantment, or as a kind of witchcraft, whose evil action has a bearing on all which goes to form the very substance of a person's life.[14]

In the presence of a situation that seems to me irremediable, whether it be my imminent death, or the closing in of the creditors to whom I owe money, or even the mechanical repetition of monotonous days, I can see no way out. I have the feeling of being in an impasse without issue, caught in a vice, incarcerated.[15] Despair has a petrifying effect on me, immobilizes me, holds me in its grip, fascinated, as it were, by the Gorgon's glance. Marcel refers to the myth of Medusa as supplying an adequate image[16], hence his reference to enchantment and witchcraft. This image underlines the obsessive character of despair. The despairing man anticipates and is immobilized by each waiting day's disappointment.

Closely connected with the obsessive and immobilizing aspects of despair is the sense of time as being closed, rather than open to future possibilities. It is as though the man in despair sees time as already consumed; he loses his sense of personal rhythm, his patience, because the time at his disposal for effective action is already used up. In his world, time no longer *passes*, or what comes to the same thing, time only passes without bearing within it the possibility of something new. Basing himself on his past experience, the despairing man anticipates nothing but the eternalization of his present situation. Time is for him a counter-eternity, an eternity turned back on itself, frozen in the hopeless present. Marcel remarks that:

---

[13] *Homo Viator*, p. 48.
[14] *Homo Viator*, p. 42.
[15] See 'Structure de l'espérance', p. 49.
[16] *Ibid.*, p. 48.

Despair seems to me above all the experience of closing or, if you like, the experience of *time plugged* up. The man who despairs is the one whose situation appears to be without exit. But this is no mere statement of fact. The man in despair is *affected* in the strongest sense of the word, by that absence of exit, and this shows that the negative term 'absence' does not give an adequate account of what is happening here. It is really as if the despairer kept hitting against a wall, the wall being faceless certainly, and yet hostile, and the result of this shock or impact is that his very being starts to disintegrate or, if you like, to give up.[17]

In the judgment of the one who despairs, his past life is an accumulation of disappointments, and it is this which he projects into the future. To the extent that the future is based on anticipation, and anticipation is an extrapolation of the past, to that extent, the future is seen as closed, as capable only of exemplifying the past. The future appears as a negation, an anticipation of future failure, and thus appears to be 'plugged up', to be an 'absence of exit'.

Another important feature of despair is a state of solitude, of being closed to other persons. Marcel links this closing in on oneself with the sense of time being closed:

Despair is hell . . . one could add that it is *solitude*. There is nothing more important than to bring out the rarely perceived conjunction between closed time and the *rupture* of *all living communication* with others.[18]

He continues:

To be enclosed in this immobilizing time is by the same stroke to lose those spontaneous communications with other people which are the most precious things in life, which are even life itself . . . In closed time friendship is no longer possible; and inversely, what is still more important, when friendship is born [*surgit*], time begins to move again, and simultaneously hope awakens like a melody which stirs in the depths of memory.[19]

Communication between persons, at any level of a relationship, involves an openness which always holds the possibility of creative development, a deepening of the relationship, mutual fulfilment. This is therefore the reverse of the situation of closed time where future possibilities are cut off. If a despairing person seeks help from another, however diffidently or with however slight expectation, this very gesture indicates that he is not yet shut up in his despair; time

---

[17] Gabriel Marcel, 'Desire and Hope' in *Existential Phenomenology*, eds N. Lawrence and D. O'Connor, Prentice Hall, Englewood Cliffs, N.J., 1967, p. 281.
[18] 'Structure de l'espérance', pp. 51–2.
[19] *Ibid.*, p. 52.

is not completely closed. The complete rupture of communication is a mark of despair which any psychiatrist could probably document. William F. Lynch sounds this theme in his *Images of Hope*. 'Perhaps', he suggests, 'it is impossible to really despair *with* someone. Perhaps it must be a private act.'[20] His analysis supports, in many respects, Marcel's interpretation of despair as solitude and the closing of the self in on itself.

The term Marcel uses for this state of closing oneself off from other persons is *indisponibilité* (non-disposability or unavailability— the English translations do not quite capture the sense of the French word). Non-disposability is a mark of the egocentric consciousness that closes itself off from others, even while it needs those others to affirm it and reflect back to it its own self-image. At the heart of the egocentric consciousness is an anxiety born of a need of others combined with a self-assertion that excludes them. The ego in its intrinsic structure is not a self-contained reality and that is why the anxiety that arises from egoism is *fundamental*. It is for this reason that Marcel can say that 'pessimism is rooted in the same soil as the inability to be at the disposal of others.'[21] If this analysis is well-founded, he goes on, 'the metaphysical origins of pessimism are the same as the origins of non-disposability.'[22]

Another characteristic of the despairing consciousness is the judgment it makes on the meaninglessness of life. The judgment about meaninglessness is closely connected with the self-centredness of a person who is closed in upon his own world of suffering:

> I can abandon myself purely and simply to my suffering, identify myself with it, and this is a terrible temptation. I can reconcile myself to my suffering which I proclaim to be completely meaningless; however, since it is the centre of my world, the world itself, centred on something meaningless, also becomes absolutely meaningless. This is not just an abstract possibility but a temptation which at times is almost irresistible.[23]

The thought of death, too, as the termination of our visible career can incite us to 'affirm that there is nothing, that nothing is of any value.'[24] Marcel often quotes in this context the lines from Claudel's *La Ville* which influenced him greatly:

[20] William F. Lynch, *Images of Hope*, New American Library, New York, 1966, p. 219.

[21] *The Philosophy of Existentialism*, p. 43.

[22] *Being and Having*, p. 73.

[23] Gabriel Marcel, *Creative Fidelity*, transl. R. Rosthal, Noonday Press, New York, 1964, p. 75.

[24] *Ibid.*, p. 172.

Nothing exists
I have seen and touched
The horror of what is useless adding the proof of my hands to what is not
The Void does not fail to declare itself by words which say: I am.[25]

To ponder these lines is to experience the vertigo of a being who discovers himself situated, as it were, between being and nothingness. If nothing *is*, then life is meaningless. This sense of the absurdity and meaninglessness of life is expressed in much recent art and literature, especially in the 'theatre of the absurd', where the function of art seems to be to sharpen anxiety and isolation. Many plays are set in an empty landscape, or in the claustrophobic encirclement of a closed room. Beckett's and Ionesco's characters, for instance, live in private fantasies, not listening to anybody else; language becomes a linguistic game without reference to external reality. In fact, the isolated consciousness is the defining concept of the theatre of the absurd. Sartre's *Huis Clos* and *La Nausée*, among others of his literary works, are striking examples of the same genre. Marcel's own plays, while not exemplifying in the same way the theme of meaninglessness, do nevertheless illustrate the effect of the 'broken world' on man in his relationships with his fellow man. 'My theatre', he says, 'is the theatre of the soul in exile, the soul suffering from a miscarriage of communion with itself and with others.'[26]

What is the root of this judgment on the meaninglessness of life? The root of it, Marcel implies, is the 'spirit of abstraction'. The spirit of abstraction is an absolutizing of objectivity, a reduction of all reality to what can be objectively explained. 'Whatever can be catalogued is an occasion for despair.'[27] Why? Because if one remains at that level, one is asserting a practical nihilism which amounts to a denial of being and value. Practical nihilism easily becomes cynical. It is the spirit of 'nothing but': love is nothing but an instinctual drive, hope is nothing but an illusion, my personal reality is nothing but a complexus of physics and chemistry, my life is nothing but a game of chance—with death at the end or the last play of the dice. Despair, indeed, seems to be the supreme wisdom! It presents itself as a kind of merciless lucidity, an exorcising of comfortable illusions. At moments of extreme discouragement which are close to despair, Marcel says:

[25] *Ibid.*, p. 172.
[26] Quoted by Roger Troisfontaines in *De l'existence à l'Être*, Vol. I, Louvain Editions Nauwelaerts, 1953, p. 35.
[27] *Creative Fidelity*, p. 70.

I seem to have suddenly rejected or torn up the veil of comforting illusions which masked life for me and by means of which I strove to provide for myself an endurable existence. It is as if life presents to me the petrifying face of Medusa; this fascinating power seems to press into its service my desire for rectitude, my desire not to let myself become deluded. This is the hour of tragic pessimism. Surely it can, if need be, emerge into a philosophy of heroism; but it can also lead either to suicide or to the surrender of a being who goes to pieces in a world of evil and suffering (*qui se défait en présence d'un monde scandaleux*).[28]

The fact that despair is possible, that suicide is possible, is, to Marcel's mind, a fundamental datum for metaphysics.

From our analysis so far, the main points that have emerged are: Firstly, hope arises out of a situation that is such that despair is also possible; secondly, hope consists in putting forth a sort of interior activity, which is 'our being's veritable response' to the trial situation. A first specification of this activity is to consider it as an active struggle against despair. We have seen that despair is a capitulation, a going to pieces before a *fatum* laid down by the judgment. It judges the future by the past and anticipates nothing but the irremediable experience of the past. The future, regarded as though it were already present is, as it were, eternalized and immobilized, so that time appears closed, frozen in the present. The despairing man is obsessed by his situation, closed in on himself, isolated from others. Finally, despair tends to transcend the particular context within which it has arisen and to pronounce on the meaninglessness of all that is, on the futility of life as a whole.

Now we must ask how we can understand hope in so far as it is an active battle against the sort of immobilizing self-dissolution that is despair. What, then, is the object of hope and what are the characteristics of hope?

The object of hope

Paradoxically the object of hope is not an object, if by 'object' we understand an empirical object or a definite and specific goal that can be characterized as 'such and such'. Referring to his 'Phenomenology and Metaphysic of Hope', Marcel says that his aim was to discover how a subject, in his actual capacity as subject ...

is related to a reality which cannot in this context be regarded as objective, yet which is persistently required to be recognized as real. Such inquiries could not be carried out without going beyond the kind of psychology

[28] Gabriel Marcel, *Presence et Immortalité*, Flammarion, Paris, 1959, p. 181 (personal translation).

which limits itself to defining attitudes without taking their bearing and concrete intention into account.[29]

He is concerned to elucidate the bearing and concrete intention of hope in its most ultimate and unconditional sense. The aim of the phenomenological analysis is to discover 'what is the nature of the affirmation that is at the heart of hope and also what is not so much its *object* but its *visée*.'[30] Hope in its fullest sense, transcends any determinate object, any particular image or representation. What, then, is it directed towards: Is hope, Marcel asks, a solution of our difficulties in this world? Or is it, on the contrary, directed to a development in the unseen which will perhaps take its start only after death?[31]

> In the first case there is always the danger that hope will meet with the direst disappointment; in the second, it passes into the sphere of the unverifiable; we shall always be entitled to see in it a mere mystification, even a sheer swindle.[32]

Marcel thus clearly sees the difficulties in his theory of hope— possible disappointment in this world and complete unverifiability in the next.

Let us first look at hopes in this world. If, as Marcel says, hope is not *essentially* to *hope that*, can it sometimes be a specific object? Surely Marcel's own examples allow for this—he speaks of the prisoner who hopes for deliverance, the sick man for restoration of health, the patriot for the liberation of his country, and so on. There are two ways of dealing with this difficulty. One is to point out that Marcel does allow for a scale of hope, admitting of various degrees, with transcendent or unconditional hope at the top of the scale. He refers to the 'coarser forms of hope' giving as an example 'hope of winning the top prize'.[33] Does not this example invalidate Marcel's whole position? Not if we realize that he has allowed for the possibility of the degradation of hope into desire when it fixes on a specific object. Our forms of speech retain the use of 'hope language' when perhaps in Marcel's terms they should be using 'desire language'. Since Marcel's concern is to clarify unconditional or transcendent hope, a different example will serve us better.

[29] *Philosophy of Existentialism*, p. 127.
[30] 'Structure de l'espérance', p. 53.
[31] Gabriel Marcel, *The Mystery of Being*, Vol. II, *Faith and Reality*, transl. R. Hague, Henry Regnery, Chicago, 1960, p. 181.
[32] *Ibid.*
[33] *Being and Having*, p. 94.

Marcel takes the example of a mother who persists in hoping that she will see her son again, although his death has been certified in the most definite manner by witnesses who found his body, buried it, etc.[34] Is not the mother's hope, in this case, illusory and irrational? First of all, Marcel maintains that no observer has the right to pass such judgment, to deny to the mother her right to hope beyond the bounds of empirical evidence. Nevertheless, is not this example calamitous for Marcel's whole argument, in that the mother would seem to have a definite and specific hope? The second point he makes is crucial: it consists in examining what is the real 'intention' of hope in this case. If the mother said 'It is possible that John will come back', meaning perhaps 'he will one day come walking through the door, I will see him and touch him', then she has fixed her mind on a specific object, and in this case her hope is illusory and she is destined for disappointment and possibly despair. But in believing that she will see her son again, in affirming that his loss is not absolute, what is she really saying? She is not talking in 'the language of prevision or making a judgment based on probabilities'.[35] What she is affirming is the indestructibility of the living bond of love that links her with her son. Her hope is 'for a communion of which [she] proclaims the indestructibility'.[36] She hopes unconditionally, and her hope amounts to a denial of the ultimacy of death. Thus hope, 'by a *nisus* which is peculiar to it, tends inevitably to transcend the particular objects to which it first seems to be attached'.[37] Marcel's phenomenological analysis of the unconditional hopes that are found in experience has elucidated the 'structure' of such hopes, namely the 'concrete intention' of the experience.

Marcel's second way of dealing with the difficulty concerning the specific object of hope is as follows. He states that even where hope is apparently for some specific object or state, such as recovery of health, or deliverance, it refuses to dwell on a particular image or representation. Let us take the case of a man who hopes to recover from a serious, even an incurable, illness. The image he might fix on could be that of himself as a healthy man in, say, a year's time. In this case, Marcel explains, there are two psychological mechanisms at work: if one is hope of recovery strong enough to

[34] *Homo Viator*, p. 65.
[35] *Ibid.*, p. 66.
[36] *Ibid.*, p. 66.
[37] *Ibid.*, p. 32.

become a positive expectation, the other (because it has fixed on a definite image) must be moving the man towards despair if he is not cured at the appointed time. If the illness is, in fact, incurable, then his hope is an illusion and despair is the more likely outcome. How can non-illusory hope be possible in this case? Here hope, says Marcel, seems to be bound up with a method of surmounting.

> From the moment when he will not only have recognized in an abstract manner, but understood in the depths of his being, that is to say, *seen*, that everything is not necessarily lost if there is no cure, it is more than likely that his inner attitude towards recovery or non-recovery will be radically changed; he will have regained liberty, the faculty of relaxing.[38]

Such a hope is a transformation of the hoped-for. Marcel seems to argue here that whereas hope arising from a specific wish may be illusory, true hope involves a deeply-felt personal insight that non-fulfilment of a specific wish is not what would matter most. The 'I hope that ...' is transformed in this process of interiorization into an absolute 'I hope' which is beyond all conditions and all representations. The transformed object of hope cannot now be specified. The 'integrity of the organism', which was originally hoped for, is as it were 'the prefiguring or symbolical expression of a supreme integrity.'[39] We might say that the person has undergone a spiritual transformation, where not bodily integrity but spiritual integrity is his concern. If this spiritual integrity takes refuge out of the body in a super-terrestrial salvation, is this not a 'treason from above'[40]—this placing of hope in an unfalsifiable position, in a zone of 'absolute metaphysical security'?[41] Ricoeur, in his book on Marcel, maintains that the transformation of the object of hope is not an escape from the dilemma—either bodily recovery or spiritual salvation:

> It is this dilemma between a wholly spiritual salvation and the restoration of a completely carnal order that hope refuses, by the undifferentiated appeal which it makes within the world and at the same time out of the world; it transcends all possible causalities, it is ready for anything, it awaits—in the very trial itself and along the margins of reality that scientific foresight does not allow for—a real though unpredictable break-through of which miracle is the limiting form.[42]

[38] *Homo Viator*, p. 46.
[39] *Being and Having*, p. 75.
[40] *Homo Viator*, p. 48.
[41] 'Structure de l'espérance', p. 51.
[42] Paul Ricoeur, *Gabriel Marcel et Karl Jaspers*, Editions du Temps Present, Paris, 1948, p. 310 (personal translation).

He concludes:

> One can understand this undividedness [*indivision*] of the *élan* of hope if one glimpses that to *transcend* the trial through recourse to the absolute is *also* to transform it interiorly, to *assume* it fully.[43]

Hope keeps all the possibilities open; it does not close the case on the basis of given evidence. In Marcel's view, this is not a mere 'wishful thinking'. The affirmation that is strong enough to overcome the temptation to despair, the evidence being what it is, requires a continuous engagement, a deliberate and sustained effort, which is far beyond the scope of any 'wishful thinking'— to transcend the trial is also to transform it interiorly, to assume it fully. The battlers live in hope, not the wishful thinkers!

It is this assuming of the trial that makes it impossible to describe hope as an evasion, an evasion that possibly characterizes certain types of philosophical optimism. The optimist who declares that everything will turn out for the best in the best of all possible worlds speaks from the point of view of the spectator, rather than the participator in life's tragedies. 'When we come down to a final analysis', Marcel says,

> ... the optimist, as such, always relies on an experience which is not drawn from the most intimate and living part of himself, but, on the contrary, is *considered from a sufficient distance* to allow certain contradictions to be ... fused into a general harmony. The optimist does not hesitate to extrapolate the conclusions which we are led to if only we are willing to consider things thoroughly, from a sufficient distance and over a wide enough stretch.[44]

This does not mean that the optimist cannot have genuine hope, but rather that hope can be understood only from within the experience itself, not through a theoretical detachment which absorbs contradictions 'into a general harmony'.

Absolute or unconditional hope transcends all particular objects. It is directed not to anything a person can have, but rather has to do with what a person *is*, with his fulfilment in being. If life is experienced as captivity, as an *épreuve*, then this fulfilment in being can be designated by the term 'salvation'. All hope, says Marcel, is hope of salvation.[45] Salvation can have no meaning except in a world which admits of real injuries[46], one in which despair is also

[43] *Ibid.*
[44] *Homo Viator*, p. 34.
[45] *Being and Having*, pp. 80 and 75; *Homo Viator*, p. 30.
[46] *Being and Having*, p. 75.

possible. If the ultimate 'object' of hope is salvation, we shall be able to fill in the content of the term—that is, what is meant by 'salvation'—only after we examine in more detail *how* hope transcends the trial.

J. Pieper's *Hope and History*[47] provides an interesting comparison with Marcel's view. Pieper describes the phenomenological analyses of the Heidelberg physician, Herbert Plügge, who in his clinic made very detailed studies of the psychological states of persons who were incurably ill or who had already attempted suicide. Plügge's analyses, like Marcel's, bring to light a difference between what are normally called hopes, hopes for specific objects (*espoirs*) and a 'different hope' (*espérance*). Plügge calls this 'different hope' the fundamental or genuine hope. This hope arises when all ordinary hopes have been disappointed; it is not a hope 'for something', but is hope *per se*. (This corresponds with Marcel's distinction.) Disillusionment, or disappointment of ordinary hopes, Plügge maintains, teaches us that

> salvation not only consists in something else entirely, but that we ourselves hope for this 'something else', hope for it with a far more vital and truly invincible force, and have always hoped for it. Disappointment then represents far more than the correction of an erroneous opinion. It represents liberation in a sense going far beyond the realm of cognition.[48]

Plügge says that possibly the experience of ultimate incurability enables the patient to experience freedom from the imprisonment of illness. Such freedom 'could not be attained before the collapse'.[49]

There are many parallels between this analysis and Marcel's. There is, however, one fundamental difference. I do not believe Marcel would maintain that absolute hope arises *only* out of the experience of disillusionment or despair although he maintains a close relationship between the two. Hope arises for Marcel only where the temptation to despair is *possible*; one has not necessarily succumbed to it.

Characteristics of hope
Hope arises out of an experience of 'captivity' where despair is possible. In the context of this basic situation, we can group together one set of the characteristics of hope that Marcel for-

[47] J. Pieper, *Hope and History*, Burns Oates, London, 1969.
[48] In Pieper, *op. cit.*, p. 26.
[49] *Ibid.*, p. 27.

mulates. They are humility, patience, non-acceptance and active waiting.

Humility is an intellectual modesty that refuses the fatalism of the judgment in adverse circumstances. The despairing man makes such a judgment as: 'There is nothing in the realm of reality to which I can give credit—no security, no guarantee.'[50] Hope refuses this statement of complete insolvency, not recognizing in itself the right to make such a judgment:

> On the level of judgment, it is quite certain that hope implies the refusal of fatalism, and in this respect it is a negation of a negation: even if the situation appears to me without issue, I do not recognize in myself the right to validate this appearance, to declare that, since the situation appears such to me, it is certainly so in fact. On the contrary I declare that this validation would be presumptuous.[51]

Hope's non-capitulation is a non-acceptance which is not revolt. It is, rather, a relaxation, as the hoping man adapts himself to the rhythm of the trial and treats it as an integral part of himself. Tension and stiffening (*crispation*), which are characteristic of the attitude of revolt, presuppose an attitude of fear that is foreign to hope. Far from capitulating before a '*fatum* laid down by the judgment'[52], the hoping man meets disaster with a non-acceptance of its finality. 'The refusal of fatalism becomes something active and positive, as if it pushed back certain limits, or as if it granted to certain favourable possibilities a vital space for development.'[53] Hope does not allow itself to pronounce on what the specific outcome will be. Even more, by pronouncing on the outcome, one prepares the conditions that bring it about. To declare that war is inevitable, for example, is to increase the chances of war.

If we introduce the element of patience into non-acceptance, Marcel says, we at once come very much nearer to hope.[54] Patience is a certain manner of adapting oneself to the duration of time. The impatient man attempts to compel time, to burn up time—witness the emphasis on speed for its own sake in modern life. The hoping man does not try to alter time's duration; he puts his confidence in a certain process of maturation in the temporal order, believing that reality is such that growth and development are possible. Patience, then, seems to suggest a 'certain temporal pluralism, a

[50] *The Philosophy of Existentialism*, p. 27.
[51] 'Structure de l'espérance', pp. 49–50.
[52] *Homo Viator*, p. 37.
[53] 'Structure de l'espérance', p. 50.
[54] *Homo Viator*, p. 39.

certain pluralization of the self in time'.[55] It therefore means allowing oneself to 'take one's time' so that this creative process may work. We can see that having patience with others includes allowing them to take their time in their own growth and development. The hope that includes patience positively fosters such a creative development in others, for 'experience undeniably shows that the hope we put in them can help to transform them.'[56] Patience with others thus reveals to us the secret of patience with ourselves.

> [Hope] is radically opposed to the act by which I despair of the other person, declaring that he is good for nothing ... That is, of course, the same despair which makes me proclaim that I shall never see the end of my captivity. It seems, strangely enough, that in hoping I develop in connection with the event, and above all through what it makes of me, a type of relationship, a kind of intimacy comparable to that which I have with the other person when I am patient with him.[57]

But patience, like hope, can be degraded when it is no longer creatively involved with the 'event'. 'Looked at from the outside', Marcel notes in his journal, 'patience reduces to passivity and hope reduces to desire.'[58] Hope can never be a passive waiting: the idea of inert hope seems to be a contradiction in terms. 'Hope underpins action and runs before it.'[59] It is much more bound up with life and action than with passive expectation. Hope is an active waiting for a future that is *open*, and it helps to prepare that future in some way by its very expectation of it. Hope is not capitulation (as with despair) but is an active waiting which is a patient non-acceptance of any determinisms.

We now move on to the characteristics that point most clearly to the metaphysical implications of hope. Marcel describes hope as trust in reality; it has a prophetic character that does not depend on categorized experience; it is rather a response to something that is offered to it; this response involves a mutuality between persons and is ultimately a response to a Thou. The hoping man has a

---

[55] *Homo Viator*, p. 40. In a conversation with Marcel in 1968, I asked if his philosophy of hope was, in fact, a disguised theology. Marcel insisted that his phenomenological analysis is quite apart from theology, especially since *he emphasizes the place of patience in hope* and the quite special relationship to time, to *duration*. He stated that he does not stand on theological grounds but on phenomenological.

[56] Gabriel Marcel, *The Existential Background of Human Dignity*, Harvard University Press, Cambridge, Mass., 1963, p. 148.

[57] *Homo Viator*, p. 40.

[58] *Being and Having*, p. 94.

[59] *The Philosophy of Existentialism*, p. 33.

basic assurance that reality in general contains a creative principle
and goes beyond the order of simple prediction. To hope is to
put one's trust in reality, *faire crédit à la réalite*.[60] Here is not the
place to ask the metaphysical question: has reality the characteristics
that Marcel assigns it? We are still at the phenomenological level,
examining the assurance that the hoping man experiences and which
enables him to hope invincibly.

> Hope consists in asserting that there is at the heart of being, beyond all
> data, beyond all inventories and calculations, a mysterious principle that
> is in connivance with me, which cannot but will what I will, if what I
> will deserves to be willed and is, in fact, willed by the whole of my
> being.[61]

In other words, reality corresponds to my demands, to my exigences, if these exigences are not superficial desires, but are constitutive of what I am ('come from the heart of my being'). As part
of reality, Marcel seems to imply, I am fundamentally related to it,
so that what makes me what I am cannot be completely unrelated
to what, in fact, *is*.

This argument of Marcel's is very similar to one used by Peter
Berger[62] and which he calls the 'argument from ordering'. Berger
maintains that within the empirically given situation, there are
'signals of transcendence' that do not depend, for their discernment,
on any 'special' experience but are incarnated in 'prototypical human
gestures'.[63] By prototypical human gestures, he means 'certain
reiterated acts that appear to express the essential aspects of man's
being.'[64] One of these is the very simple example of a mother's
assurance to a child, who wakes crying in the night, that everything
is all right, everything is 'in order'. Berger asks the question: Is the
mother lying to the child? If the 'natural', that is, the 'empirically
given' is the only reality there is, then the mother *is* lying to the
child, not consciously of course, but in the final analysis lying just
the same. Why? 'Because the reassurance, transcending the immediately present two individuals and their situation, implies a
statement about reality as such.'[65] The statement that 'everything
is all right, everything is in order' can be translated, Berger says,
into a statement of cosmic scope—'Have trust in being', or in

[60] *Being and Having* p. 74.
[61] *The Philosophy of Existentialism*, p. 28.
[62] Peter Berger, *Rumour of Angels*, Penguin, Harmondsworth, 1971.
[63] *Op. cit.*, p. 70.
[64] *Ibid.*, p. 70.
[65] *Ibid.*, p. 73.

Marcel's terms *'faire crédit a la réalité'*. At the core of our humanity, Berger maintains, we find an experience of trust in the order of reality. Thus man's ordering propensity implies a transcendent order, and each ordering gesture is a 'signal of transcendence'.[66] The parental role, therefore, is not based on a loving lie, but is a witness to the ultimate truth of man's situation in reality. This argument of Berger's almost exactly corresponds to Marcel's argument that trust in reality lies at the heart of hope.

Needless to say, there is no empirical method by which this hope can be tested since it is not confined to empirically testable experience. The notion of experience is itself ambiguous, according to Marcel. 'On the one hand there is an established and catalogued experience ... On the other hand, there is an experience in the making'[67] that does not necessarily rely on what has happened in the past. This is what Marcel means when he says that hope is *creative*; 'it is engaged in the weaving of experience now in process'[68]; it is not chained to the categories of past experience[69] as a basis for projecting into the future. Free from 'the calculation of possibilities on the basis of accepted experience[70], it can create its own experience afresh:

> In hoping, I do not create in the strict sense of the word, but I appeal to the existence of a certain creative power in the world ... Where, on the other hand, my spirit has been tarnished by catalogued experience, I refuse to appeal to this creative power, I deny its existence; all outside me, and perhaps within me (if I am logical) appears to me as simple repetition.[71]

The hoping man, therefore, is not chained down to the closed time of repetition which we saw to be the characteristic of despair. Despair, Marcel says, 'encloses me within time as though the future, drained of its substance and its mystery, were no longer to be anything but the place of pure repetition.'[72] If despair is in a certain sense the consciousness of time closed, hope appears as a 'piercing

[66] *Ibid.*, p. 74.
[67] *Homo Viator*, p. 51.
[68] *Ibid.*, p. 52.
[69] *The Philosophy of Existentialism*, p. 43.
[70] *Homo Viator*, p. 51.
[71] *Ibid.*, p. 52.
[72] *Ibid.*, p. 60.

through time', a 'kind of memory of the future.'[73] Let us examine this last striking phrase. Memory refers to the past, yet hope is a 'memory' of the future. This can only mean that my past experience holds within it the promise of what I hope for. Marcel, indeed, refers to those 'experiences of inner renewal'[74] when one is conscious of a creative power at work in one's life, which offer us as it were a token of reconciliation, a promise of restoration. This past is not the past that is in the record books, this future is not the future that is in the statistical tables. The future that is in the statistical tables is not the future at all: drained of its mystery and its substance, it is the time of pure repetition, based on the calculation of probabilities. Thus the relationship of hope to time is established in a curiously dialectical fashion: hope implies at once the idea of a return, of a restoration, and the expectation of pure nowness, unforeseeable and yet awaited. It appeals ingenuously to a 'certain creative power in the world'[75] on which it can rely since it considers that nothing is finished but the future lies open.

This is what Marcel means by the *prophetic* character of hope, understood as a 'kind of radical refusal to reckon possibilities.'[76]

> It is as though it carried within it as a postulate the assertion that reality overflows all possible reckonings; as though it claimed, in virtue of some secret affinity, to touch a principle hidden in the heart of things ... which mocks such reckonings.[77]

Beyond all probability, all statistics, 'I assert that a given order shall be re-established, that reality is on my side ... such is the prophetic tone of true hope.'[78] Hope refuses to rest all on the security of calculation, on the inventory approach to reality. Despair is the place where one can make an inventory, but being is beyond all inventories, reality overflows all possible reckonings.

At this point, we may well ask the question: is there no relation between hope and reasons for hoping? Can one hope when reasons

---

[73] *Ibid.*, p. 53. In 'Structure de l'espérance' Marcel fills out the content of this 'memory of the future': 'Hope transcends the ordinary or pragmatic (if I may so call it) opposition between the past and the future: what is hoped for is always in a certain sense of the past, inasmuch as paradise perhaps is of the past, but more profoundly it is of the future, for what has been lost could not simply be restored, but, rather, renewed and as it were promoted to a higher ontological dignity.' (p. 54)

[74] *Homo Viator*, p. 67.

[75] *Ibid.*, p. 52.

[76] *Being and Having*, p. 79.

[77] *Ibid.*, p. 79.

[78] *The Philosophy of Existentialism*, p. 28.

for hoping are insufficient or completely lacking?[79] The question is misleading, for it is posed from the viewpoint of an observer, even if it is I who am observing my own hope. To ask the question is to detach oneself in some degree from one's own hope. For if a person 'truly recognizes in all sincerity that these reasons are non-existent or insufficient, he himself admits that he does not really hope.'[80] In so far as he hopes, the question does not arise for him, for 'hope and the calculating faculty of the reason are essentially distinct.'[81] If he asks himself if he has reasons for hoping, he is entering into the process of a calculation of possibilities and to that extent he is not hoping.

Is hope then irrational or fideistic? Hope is irrational only in so far as the rational is identified with reflection on a world of objects. Such reflection on the grounds for hoping will turn only on empirical evidence that can be tested. Hope's intelligibility, Marcel says, is the 'very movement by which it challenges the evidence upon which men claim to challenge it itself.'[82] Hope is in a sense supra-rational; its intelligibility is immune to critique on the level of objective impersonal evidence, since it does not claim to be factual knowledge.

> There is room for hope when the soul manages to get free from the categories in which consciousness confines itself as soon as it makes a clear line of demarcation between what it knows for a fact on the one hand and what it wishes or hopes on the other. Perhaps hope means first of all the act by which this line of demarcation is obliterated or denied ... hope is a knowing which outstrips the unknown—but it is a knowing which excludes all presumption, a knowing accorded, granted, a knowing which may be a grace but is in no degree a conquest.[83]

Hope's intelligibility, therefore, is not expressed in an affirmation made in the void; rather 'at the root of hope there is something which is literally offered to us.'[84] This is the heart of the matter: Marcel has designated an 'experiential' source of hope. It is akin to the 'hold on the real at root of intelligence' for which no epistemology can account, for it continually presupposes it. 'It may be', Marcel says, 'that genuine hope always consists in awaiting a certain grace, the nature of whose power we may not clearly define to

[79] See *Homo Viator*, p. 63.
[80] *Ibid.*, p. 64.
[81] *Ibid.*, p. 65.
[82] *Ibid.*, p. 67.
[83] *Ibid.*, p. 10.
[84] *Ibid.*, p. 63.

ourselves, but to whose bounty we think we can assign no end. Hope is centred on our consciousness of this beneficent power.'[85]

The hope that looks to this 'beneficent power' sees itself as called to respond actively rather than to receive in a passive sense. I can refuse hope, I can refuse to give credit to reality, and in this sense hope depends on me. On the other hand, because it is something I receive, there is a real sense in which hope does not depend on me. Rejecting the ancient Stoic distinction between things that depend and those that do not depend on ourselves, Marcel states that hope transcends this opposition. Hope is the willed response to a reality which appears to it as 'gracious'. Hence it has affinities not with desire, but with the will and with freedom. Far from being a passive expectation of something desired, hope is 'the prolongation into the unknown of an activity that is central—that is to say, rooted in being.'[86]

A defence of hope, a case for the intelligibility of hope, must rest on the decision (as Sam Keen points out[87]) to accept the inner logic of the experience as cognitive. A theory of hope that treats it merely as a subjective disposition is dealing with hope from the outside, classifying it according to the categories of primary reflection. Hope by its inner logic is directed towards a 'beyond' which it regards as real. This ordination to the transcendent is in no way assimilable, in Marcel's view, to a subjective disposition: 'Wherever a subjective disposition exists, it is interpreted as the *sign* of a soul inhabited by hope.'[88] Hope, he says,

> can in no case be reduced to a simple interior disposition; I shall say that it is much more than a psychological state—and even that the psychological as such is perhaps incapable of discerning its nature—Hope is a life and, I might add, a radiant life [*une vie rayonnante*], not at all a life bent back on itself. This radiating aspect [*rayonnement*] is translated into relationships with the neighbour.[89]

Here we discover what Marcel regards as one of the most fundamental aspects of hope, namely its intersubjective character. Hope is always in some way related to a 'thou'. In this it differs from desire, which is egocentric, and from despair, which cuts itself off from relationships with others.

[85] *Being and Having*, p. 91.
[86] *The Philosophy of Existentialism*, p. 33.
[87] S. Keen, *Gabriel Marcel*, Routledge, London, 1966, p. 43.
[88] Gabriel Marcel, *Presence and Immortality*, transl. M. Machado, Duquesne University Press, Pittsburgh, 1961, p. 145.
[89] 'Structure de l'espérance', p. 79.

Hope is always linked to intersubjectivity and vice versa. Clearly this means that hope is always centred on a *nous*, on a living relation, and if we do not realize it, that is because all too often we use the word hope when it is really a matter of desire.[90]

As an example of this, Marcel goes back to the situation which occasioned many of his reflections on hope, the situation of prisoners in concentration camps during the last war. Not all of them would have been animated by hope; for a good many of them, their time in prison would have been a period of inert waiting, a dead time.

... let us even say a time of death, for each individual would have been literally decomposed into impotence and depression.[91]

But there were others who knew the active waiting that is characteristic of hope. What is it that would have enabled these prisoners to wait actively, to retain their hope in spite of external restraints and even dehumanizing conditions? It was, Marcel says, because it was 'a hope for all of us, a hope which went far beyond the desire which each one could feel for himself.'[92] Because they hoped, they 'remained open to one another; a real communion was established among them.'[93] Hope, therefore, seems to involve a spiritual bond in which there is mutual interaction: hope generates openness to others or communion with them; reciprocally, this communion itself generates a hope that keeps the soul in a sort of active readiness to believe, trust, take action, overcome despair.

If hope is generative of action this is primarily because it creates or implies a communion, and this word should be taken in its strongest sense. If a real bond is established between me and my companions in captivity ... a 'we' is constituted, which is not simply the functional we of the crew, but rather an interiorized, spiritualized expression of it.[94]

Marcel believes that hope is impossible for the isolated consciousness. On the basis of the example he has given of prisoners inspiring hope in one another and being themselves inspired to hope as a result, he states that a 'spiritual economy' has been established that

[90] 'Structure de l'espérance', p. 52.
[91] 'Desire and Hope' in *Existential Phenomenology, op. cit.*, p. 282.
[92] 'Structure de l'espérance', p. 52.
[93] 'Desire and Hope', p. 282.
[94] *Ibid.* In this article, Marcel gives a commonplace enough example of the sort of external activity in which the underlying 'active waiting' of hope would have expressed itself. In the concentration camps, those who had faith and hope 'must have constituted frequently, and perhaps in the majority of cases, the centre around which the cultural life of the camp (lectures, theatrical productions etc.) was organized.'

changes for each one the value of his own existence and involves him in the fate of his brothers. This is true, Marcel believes, with a universal truth that overflows the particular example chosen.

In *Homo Viator*, he speaks of a 'spiritual interconnection' which confers meaning and value on human existence:

> We are not dealing here with an abstraction, an impersonal order: if I inspire another being with love which I value and to which I respond, that will be enough to create this spiritual connection. The fact of the reciprocal love, the communion, will be enough to bring about a deep transformation in the nature of the bond which unites me to myself ... we might say ... that my relationship to myself is mediated by the presence of the other person.[95]

Hope and love are intimately connected. Hope is not only an interior resource, it is a gift from another. We can speak of hope, Marcel says, only where 'the interaction exists between him who gives and him who receives, where there is that exchange which is the mark of all spiritual life.'[96] In the example given of prisoners, for example, for each one of them isolation and despair were possible:

> When I am alone and on trial, or more exactly when I treat myself as alone or on trial, the question of knowing what will happen to me seems almost bare of interest or significance ... It is not the same if I know that in one way or another the one I love depends on me, is vitally affected by my fate.[97]

The 'one I love' need not refer to the other prisoners, even though a level of communion has been established among them, but to the 'someone' or 'someones' who are waiting for me at home. Completely isolated from any attachment to anybody or anything, man has little reason to hope. Hope, Marcel says, is primarily centred on a 'we' and not an 'I'.

The hoping man is *disponible*, open to others. The more *indisponible* a man is, the less room there is for hope in him. *Disponibilité* 'is realized not only in the act of love but also in the act of hope'[98], so that the hoping man is at the same time the most fraternal, for to love one's brothers is at the same time to have hope in them.'[99]

---

[95] *Homo Viator*, p. 49.
[96] *Ibid.*, p. 50.
[97] 'Desire and Hope', p. 283.
[98] *Creative Fidelity*, op. cit., p. 47.
[99] *The Existential Background of Human Dignity*, op. cit., p. 147; cf. *Homo Viator*, p. 49.

Isolated, man is delivered to despair believing himself fixed in the inner determinism of closed time.

Disponibilité therefore takes on a double significance: it is not only openness to the other person, it is a sort of cosmic openness to reality as a whole, an openness that discovers on the 'borders of experience, all manner of alliances, all manner of promises of a deliverance, of a dayspring beyond our power to imagine.'[100] Being open-minded, hope is intrepid; it is intrepidity itself for 'inevitably laying itself open to mockery, even to the sarcasms of those who base their invariably discouraging forecasts on carefully catalogued precedents'[101]; it nevertheless 'with scandalously care-free grace' undertakes to take its stand against these assertions. Hope, Marcel says, is identical with [*se confond avec*] open thought at its extreme point of dilatation[102]; as such it stands against all *isms*, whatever they be, in which thought encloses itself to ostracize contrary positions.

> I draw from this the surprising conclusion that any ideology whatever is invariably turned against hope, even if in appearance it adopts its language, for there is in every ideology something that is turned against love, but love and hope are one.[103]

If we hear here an echo of Marcel's critique of the 'spirit of abstraction' and of the 'fanaticized consciousness', that is not surprising. What is interesting is that there seems to be emerging a relationship between the openness of hope, the openness of thought and Marcel's epistemology of mystery. The 'intelligibility' of hope consists in opening the system of closed thought. Summing up the essential elements of his phenomenology of hope, Marcel concludes his essay with a definition that brings together the points made in this paragraph.

> Hope is essentially the availability of a soul which has entered intimately enough into the experience of communion to accomplish the act transcending the opposition between will and knowledge—the act by which it affirms the vital regeneration [*perennité vivante*] of which this experience affords both the pledge and the first fruits.[104]

If the 'object' of hope is salvation, and if hope and love are strictly related, then hope demands the '*perennité vivante*' of a communion of love.

---

[100] *Being and Having*, p. 138.
[101] 'Structure de l'espérance', p. 53.
[102] *Homo Viator*, p. 51.
[103] 'Structure de l'espérance', p. 55.
[104] *Homo Viator*, p. 67. (I have revised the translation of this key text.)

The ultimate and authentic formula for hope is, according to Marcel, 'I hope in thee for us.'

> 'In thee—for us': between this 'thou' and this 'us' which only the most persistent reflection can finally discover in the act of hope, what is the vital link? Must we not reply that 'Thou' is in some way the guarantee of the union which holds us together, myself to myself, or the one to the other, or these beings to those other beings? More than a guarantee which secures or confirms from outside a union which already exists, it is the very cement which binds the whole into one.[105]

The passage from giving 'credit to reality' to discovering a 'thou' at the heart of reality has been effected *via* reflection on the relationship between love and hope. Notice that Marcel says that 'only the most persistent reflection' can finally discover the Thou who is the transcendent source and guarantee of absolute hope. The phenomenology of hope reveals an unconditional element at the heart of hope, a demand that love should have an absolute foundation. Since hope seeks its fulfilment in love, then hope also requires faith in an absolute Thou who secures and confirms the communion of love. In hope, love and faith are united.

Marcel's last word on hope is that hope is a risk, but not to hope is riskier still. 'Unhope' leads to despair and despair is the ultimate undoing.

> Perhaps the human condition is characterized not only by the risks which go with it and which after all are bound up with life itself ... but also, and far more deeply, by the necessity to accept these risks and to refuse to believe that it would be possible ... to succeed in removing them. Experience teaches us ... that we can never refuse to take risks except in appearance, or rather, that the refusal itself conceals a risk which is the most serious of all.[106]

The hoping man, therefore, like the hero in Marcel's play *L'émissaire* is *Homo viator* who can only say that in life's journey we are on the way to a goal that we both see and do not see. If we saw perfectly clearly, we would not hope; conversely, if we did not see at all we could not hope. In either cases we would be immobilized. It is hope that makes the journey more than a mere wandering, and establishes man's status as that of *Homo viator*.

[105] *Homo Viator*, pp. 60–61.
[106] *Ibid.*, p. 55.

Genesis of Hope:
The Case of Alcoholics Anonymous

Ross Fitzgerald

There is no more despairing human being than the obsessional alcoholic condemned by a condition of mind and body to continue to drink. Despite knowing the disastrous consequences involved in drinking, time and time again the alcoholic of whatever class or station will resort to alcohol. This is often directly against the person's will and contrary to promises sincerely made to the self and others. Sometimes, however, alcoholism has a human being so much in its grip that although the complaint may be obvious to others, the alcoholic cannot see the nature of his or her condition or the possibility of a way out. So strong is the process of denial that often alcoholics are the last to realize that drinking is a problem, if they come to this realization at all.

Alcoholism is the third greatest killer in the Western world and the physical and psychic damage it inflicts on individuals, families and society is incalculable. Although the percentage of alcoholics who recover is still pitifully small, almost all of them have done so via Alcoholics Anonymous. This informal, non-professional fellowship keeps no official records. However, it is estimated that A.A.'s programme of recovery has helped more than a million men and women in more than 30,000 groups throughout the world to lead healthy and productive lives without the need to use alcohol or other drugs.[1] Coming from every walk of life, these people have usually resorted to numerous 'remedies' and tried many other forms of treatment before contacting Alcoholics Anonymous, which remains the place of last resort for many compulsive drinkers.

In the health care field A.A.'s success is an amazing achievement by any standards. Yet despite increasing acceptance within the medical and nursing professions, A.A. is still unfashionable in psychiatric circles and its recovery programme has seldom been subject to detailed scrutiny. The aim of this essay is to explore the therapeutic mechanisms of Alcoholics Anonymous in order to explain why and how it is that a very large number of despairing, hopeless people have, by their participation in A.A., come to lead lives free of the compulsion to drink and characterized by hope and a sense of meaning.

The illness of alcoholism

Since its inception, A.A. has regarded alcoholism as an illness. While the 'disease concept' of alcoholism unfortunately is still not universally accepted in medical circles, A.A. treats alcoholism as fundamentally a health problem and not a moral problem or a question of willpower. Just as there is no point in blaming the victim of diabetes or cancer for a lack of willpower or moral fortitude in becoming ill, it is useless to condemn an alcoholic for his illness or to regard alcoholic drinking as a vice. The alcoholic is a sick person, not a bad or weak one.

While there is no formal 'A.A. definition' of alcoholism, most members agree that for them, when they were drinking, the disease could be most simply described as a physical compulsion coupled with a mental obsession to drink. In A.A. the alcoholic is regarded as suffering from a progressive illness for which there is no known cure—that is, no cure in the sense that he or she will ever be able to drink moderately or socially for any sustained period. However, while the illness cannot be 'cured', like some other illnesses (most notably diabetes) the disease can be arrested if the alcoholic can learn to abstain completely from alcohol in any form.

Despite a host of conflicting theories, how and why alcoholism begins is still not known, but later adult relationships apparently have little effect on its severity or progression. It now seems clear

---

[1] This estimate, given by the Central Service Board of Alcoholics Anonymous, New York, in a personal communication to the author, 21 April 1978, is supported by World Health Authority figures.

that the alcoholic, once he or she becomes an alcoholic, is physio-logically different from moderate or social drinkers, but nobody is certain of the cause (or of the relative importance of genetic and environmental factors). A.A. suggests that as far as recovery is concerned the causes of alcoholism are unimportant and indeed that searching for causes could well be counterproductive. What matters is not what may have precipitated the condition, but whether one is an alcoholic *now* and whether one wants to do something about it—namely stopping drinking. This (existential) approach is quite different from the classic psychoanalytical approach, for example, which falsely believes that once the alcoholic has uncovered and come to terms with the underlying cause(s) of his or her condition, then he or she will be able to drink in a moderate or controlled manner. While the latter approach may sound theoretically promising, it has proved disastrous in practice.

A.A. regards all forms of alcoholism as being manifestations of the one disease, despite the differences in alcoholic drinking patterns. Some A.A. members drank in an out-of-control fashion from their very first drink. Others slowly developed after many years of controlled social drinking to compulsive alcoholic drinking. Some alcoholics are daily drinkers. Others can abstain for periods ranging from days to months or years. But once they start again their drinking becomes uncontrolled. The latter are called 'periodic' or bender drinkers. Some alcoholics drink only beer, while others will literally drink anything. Many members of A.A. had been drinking only for a few years or only relatively small quantities of alcohol, but they soon found themselves as helpless as those alcoholics who had been drinking for thirty years or who drank copious amounts. It is not the quantity of alcohol consumed, but the effect that determines whether one is alcoholic.

Some alcoholics have been committed many times to jails and mental hospitals, while others have never lost a day's work and arrive at A.A. with their families and occupation intact. Because the illness progresses in stages, some alcoholics show more extreme symptoms than others, but in A.A. language they are all equally alcoholic. If a person is alcoholic and continues to drink, over any considerable period the condition gets worse, never better. Despite some current claims of behavioural therapists to 'train' problem drinkers to drink moderately, no reliable evidence whatsoever exists that any real alcoholic (as opposed to the heavy drinker) has been able to return, for long, to normal social drinking. Once a problem drinker has crossed over the line from controlled drinking into the state of compulsive alcoholism, there is no way that that person can *ever* regain control of his drinking. If the person is to recover, the alcoholic must face the fact that he cannot drink normally and that he can no longer safely take even one drink.[2]

Because the alcoholic is physically and mentally different from his fellows, A.A. suggests that it is the first drink, not the fifth or the fifteenth one, that does the damage. Just as when sugar enters the diabetic's system, his metabolism craves more sugar, so when alcohol (in any form) enters the alcoholic's system, a craving mechanism develops, sometimes quickly, sometimes over a long period, over which the alcoholic's will is powerless. And because alcoholism is an illness of the whole person, in an alcoholic the physical compulsion is coupled with a mental obsession to drink. This is why some time after taking the first drink the alcoholic is forced to continue, despite the consequences. Some alcoholics can *appear* to get away with controlled drinking for a time. But just as with those addicted to other drugs, uncontrolled drinking can always be traced back to the first intake of alcohol—the alcoholic's primary drug of addiction. A.A. has a way of expressing this: For an alcoholic, one drink is too many and a hundred are not enough.

The alcoholic must therefore learn to stay away from the first drink. But bitter experience with thousands of alcoholics of all types strongly suggests that knowledge on its own is not enough to change or remedy the situation in any lasting fashion. Just as the classic psychoanalytical fallacy is that once the alcoholic *knows* why he acts in such a self-sabotaging manner he will cease so to act, so a common rationalist fallacy is that once a person *knows* he is an alcoholic he will simply stop drinking. The facts of the matter are otherwise. With hardly an exception the alcoholic (whatever his degree of enlightenment, standard of education or personal resolve) is absolutely unable to stop drinking, and stay stopped, on the basis of self-knowledge and willpower. The alcoholic, with extremely rare exceptions, cannot recover alone.

---

[2] See, for example, Harry M. Tiebout, 'The role of psychiatry in the field of alcoholism, with comment on the concept of alcoholism as symptom and disease', *Quarterly Journal of Studies on Alcohol*, 12, 1, 1951, pp. 52–57; and J. Ross, 'Alcoholics Anonymous: A Neglected Adjunct to Hospital Treatment', *Kansas Medical Society Journal*, Vol. 66, January 1965, pp. 23–27.

During their drinking days many alcoholics make numerous promises never to drink again. Almost universally the results are not lasting. In contrast to the notion of not drinking for ever, the A.A. approach is based on the idea that virtually every alcoholic, at one time or another, has gone for at least 24 hours without a drink. Consequently it is suggested that A.A. members do not swear off alcohol for ever or for any other extended period, but rather that they try staying sober *today*—during *these* 24 hours. A.A.'s suggested method of not drinking is again an existential one of concentrating on not taking one drink just for today, or, if initially this is too difficult to manage, on not drinking for this hour, or on not drinking *now*, this minute.

However, while this one-day-at-a-time idea is an extremely useful technique, recovery almost always requires the help of others, and especially of others fundamentally like oneself.[3] Thus regular attendance at A.A. meetings, where members share their experiences with each other, plays an essential part in the continued sobriety of most alcoholics. In every A.A. meeting, the suffering alcoholic can see living examples that the A.A. recovery programme works. In these meetings he can see and hear for himself how other alcoholics have managed to get well, no matter what their particular background or drinking pattern may have been. A.A. experience has shown that however 'hopeless' the new member may seem, or however far down the ladder of alcoholism drinkers may have gone, very few have passed beyond the hope of recovery in A.A.— that is, providing they *want* to stop drinking.

The structure of A.A.
The nature of the A.A. fellowship goes a long way to explaining its unique success with alcoholics. As in its beginning in May 1935— when Bill W., a New York stockbroker, regarded six months earlier as a hopeless alcoholic, met Dr Bob S., an Akron physician, also considered to be a hopeless case—one alcoholic helping another

---

[3] The notion of a fellowship of those who have had similar experiences, and the just for today/day-at-a-time idea, also applies to all the offshoots of A.A. (for example, Narcotics Anonymous, Gamblers Anonymous, Drugs Anonymous, Overeaters Anonymous) which have also adopted A.A's 12 suggested steps of recovery.

remains the basic foundation of the fellowship.[4]

The most useful brief description of what Alcoholics Anonymous is and what it does is this short 'preamble', usually read at the beginning of every A.A. meeting:

> Alcoholics Anonymous is a fellowship of men and women who share their experience, strength and hope with each other that they may solve their common problem and help others to recover from alcoholism.
>
> The only requirement for membership is a desire to stop drinking. There are no dues or fees for A.A. membership; we are self-supporting through our own contributions.
>
> A.A. is not allied with any sect, denomination, politics, organization or institution; does not wish to engage in any controversy; neither endorses nor opposes any causes. Our primary purpose is to stay sober and help other alcoholics to achieve sobriety.[5]

What A.A. does not do is equally as instructive as what it does. Contrary to some misconceptions, it does not furnish initial motivation for alcoholics to stop drinking, solicit members or try to persuade anyone to join A.A. The movement is in no way opposed to the consumption of alcohol in the community at large. What other people do with regard to drinking is of no concern to A.A. members. In A.A., no membership records or case histories are kept, and no attempt is made to follow-up or control those who attend A.A. meetings. Apart from the above, A.A. does not engage in or sponsor research; make medical or psychological diagnoses or prognoses; provide drying-out or nursing services, hospitalization, drugs, or any medical or psychiatric treatment; offer spiritual or religious services; engage in education or propaganda about alcohol; provide housing, food, clothing, jobs, money or any other welfare or social services; or provide domestic or vocational

---

[4] After the meeting of Bill and Dr Bob, it became apparent that one alcoholic, talking about his own experiences and relating how he had become sober, could help another to stop drinking, even those that seemed, to medical authorities and to themselves, to be beyond help. In 1939 when the movement numbered a little more than 100 they put together a record of what had happened to them and what they found necessary for themselves to do in order to get and to remain sober. This record was a book entitled *Alcoholics Anonymous* from which the fellowship got its name. The foreword to the first edition of the book began as follows: 'We, of Alcoholics Anonymous, are more than 100 men and women who have recovered from a seemingly hopeless state of mind and body.' See *Alcoholics Anonymous: The story of how many thousands of men and women have recovered from Alcoholism*, third edition (new and revised), Alcoholics Anonymous World Services Inc., New York, 1976.

[5] The A.A. Preamble is reprinted with permission of the A.A. Grapevine Inc., copyright owners.

counselling. An individual may do some of these things on a private basis, but this is not part of his A.A. membership. Many professionals in the field of alcoholism are also members of A.A.; their professional work, however, is quite separate from their A.A. membership.

It is crucially important to emphasize that the *only* requirement for A.A. membership is a desire to stop drinking. And nothing more. A.A. demands no dues or membership fees and asks no pledges or personal commitments of any kind. A.A. is open to anyone with a drinking problem and no person of whatever type of background who desires to stop drinking can be excluded or barred from the fellowship. Membership in A.A. is purely personal and is essentially a subjective experience. The common expression of this is 'Anyone is a member who says he is'. No one can dispute the membership of another, for in A.A. the individual diagnoses himself as being alcoholic. No one else has the authority to say that one is, or one is not, alcoholic.

A key characteristic of this loosely knit anarchistic fellowship is that there are no bosses, or privileged classes or hierarchies. In A.A. no one is 'above' or 'below' anyone else. There are no formal officers with any governing power or authority whatsoever and no one is empowered to speak 'for' the movement. A.A. is therefore not an organization in the usual sense of the word. Instead it is a fellowship of persons with a common problem where everyone calls everyone else by their first name. If they want to, members take turns doing the services needed for group meetings and other functions (for example, being secretary, opening the mail, paying the rent, making tea or coffee) but for these temporary duties no particular professional skill or education is needed or required.

A.A. remains staunchly unaffiliated with medicine, religion, politics, lay foundations or government sponsors. Not only does it not accept money for its services, it refuses to accept any donations or contributions from non-A.A. sources and even limits the amount that members themselves can bequeath to the fellowship to 300 dollars. In A.A. there is no accumulation of money or property, no seniority and no experts on alcoholism.

In A.A., members do not *tell* other people what to do, but instead talk about themselves and about what *they* had to do in order to get and to remain sober.

In A.A. meetings and often in face-to-face encounters with new members, sober alcoholics relate their own personal experiences.

Usually they explain in a general way what they were like, what happened and what they are like now. The reason they talk about themselves and what they did is basically to reinforce their own sobriety, and in the hope that new persons can identify themselves as being alcoholic and see the possibility of recovery in A.A. Most importantly, A.A. doesn't tell people *not* to drink, but explains to the person who wants to stop drinking that they themselves try not to drink today. The prime suggestion is that the essential foundation of recovery is for an alcoholic not to pick up the first drink one day at a time.

The fact that no alcoholic person can be excluded from the fellowship, that there are no rules or coercive powers, and that no one tells anyone else what to do is especially important, given the personality characteristics of many alcoholics; defiance and rebelliousness being very much in the forefront.[6]

If you *tell* an alcoholic to do or not do something, the chances are that he will resentfully do the opposite. But when a recovered alcoholic talks about himself to a new person, a very special relationship of trust can develop. Unlike many members of his family (and often physicians, friends and employers as well) the sober alcoholic does not condemn the newcomer, and therefore is not threatening. Moreover the A.A. member seems to understand and accept him as he is. When sober members talk about their own alcoholic behaviour, the new person can identify himself with them and if, as is usually the case, they have had similar experiences, he can feel, often for the first time, that his own actions are not particularly unique or reprehensible. At an A.A. meeting, newcomers will often hear people talk about the very things they thought were unique to themselves and were afraid to tell anyone else—in particular their fears, anxieties and acts of irrationality and insanity. Moreover they can see that these people, fundamentally like themselves and who talk a language they understand, do not need to drink. This is why a sober alcoholic can win the confidence of a sick alcoholic when often a professional, no matter how studied or highly trained, cannot.

---

[6] Other personality characteristics common to many alcoholics are hypersensitivity, extreme egocentricity (that is, the make-up of a child who wants people to think his way and the world to be his way), extreme impatience, demand for instantaneous gratification of desire, very low tolerance of frustration or stress, and a high potential for entering dependency relationships. All of these, it might be noted, are infantile characteristics.

The discovery that the alcoholic is not alone, that he or she is not so unlike everybody after all, that there really are people who understand, is often an amazingly powerful therapeutic experience. At their very first contact many alcoholics sense, before they can articulate it, that they really do belong somewhere and that there is hope that they can get well. Apart from actual A.A. meetings, there is an extensive network of informal social contacts among A.A. members in which the newcomer can participate.

Acceptance by the self and others

Treatment of the alcoholic condition primarily involves not taking a drink or any other mood-changing drug. In practical matters, this means that alcoholics must take whatever steps are necessary, however radical, in order not to drink or to use any other drugs to which alcoholics, because of a physiological and psychological predisposition, readily become addicted. Alcoholic drinking for most alcoholics is part of a whole pattern of living and behaving. This consequently involves the alcoholic in changing his or her way of life and manner of dealing with situations if they are not to drink. It also means a radical change in the alcoholic's perception of the self and of others.

In terms of the self-perception of alcoholics when drinking, one personality characteristic stands out above all others. Despite their apparent surface differences (for example, extrovert, introvert, loud, quiet, rich, poor, etc.) a deeply felt sense of inadequacy and lack of worth seems always present in alcoholics by the time they arrive at A.A. While often confused with guilt and shame over drinking, and its secondary effects, this negative self-perception very often antedates drinking. In this sense many alcoholics are predisposed to alcoholism in terms of personality factors as well as of physiology. In such people earliest childhood memories frequently centre on themes of being unworthy, damaged, abandoned, or helpless. As Garitano and Ronall point out, often the alcoholic compensates for these feelings of inadequacy by 'ascribing to himself special qualities or talents, and by setting grandiose goals for himself to prove (his) worth ... However, vaguely aware of the discrepancy between these goals and his ability to perform, he is self-critical and easily discouraged. He is hypersensitive to criticism by others which he easily interprets as hostility, thereby proving to himself that others are against him. He suspects even praise and genuine concern, thus creating an ever-growing distance between himself and others, and between his wish to be acceptable to and accepted by others, and the possibility of its being fulfilled. He becomes less and less able to tolerate tension or to work steadily toward a goal. To insure himself against failures, he becomes increasingly passive. In short, [the alcoholic life style is typically one] of flight; from tasks, from others and eventually from oneself.'[7] Certainly by the time an alcoholic seeks out the help of Alcoholics Anonymous, almost invariably he or she has a deep problem with self-esteem. In many ways this negative self-perception can be changed by the understanding and acceptance of others in A.A. Many new members go to meetings on a daily basis, and to be accepted, indeed welcomed, as one is day after day, is a powerful first step to self-acceptance, esteem and the end of isolation. For this reason, and a host of others, one must never underestimate the therapeutic significance of attendance at A.A. meetings in the generation, and regeneration, of hope.

The thought of a life without alcohol is a terrifying prospect for most alcoholics. Many who tried to abstain on their own before coming to A.A. felt lost and stranded in what was perceived to be an empty and hostile universe. That is, the old feelings and perceptions of the self and others remained; indeed they were left in a more acute and disturbing form as the anaesthetizing effect of alcohol was withdrawn. The early period of adjustment to a life without alcohol (before the person has come to rely on the A.A. programme), is when the friendship and support of others in the fellowship is crucial.

The A.A. programme

While acceptance by others is extremely important, changing one's self-perception and way of life, so that the alcoholic will not have to drink again, involves action on the part of the alcoholic. Part of

---

[7] See W.W. Garitano and R.D. Ronall, 'Concepts of Life Style in the Treatment of Alcoholism'. *The International Journal of the Addictions*, Vol. 9, No. 4, 1974, pp. 588–92. The quotation is from p. 588. The authors correctly point out that, in treatment, 'alcoholism must be seen as the patient's primary problem, and not—as is so often the case—"only" as the presenting complaint and as a cover-up for the essential underlying pathology. This failure to give the alcoholism its proper weight has been one of the most frequent pitfalls of therapy. Only when the therapist himself is deeply convinced that the alcoholism is not "just a symptom", which somehow will disappear as the underlying neurotic problems are dealt with, can he hope to convey this to the patient.' pp. 589–90.

the recovery programme that A.A. suggests is set forth in the Twelve Steps which are listed in the appendix. Based on the experience of A.A.'s earliest members, the steps are a record of the principles and practices they developed, to gain and maintain sobriety, after many other approaches had failed. However, like everything else in A.A., the steps are not compulsory; they are suggested as a programme of recovery. Although experience shows that many A.A. members' continued sobriety depends, to a considerable extent, on their understanding and acceptance of the steps, no A.A. member is forced to accept—or even read—them. It is up to each individual to decide when and how the steps will be used.

Listening to other alcoholics relating their own personal experiences and explaining what they did in order to get and stay sober, allows the new member to realize that he too is an alcoholic and that he can get well. Hearing others talk about themselves, plus the realization that alcoholism is an illness, offers the new person an *explanation* for his past behaviour, indeed an explanation of the nature of himself. The act of *naming* himself an alcoholic gives the person a sense of identity. Coupled with the example of others fundamentally like himself, who no longer need to drink, the process of self-identification is itself a great source of hope. It is not accidental that in many societies, the act of naming has magical qualities attributed to it—that naming a thing or quality is an integral part of being released from its power. A.A. therapy keeps the name 'alcoholic' in the forefront. Thus at every A.A. meeting, each speaker will ritualistically begin by saying 'My name is---. I am an alcoholic.' Apart from self-identification, the goal of continued sobriety one day at a time and personal growth by way of the twelve suggested steps gives the alcoholic's life *meaning* and enables him to be *useful* in a unique way—to help others who are in a similar situation (just as he has been helped himself). But the success of A.A. is not simply to be explained by human beings sharing similar experiences. There is more to the movement than group therapy.

The A.A. programme emphasizes that continued abstinence (or sobriety as A.A. members prefer to call it) depends on a complete reorientation of the individual in which he sees society and himself in a different light, refracted through a quite different set of values, perceptions and criteria of judgement. This implies in effect some kind of fundamental psychic change that one can term a conversion experience, though not of the religious variety. It is therefore not surprising that many members regard their involvement in A.A. as comprising a way of life.

The mechanism of surrender

If there is any one aspect of the therapeutic process of Alcoholics Anonymous that best explains the transition from hopelessness to hope in alcoholic persons, it is what can most usefully be called the mechanism of surrender.[8]

Instead of telling the alcoholic to use his willpower, control his drinking or pull up his socks, A.A. suggests to the alcoholic that he give in and admit he is beaten. The shared experience of sober members strongly suggests that it is only by surrendering that the alcoholic is freed from the compulsion to drink.

By accepting defeat in depth, the alcoholic is able to undergo the psychic turn-about referred to above as a 'conversion experience', sometimes quickly, sometimes slowly. This major shift in attitude is able to unlock (psychic) forces which produce new positive affirmative feelings, especially hope.[9] Whereas before the shift the alcoholic is governed by a set of predominantly hostile, negative, self-punishing attitudes and feelings, afterwards the person develops a set of positive, affirmative feelings. This major shift may take place suddenly, or, most usually, it may occur slowly over a period of time. Almost always it is not consciously willed. But the act of surrender is the key to, and the source of, the conversion experience, without which it is highly unlikely that the alcoholic will maintain his sobriety. (As useful and important as

[8] The crucial importance of the act of surrender was documented early in A.A.'s history by Dr Tiebout. See Harry M. Tiebout 'Therapeutic Mechanisms of Alcoholics Anonymous', *American Journal of Psychiatry*, Vol. 100, 1944, pp. 468–73 and 'The Act of Surrender in the Therapeutic Process with Special Reference to Alcoholism', *Journal of Studies of Alcohol*, Vol. 10, 1949, pp. 48–58. See also Tiebout, 'Psychological Factors Operating in Alcoholics Anonymous', *Current Therapies of Personality Disorders*, ed. Bernard Glueck, Grune & Stratton, New York, 1946, pp. 154–65.

[9] The most important recent paper dealing with the shift in attitude consequent upon the acceptance of defeat is Gregory Bateson, 'The Cybernetics of "Self": A Theory of Alcoholism', in Gregory Bateson, *Steps to an Ecology of Mind: Collected Essays in Anthropology, Psychiatry, Evolution, and Epistemology*, Chandler Publishing Co., San Francisco, 1972, pp. 309–37. Bateson rightly points out that alcoholics who attempt to use 'self-control' to fight alcoholic addiction 'will not, or cannot, accept the premise that *drunk or sober*, the total personality of an alcoholic is an alcoholic personality which cannot conceivably fight alcoholism', p. 312, my emphasis.

they are, techniques like 'a day at a time', avoiding the first drink, etc., will not avail for long if the alcoholic has not accepted defeat.)

An example of the conversion shift is the disappearance or diminution of the tense, anxious, driven state so characteristic of the practising alcoholic. Other examples are the reduction of the manipulative and egocentric power drive, the disappearance of infantile rage and hostility, and the reduction of the perfectionist drive. Almost always there is a major shift in the feeling of guilt. Before the conversion the alcoholic is burdened by a sense of guilt, which can be called truly sadistic and punishing, whereas afterwards he is much more likely to regard himself (and other people) as human beings who are liable to err. Finally the defiant grandiosity, so typical of the drinking alcoholic, gives way to the reality of the situation and produces an acceptance of the need for help. In fact, the act of surrender can be viewed as a moment when the unconscious forces of defiance and grandiosity (and of denial) cease to function effectively. At that time the alcoholic sees himself as he actually is—helpless with regard to his disease.[10]

Surrender in A.A. is the acceptance of defeat. It involves the letting go of control. Thus at meetings of Alcoholics Anonymous, one often hears a speaker say 'I'm not a retired alcoholic, I am a defeated one. I've thrown in the towel.' To let go in surrender is totally different from fighting alcohol (or life). It is a giving up of the battle. Despair and hopelessness, not personal strength, is at its source.

The feeling 'I cannot go on', 'I've had it', is so very often an integral part of the crisis experience that leads an alcoholic to seek the help of A.A.—usually when all other avenues have failed. Rather than being denied, this feeling is reinforced by the first and most basic of A.A.'s Twelve Steps. The First Step reads: 'We admitted we were powerless over alcohol, that our lives had become unmanageable.'[11] It expresses with clarity the life experience of nearly all alcoholics by the time they reach A.A., and verbalizes a surrender at depth in which volitional consciousness plays a very small part. In terms of 'letting go', few alcoholics who have been released from the obsession to drink would agree that they could have made it happen or consciously willed it to happen themselves. The experience of letting go in surrender is not the 'doing' of anything, so

---

[10] See Harry M. Tiebout, 'Psychological Factors Operating in Alcoholics Anonymous', *Current Therapies of Personality Disorders*, pp. 154–65.
[11] See Appendix on p. 86.

much as it is a not doing. With regard to the alcoholic, it is a giving up. This shift from the level of 'making' things happen to the realm of allowing them to happen, is almost always part of the conversion change.[12] While the act of surrender cannot be consciously willed, the total experience of an A.A. meeting can, however, often induce a new member who has come to seek help to surrender.

In contrast to the false (Western) sense of self-power which suggests that the individual has (or should have) the 'will' or 'control' to fight the 'temptation', the first step demands that the alcoholic agree that he is powerless over alcohol. Acceptance of the first step represents a fundamental change in attitude. Moreover it is a change from an incorrect assessment of the situation ('I can fight the bottle') to a correct one ('I am beaten, I cannot overcome this on my own').[13] In A.A. language, the person has accepted the need for some power greater than himself. As will be stressed, the way in which this power is conceptualized is, in A.A., quite unimportant. What matters, if he is to remain sober, is that an alcoholic comes to rely on something other than his isolated ego. The Second Step reads: 'We came to believe that a power greater than ourselves could restore us to sanity.' Implicit in the combination of the first two steps of A.A., Bateson argues, is an extraordinary (and, he believes, a correct) idea: 'The experience of defeat not only serves to convince the alcoholic that change is necessary: it *is* the first step in that change. To be defeated by the bottle and to know it is the first "spiritual experience". The myth of self-power is thereby broken by the demonstration of a greater power (that is, alcohol).'[14]

Acceptance of defeat and the shift in psychological orientation consequent upon it have been basic pillars of A.A. from its beginning.

According to Bill W., the movement's co-founder, the chain of events that led to the foundation of Alcoholics Anonymous had its origin in 1932 in the Zurich office of Carl Jung, during a conversation the psychiatrist had with an American alcoholic named

---

[12] cf. Leslie H. Farber, *The Ways of the Will: Essays Toward a Psychology and Psychopathology of Will*, Constable Publishing Co., London, 1966, especially 'The Two Realms of Will', pp. 7–15.

[13] See Gregory Bateson, 'The Cybernetics of "Self": A Theory of Alcoholism', *op. cit.*, pp. 318–20.

[14] *Ibid.*, p. 313, his emphasis. A.A. employs the word 'spiritual' in the widest possible sense and draws a crucial distinction between 'spiritual' and 'religious'. As has been already noted A.A. is not associated with religion in any way.

Roland H. Instead of offering Roland any encouragement, Jung told his patient there was nothing he could do for him and stressed his utter hopelessness so far as any further medical or psychiatric treatment might be concerned. Coming from a physician he so much admired, the impact upon Roland was immense. When he then asked if there was any other hope, Jung told him that there was a possibility if he could become the subject of a spiritual experience. This, Jung pointed out, might change him when nothing else could. But he cautioned that while such conversion experiences had some-times brought recovery to alcoholics, they were indeed rare. The substance of Jung's advice was that Roland place himself in a religious atmosphere and hope for the best.[15]

As a result, Mr H. joined the Oxford Groups, an evangelical movement then at the height of its success in Europe. This move-ment, led by a one-time Lutheran Minister, Dr Frank Buchman, stressed meditation and prayer and emphasized the principles of self-analysis, confession, restitution and the giving of oneself in service to others. In this atmosphere Roland H. did find a conver-sion experience that temporarily released him from his obsession to drink. Feeling that he could especially help other alcoholics, Roland and another Oxford Grouper chanced upon an old school friend of Bill W's named Ebbie (Edwin T.) who had been threatened with life commitment to an institution. With Roland's help Ebbie became sober, also temporarily, with the Oxford Groups.

At this time (1934) Bill was threatened with permanent commit-ment himself. Fortunately he had fallen under the care of a phy-sician, Dr William Silkworth (of the Charles B. Towns Hospital in New York City), who had a great understanding of alcoholics. Bill had been dried out under his care a number of times. For years Dr Silkworth had been proclaiming alcoholism as an illness. It was his theory that alcoholism had two components—an obsession of

[15] Jung later wrote of Roland H. 'His craving for alcohol was the equivalent, on a low level, of the spiritual thirst of our being for wholeness, expressed in medieval language; the union with God ... You see, Alcohol in Latin is "spiritus" and you use the same word for the highest religious experience as well as for the most depraving poison. The helpful formula therefore is "spiritus contra spiritum".' Carl Jung to Bill W., 30 January 1961. (See 'The Bill W.–Carl Jung Letters', *The A.A. Grapevine*, Vol. 24, No. 8, January 1968.) By this time, Jung had come to believe that for an alcoholic, the ultimate sources of recovery are spiritual sources and are to be found in the conversion experience.
(Elsewhere Jung had written 'It is not through sheer perversity that the alcoholic pursues alcohol, for he finds in it a dim glimmer of the spiritual experience for which he so much hungers.')

the mind that compelled the sufferer to drink against his will and interest, and some sort of metabolism difficulty which he then called an allergy.[16] The latter, he suggested, explained the phenomenon of craving. Though initially he thought it possible to be of help, he was finally obliged to tell Bill of the hopelessness of his condition. To Bill this was a shattering blow. Just as Roland had been made ready for his conversion experience by Carl Jung, so had Dr Silkworth prepared Bill.

Bill left hospital and, despite all his efforts, drank again more compulsively than ever. Hearing of Bill's plight, Ebbie came to see him. Bill, who had long regarded Ebbie as a hopeless case, was tremendously convinced by his friend's obvious state of 'release' from alcohol. Because he was a kindred sufferer, Ebbie could communicate with him at depth in a way no other could.

Over and over, Ebbie repeated phrases like 'I found I couldn't run my own life.' 'I had to ask God for help even though I wasn't sure there was any God.' 'When I asked God's help, the craving for alcohol left.' Bill reports that Ebbie communicated these simple ideas with great clarity and force.

After another three weeks of uncontrolled drinking, Bill returned to hospital on 11 December, where he was again dried out. During his stay, Ebbie came to see him and again recounted his experience. Clear once more of alcohol, Bill found himself deeply depressed. The realization of the utter futility of his own efforts, Dr Silkworth's repeated message concerning the nature of his condition, coupled with his inability to gain the slightest faith, produced in Bill an emotional state of hopelessness that he later termed 'hitting bottom'.[17]

Bill reports that in utter despair he cried out for help: 'If there be a God, will he show himself.' There came upon him an experi-

---

[16] Technically this is a misuse of the term, but as a metaphor it does draw attention to the peculiar physiological/biochemical reaction of the alcoholic to alcohol, which is quite different to the non-alcoholic. Similarly, the diabetics' metabolism reacts atypically to sugar, the asthmatic to pollen, etc.

[17] The importance of the need for alcoholics to hit an emotional bottom as a prelude to recovery is now quite widely accepted. But at the time of A.A.'s formation, it was a revolutionary idea. Certainly the notion of letting an individual suffer until he cried for help had very little sanction in psychiatric circles. As Dr Tiebout explained, 'The psychiatrist was (perceived as) a source of love and support even though that support carried the (alcoholic) patient upright to his grave. For a psychiatrist to say "He has to hit bottom" was new and horrifying.' 'Alcoholics Anonymous: An Experiment of Nature', *Quarterly Journal of Studies in Alcohol*, Vol. 22, March 1961, pp. 52–68. The quotation is from p. 55.

ence of enormous impact and dimension which he describes in the language of mystical illumination. Immediately he was released from the alcoholic obsession and never drank again.[18] (He died in January 1971.)

Dr Silkworth took great pains to convince Bill that he was not hallucinated. The doctor said 'Something has happened to you I don't understand. But you had better hang on to it. Anything is better than the way you were.' Soon after, Bill read William James' *Varieties of Religious Experience* which had been left by his bed. The book confirmed the immense importance of what had happened to him. James explained that such spiritual experiences had transformed men and women so that they could do and feel what had hitherto been impossible to them. James said it mattered little whether these awakenings were sudden or gradual, their variety could be almost infinite. But to Bill the greatest point of contact with the book was that in most of the cases described those who had been transformed were hopeless people. In some controlling area of their life, they had met absolute defeat.

While in hospital, Bill decided to try to pass on this message to other suffering alcoholics, who in turn might help others. On his discharge, Bill devoted himself exclusively to 'saving' alcoholics, to the consternation of the Oxford Group. After six months of spiritual and moral exhortation, he met with no success at all. Almost to a person all the alcoholics he encountered found his emphasis upon 'spirituality' extremely disagreeable. But by working with other alcoholics he had remained sober. Dr Silkworth took Bill aside and suggested that, rather than stressing his spiritual experience, he first explain the fatal and progressive nature of his own condition and carry the news of the hopelessness of alcoholism to each new person.

---

[18] After seeing Bill's recovery, and that of a number of other alcoholics he had regarded as hopeless cases, Dr Silkworth became an enthusiastic supporter of A.A. and wrote a medical testimony to the first edition of the book *Alcoholics Anonymous* entitled 'The Doctor's Opinion'. Like Jung, by this time he became convinced of the alcoholic's need for a conversion experience. Thus he wrote ' . . . unless the (alcoholic) person can experience an entire psychic change, there is very little hope of his recovery.' In the same piece Dr Silkworth also expressed something that he had long been advocating: '(Alcoholics) cannot start drinking without developing the phenomenon of craving. This phenomenon . . . differentiates these people, and sets them apart as a distinct entity. It has never been, by any treatment with which we are familiar, permanently eradicated. The only relief we have to suggest is entire abstinence.' See *Alcoholics Anonymous*, third revised edition, 1976, pp. xxii–xxx.

Shortly thereafter, Bill found himself in Akron, Ohio, on a business venture which collapsed. Afraid that he would drink, he sought out another alcoholic. The person he found, a physician, was in a perilous condition. Dr Bob had also been in touch with the Oxford Groups, but all his attempts at staying sober had failed. When Bill, following Dr Silkworth's advice, told from his own experiences of the hopelessness of alcoholism, Dr Bob accepted defeat and after a brief relapse stayed sober until his death in 1950. In 1939 when his story appeared in the book *Alcoholics Anonymous*, along with the experiences of the first 100 members, Dr Bob put one paragraph of it in italics. Speaking of his meeting with Bill he said 'Of far more importance (than the medical information Bill gave) was the fact that he was the first living human with whom I had ever talked, who knew what he was talking about in regard to alcoholism from actual experience. In other words he talked my language.'[19]

The meeting between Bill and Dr Bob proved to them both that one alcoholic could affect another as no non-alcoholic could. Since May 1934, more than a million alcoholics have achieved sobriety in A.A. As has been seen, the foundation of this remarkable movement can be traced back to Carl Jung's consulting room where Roland was told of the physician's inability to help and that his only hope lay in some spiritual source.[20]

Although the notion is unpalatable to many alcoholics, it seems clear that if the alcoholic is to recover, he has to ask for the help of something other than his isolated self. The acceptance of defeat at depth is crucial. However, the initial act of surrender needs constantly to be reinforced or the alcoholic will revert to old ways of thinking, feeling and responding, and hence will eventually drink again. There is a pronounced tendency for alcoholics who have stopped drinking for a time to come to believe that they can manage their own affairs and that they can control their drinking. Alcoholic 'pride' suggests that the individual is not 'really' beaten. Instead of encouraging notions of 'self-sufficiency', 'self-reliance' and 'self-control', A.A. restructures the whole context and asserts over and over again that, with regard to alcoholism, the person is

---

[19] *Alcoholics Anonymous*, third edition, p. 180.
[20] For the history of the movement see *Alcoholics Anonymous*, especially Foreword and Chapter 1; *Alcoholics Anonymous Comes of Age* by a co-founder (Bill W.), Harper, New York, 1957; 'The Bill W.–Carl Jung Letters', *op. cit.*; and 'A Fragment of History' by Bill W., *A.A. Grapevine*, July 1953.

defeated. The A.A. proposition 'Once an alcoholic always an alcoholic' reinforces a fundamental fact. Thus in A.A., members never use the past tense about their alcoholism. No matter how long an alcoholic has been sober, he or she will always begin by saying 'My name is --- and I *am* an alcoholic.' Moreover, as opposed to placing alcoholism 'outside' the self (with the subsequent implication that the self can fight the problem), A.A. tries, as Bateson explains, 'to have the alcoholic place alcoholism within the self, much as a Jungian analyst tries to have the patient discover his "psychological type" and to learn to live with the strengths and weaknesses of that type. In contrast, the contextual structure of alcoholic "pride" places the alcoholism *outside* the self: *I* can resist drinking.'[21]

A.A.'s only theological conception is that of a Power greater than the self. This Power, however conceived, is intimately linked with each person. It is 'God as *you* understand Him to be'.

Just as the traditional stereotype associated with the word 'alcoholic' (often an old man in a raincoat drinking methylated spirits) blinds victims of the disease to the reality of their condition, so does the traditional stereotype associated with the *word* 'God' lead to confusion and resistance.[22] But once the deistic, Christian (or any other) stereotype is done away with, it becomes clear that the notion of a power greater than oneself makes room for all alcoholic persons, including atheists and agnostics, as long as they are willing to accept and rely on something outside or other than the self—if only the A.A. group. Conceptions of the nature of a power greater than oneself are as diverse as A.A. members, but all alcoholics who have been sober for any length of time would agree that when they were drinking, *alcohol* was certainly a power greater than themselves. Hence the need, in recovery, to seek the aid of some force or power outside the isolated self.

At some time during almost every A.A. meeting in the world, the new person will hear the following phrase: 'You may leave this meeting today (tonight) and need never drink again.' Often it is a conception that he or she has never considered before. The remarkable fact is that hundreds of thousands of alcoholic people have done just that; that is, if they are able to accept defeat and continue

---

[21] Gregory Bateson, 'The Cybernetics of "Self": A Theory of Alcoholism', *op. cit.*, p. 322. His emphasis.

[22] Typically the word/symbol for God is that which has no name, for example, Yahweh—the nameless one.

to surrender. It is my contention that all the elements that comprise A.A. (attendance at meetings, the notion of alcoholism as an irreversible condition, working with other alcoholics, the Twelve Steps) are part of a continual process of surrender which offers the alcoholic not only freedom from the obsession to drink, but a sense of meaning and an entirely new and positive way of life. 'Surrender to be Free' is an ancient spiritual truth. In A.A. the sources of hope, paradoxically, spring from an alcoholic's acceptance of the utter hopelessness of his or her condition and the need for the help of something other than the self. By accepting, at depth, one's individual powerlessness with regard to alcoholism, the alcoholic opens the way for the working of this power greater than the self. Maintenance of the state of self-surrender is at once the guarantee of personal recovery and the continuing mainspring of hope.

APPENDIX

The Twelve Suggested Steps of Alcoholics Anonymous

1. We admitted we were powerless over alcohol—that our lives had become unmanageable.
2. Came to believe that a Power greater than ourselves could restore us to sanity.
3. Made a decision to turn our will and our lives over to the care of God as we understood Him.
4. Made a searching and fearless moral inventory of ourselves.
5. Admitted to God, to ourselves and to another human being the exact nature of our wrongs.
6. Were entirely ready to have God remove all these defects of character.
7. Humbly asked Him to remove our shortcomings.
8. Made a list of all persons we had harmed, and became willing to make amends to them all.
9. Made direct amends to such people wherever possible, except when to do so would injure them or others.
10. Continued to take personal inventory and when we were wrong promptly admitted it.

11. Sought through prayer and meditation to improve our conscious contact with God, as we understood Him, praying only for knowledge of His will for us and the power to carry that out.

12. Having had a spiritual awakening as the result of these steps, we tried to carry this message to alcoholics, and to practice these principles in all our affairs.

The Twelve Traditions of Alcoholics Anonymous

1. Our common welfare should come first; personal recovery depends upon A.A. unity.

2. For our group purpose there is but one ultimate authority—a loving God as He may express Himself in our group conscience. Our leaders are but trusted servants; they do not govern.

3. The only requirement for A.A. membership is a desire to stop drinking.

4. Each group should be autonomous except in matters affecting other groups or A.A. as a whole.

5. Each group has but one primary purpose—to carry its message to the alcoholic who still suffers.

6. An A.A. group ought never endorse, finance or lend the A.A. name to any related facility or outside enterprise, lest problems of money, property and prestige divert us from our primary purpose.

7. Every A.A. group ought to be fully self-supporting, declining outside contributions.

8. Alcoholics Anonymous should remain forever nonprofessional, but our service centers may employ special workers.

9. A.A., as such, ought never be organized; but we may create service boards or committees directly responsible to those they serve.

10. Alcoholics Anonymous has no opinion on outside issues; hence the A.A. name ought never be drawn into public controversy.

11. Our public relations policy is based on attraction rather than promotion; we need always maintain personal anonymity at the level of press, radio and films.

12. Anonymity is the spiritual foundation of all our traditions, ever reminding us to place principles before personalities.

Hope for the Triumph of Truth about 'Life'

David Holbrook

Over the last decade it has been difficult to be hopeful about man's future. I switch on the radio and listen to the news. A nuclear satellite, put into space by the Russians, is about to fall, no one knows where. There are many of these objects in space, and the Americans confess to have lost one which caused world-wide radioactive pollution. In France, hundreds of thousands of tonnes of crude oil pollute the shores of Brittany. In France, too, the primary cause of death among young people is suicide. Everywhere terrorists deliberately attack and kill children, and set out to destroy democratic political life, as in Italy, by murders and kidnappings. In the world of culture, not only does one read of films showing the most extreme forms of sexual perversion, such as bondage and the mutilation of sexual organs, but liberal critics still continue to applaud such developments, and claim that we must have more of them, even as the consequences of this kind of pollution of consciousness become clear in hooliganism and vice. In sex clubs in America there are special floor areas where people can copulate in public; at parties in California not only 'pot' is handed round, but cocaine to sniff, as a matter of course. Yet people wonder at intellectual confusion and decline! Cuban troops gather in Ethiopia in tens of thousands, while the Soviet Union cynically exploits every episode in the world, from Northern Ireland to Rhodesia, indifferent to the consequences, so long as each episode takes Russia closer to world domination. Yet every university contains a large core of Marxists who continue to promote communist ideas without any reference to the Gulag, and the death and suffering of millions, under the righteous moral fervour of Marxism in action, which tortures and kills children in the Horn of Africa and continues to build up its armed forces everywhere. Crime rises at a disastrous rate in Britain while theft and fraud are now simply a way of life for the majority, it seems. 'Progressive' ideals go sour; enforced comprehensive education, without provision for special training for teachers, has undermined standards and contributed to social chaos; the health service is in difficulties; the economy is in decline. Unemployment stands at a million and a half, while five million is promised for the mid 1980s. Sexual casualties escalate as 'liberation' progresses: there are more rapes than ever, more divorces, more people with sexual diseases, more child prostitutes, more battered wives and babies. Under a socialist government, the Arts even though trivial and obscene, are given state support, while in education there is a new movement towards utilitarianism and formal instruction—to the danger of those genuine movements of the last three decades that sought a more humane content. In the field of ideas dogmatism and false polarisations are the order of the day, while dissent is suppressed.

How can anyone be hopeful of the future, as the 1970s draw towards such a decadent and disturbed close—as if man's mind were becoming seriously disturbed, by hate, false · values and nihilistic despair? I say nothing of religion, because I see no hope there, despite various pronouncements from the Church about a possible revival. There is, evidently, a vacuum in the sphere of meaning, which is filled with various irrational beliefs, from occultism to the new commercial myths about space travel and visits from other planets. Superstition finds its way even into scientific discourse, as when I heard a scientist on the radio declare that we might obtain energy from 'black holes' by turning them round with some 'new technology'! Both this kind of 'science fiction' and talk of a religious revival seem to me to be part of the general collapse of consciousness into disorder. Every development, of the kind I have outlined, which seems to make hope seem futile, originates in one central problem; do we have anything to believe in? Does life have any meaning? Must we not agree with those who declare that everything is merely 'matter in motion'? That man's existence is an accident? That we are essentially at the mercy of impersonal 'forces' beyond our control? And that these are the conclusions to which we are forced by 'modern science'?

My own feelings of hopefulness, despite all these ominous trends, attach themselves to a sentence from Professor E.A. Burtt's book, *In Search of Philosophical Understanding:* 'in the long run, truth wins the race with falsehood and error—and it wins because it is the truth.'[1] There is a philosophical revolution afoot which has been going on for a hundred years, and it seems clear from the work of many thinkers in this tradition that the nihilistic view, that 'science has demonstrated' life is an accident and man's quest for meaning is futile, is based on misconceptions of what science says. Some even argue that in its more extreme views—that Mozart's music came into existence through various accidental mutations originating in sun-warmed mud, to caricature the position some-what—this view is insane, psychotic and certainly schizoid.[2] I believe that there will be a hopeful change, when it becomes clear that the 'matter-in-motion' view of the universe, when the philosophy known as mechanism, is exposed as both *false* and *mad*. Moreover, I believe that when this revolution in philosophical anthropology begins to *offer something in which to believe* there will be a radical change in the world.

This philosophical revolution examines the 'reality' with which the nihilistic materialistic view of the universe presents us, turns back from it, and demonstrates that what is in question is not that 'reality', but our *way of knowing*. The bleak, inhospitable and pointless view of the universe and man in it which dominates Western thought, it shows, is the product of an erroneous concept of *what thinking is*, of *knowledge* itself. It challenges the very way in which we make up our view of the cosmos. The predominant view depends upon the artificial exclusion of certain important realities—not least that of the knowing mind itself. Once our concept of man's mind is altered, to include man in the universe he knows, the universe itself alters and is relieved of its alien blank-ness. It is no longer a universe that is meaningless, but rather one that is full of meaning: and so it becomes possible to move towards

---

[1] E.A. Burtt, *In Search of a Philosophical Understanding*, Allen and Unwin, 1967.
[2] See, for example, Karl Stern, *The Flight From Woman*, Allen and Unwin, London, 1966; and Professor E.W.F. Tomlin in *The Encyclopaedia of Ignorance*, eds Ronald Duncan and Miranda Weston-Smith, Pergamon Press, Oxford, 1977.

something in which to believe. We are part of its meaning, as is our knowing, which brings terrible responsibilities.

So, I believe, changes in ideas can bring us new hope: and (strangely enough) the greatest hope comes in the area of *biology*, in our concept of 'life'.

The many torments of the world today are, if we examine them deeply enough, consequences of certain ideas, and the trouble is that these ideas lead to nihilistic conclusions. Michael Polanyi, the sometime chemist who became a leading philosopher, explored the way in which certain scientific ideas came to predominate in the West.[3] The plague of our time is the combination of extreme righteousness with scientific scepticism and moral inversion based on it. Thus, in Ethiopia, it becomes of the highest good to torture a child to death in order to overcome reactionary opponents of the 'revolution'—because the ultimate dictatorship of the 'proletariat' is a heavenly goal of all human action and to this magical era all present values must be sacrificed, even if the opposition (in this case) is also Marxist, with roughly the same goal! Ludicrous as many acts of terrorists are today, from the Italian Red Brigades to the Baader-Meinhof gang in Germany, they show a fanatical adherence to ideas; and thus, however contradictory it may seem, they indicate that if only the predominant ideas could change, then many other manifestations could change, too. The life of Eldridge Cleaver indicates that if only the ideas change to which a man gives allegiance, he may cease to be a fanatical terrorist and may become a man governed by humane considerations. At the time of writing M Jean Genet, Sartre's 'saint', writes in *Le Monde* approving of the terrorist acts of the Baader-Meinhof gang. Of course, we hear nothing from the craven intellectuals who approve of destructiveness on such a matter: they simply run with the herd. But some do not: and it could also be possible to persuade someone like M Genet to adopt other ideas. The problem becomes one of exposing the wrongness of ideas that are freely chosen. It is possible for men like M Genet to chose wrong ideas; but it is also possible, as Professor Burtt indicates, for them to choose right ones. The hope may seem a faint one: but it impels all our engagement with the question of the truth, and Professor Burtt's position seems the only possible stance.

[3] See the essay 'Beyond Nihilism' in Polanyi's *Knowing and Being*, Routledge, London, 1963.

There is also a central psychological problem here, which is the strong appeal to certain kinds of individuals of ideas that invert positive values based on love, to base their structure on hate. These are the schizoid elements in the field of ideas, and these perhaps represent the greatest danger of all, since they lead people to endorse evil. According to Karl Stern, the psychotherapist referred to above, the original scientific revolution was made possible by the somewhat schizoid ideas of René Descartes. It was he who substituted mathematical structures for real things, and divided the *res extensa* of things from the *res mensa* of mind, which thus became ineffectual. Despite the effectiveness of his dualism, which enabled men to manipulate the world with cold detachment, his influence contains a psychopathological element. Descartes lost his mother at an early age, and so his universe is one in which man is alienated from Mother Earth. Karl Stern traces the development of such concepts of the universe through Schopenhauer to Sartre, and suggests that the dread and horror of the mother deepens, until we are plunged with Sartre into total nihilism, utter revulsion from the breast, behind which there is a total failure to find the kind of at-oneness that the normal individual experiences with the mother, seeks in woman, and finds in his being-in-the-world: in *Being*. It is certainly very strange that the modern age, as it loses its faith, plunges more and more deeply into a sense of total alienation from the universe, whose psychological undercurrent is failure of relationship with woman and with the mother. The whole catastrophic state of consciousness which we are experiencing (Stern suggests) originates in fear of woman; and, since woman is the focus of being, in fear of being. There is (in both men and women) in this civilization a fear among all of feminine elements in themselves—fear of sensitivity, of quietness, of creativity, of the *attention to meaning itself*. We only have to compare our civilization with Eastern civilizations of the past to see this: Eastern philosophies have never fallen into that kind of exploitation of male capacities such as analysis and intellectualism, at the expense of the more feminine qualities. Yet such a separation has reduced Western philosophy to triviality and mentalized irrelevance, with the consequent loss of the capacity to engage with moral issues and questions of meaning.

What gives me hope is that the revolution in philosophical anthropology of which I have spoken is a profound reaction against this pseudo-male, intellectualized, alienated attitude to life of our civilization. In the spirit of Kierkegaard it regards as 'blasphemy' the application of natural scientism to the realm of man's spirit. It is concerned with Being, and it recognizes that it is concerned to restore attention to 'the still centre', to love, and to the feminine. Moreover, it has enormous strength, not least because it is not concerned merely to erect an intellectual structure: it is rather concerned to help individuals to realize their potentialities. This philosophical movement is associated with existentialism, and so with the impulse to include man's subjective needs in its scope: but also with biology—so that it originates in science itself, and thus offers to build bridges between science and poetry, between objective and subjective disciplines.

Here the philosopher to whom I have already referred, Professor E.A. Burtt, is an important figure. One of his most significant declarations is that philosophy must take account of the findings of psychoanalysis, and he devotes a chapter to existentialism, which he finds to be not only a valid philosophical mode of enquiry but also an attitude to existence concerned with finding a way of life, a way to personal fulfilment. In Burtt's work 'knowing' and finding the truth of the world are evidently inclusive of unconscious, bodily, inward modes—and so of those areas of perception and awareness that are excluded too much from Descartes' conception of how the mind works. (As Marjorie Grene says, 'there is no aspect of our lives which is not essentially process'.)

The whole problem of what knowledge consists of is, of course, an enormous one. Many people are more or less acquainted with the kind of account of what constitutes scientific knowledge as put forward by Karl Popper. His is perhaps the clearest account of the empirical view. Marjorie Grene, however, finds 'Popper's concept of knowing inadequate; in his view, she declares there is 'no such thing as learning'. If knowledge is conceived of as it is in his account, only in terms of whether or not hypotheses can be falsified, this does not provide an adequate enough concept of the *active knowing* we all experience. Popper's concept of knowledge is too preoccupied with what is explicit, what is present to the mind at the centre of attention. Marjorie Grene invokes a question by Meno in a dialogue of Plato's: 'Why, on what lines will you look, Socrates, for a thing of whose nature you know nothing at all? . . . Or even, supposing, at the best, that you hit upon it, how will you know it is the thing you did not know?'[4] In Popper's philosophy,

---

[4] Marjorie Grene, *The Knower and the Known*, Faber, London, 1966.

she argues, as in much of the theory of modern science and psychology, there is no adequate account of the kind of learning we experience every day—when we come upon realities we suspected were there and recognize them as the unknown truths we believed they might be, when we arrived at them and (mysteriously) recognized them for the truth.

Here we encounter a whole area of divergence between established philosophies and the newer ones. The Cartesian tradition continues to believe in 'clear and distinct ideas'. But psychoanalysis, post-critical philosophy and phenomenology do not accept this faith. One important book in the exploration of such elements in knowing is Maurice Merleau-Ponty's *The Phenomenology of Perception*.[5] The marvellous relevance of this French thinker's engagement with the realities of our knowledge of the world is clear from almost every page of Marjorie Grene. She uses dense and penetrating paragraphs from Merleau-Ponty at the end of her chapter on Descartes, to show that the latter's account of the way we live in the world, and 'find' it, is seriously inadequate. Where in life are those 'clear and distinct ideas'? Much of our learning and knowledge is shadowy and half-formed: much of reality is impossible to grasp, by the paradigms of empiricism. There is much about knowing we simply cannot yet account for.

Merleau-Ponty writes about the existence of the self in time in a way the poet can readily understand. The scientist finds it more difficult, because his concepts of mind and time are comparatively naive. They belong to the Cartesian 'string of bead-like instants' which is a falsification of how things are, and to the Humean fragmentation of everything into dissociated bits with no 'I' to unite them. Merleau-Ponty's conception of perception is more fluid, more embodied, and hence more 'human'. Learning becomes a process that changes human beings: 'Knowledge is an achievement, but like every living achievement a stage in history, neither an end nor simply a beginning, but a "stage on life's way".'[6] Incidentally, this kind of concept of human knowledge seems far more democratic than that which emerges from the Cartesian tradition, because it embraces man's aspirations and desires, and allows his autonomous freedom: his primary reality in his creative 'I'. The strict Cartesian tradition which generates a concept of man as a

[5] M. Merleau-Ponty, *The Phenomenology of Perception*, Routledge, London, 1962.
[6] Marjorie Grene, *op. cit.*

pure cognition attached (absurdly) to a machine seems by contrast to belong to the machine age. Merleau-Ponty speaks of us in terms that embrace our spontaneity, 'because we are the upsurge of time'. There are important political implications here.

The other important figure in the developing concepts of knowledge in philosophical anthropology is Michael Polanyi, whose attention to the 'inexplicit' and 'tacit' elements in knowledge runs parallel to Merleau-Ponty's thinking. Polanyi was a great chemist who turned philosopher, and there is certainly nothing in him of the cult of irrationalism or of mysticism. Scientists too often react to any criticism of their 'objective' paradigms by cries of 'mysticism' and 'animism'—when in fact one often finds it is they who are being obscurantist, since they have made a dogma out of their assumptions and hypotheses. The book to read here is Thomas Kuhn's *The Structure of Scientific Revolutions.*[7] There is an interesting introductory note of this book in Dr Roger Poole's *Towards Deep Subjectivity.*[8] It was Polanyi's conclusion that science had gone seriously wrong by adhering to the paradigm of strict 'objectivity'. Scientists fail to recognize that this essential position of their work, its positivism, is a paradigm, based on certain assumptions and hypotheses which can only be upheld until a better paradigm replaces them. 'Objectivity' as Poole argues, 'may one day be forced to suffer the ignominious defeat of so many of its predecessors.' The very idea that this could be so fills many scientists with terror, since they feel that if they could not passionately believe in 'objective science' they would be left high and dry. But Poole refers to a number of thinkers who are arguing that 'the Popperian orthodoxy has been challenged, and the paradigm of scientific objectivity which has reigned up to now is about to be deposed.'

This impulse, of which the new existentialism is also a part, is far from being an impulse towards irrationalism or mysticism. On the contrary, it has its origins in the perception that much in modern rationalism has itself become mumbo-jumbo: Poole, for instance, finds much in behaviourist psychology to be 'alchemy', since it involves the mathematical quantifying of experiences, emotions and attitudes that defy quantification.

---

[7] Thomas Kuhn, *The Structure of Scientific Revolutions*, University of Chicago Press, 1970.
[8] Roger Poole, *Towards Deep Subjectivity*, Allen Lane, London, 1972.

The existentialist and phenomenological movements to which I am trying to draw attention begin within science itself. This philosophical revolution may seem challengingly new to many, but in fact it is more than a hundred years old. One original figure is a psychologist, Wilhelm Dilthey (1833–1911). His name is coupled with that of Theodore Lipps (1851–1919) in Michael Polanyi's *The Tacit Dimension*:[9]

> At the turn of the century, German thinkers postulated that indwelling, or empathy, is the proper means of knowing man and the Humanities. I am referring particularly to Dilthey and Lipps.

Dilthey thought that the mind of a person can be 'understood only by reliving its workings' while Lipps represented aesthetic appreciation as 'an entering into a work of art and thus dwelling in the hand of its creator.'

> I think that Dilthey and Lipps described here a striking form of tacit knowing as applied to the understanding of man and of works of art, and that they were right in saying that this could be achieved only by *indwelling*.[10]

As early as 1865 Dilthey was searching for a *reale Psychologie* that could serve as the foundation for the human studies (*Geisteswissenschaften*)—a radically new psychology. In his *Ideen* of 1894 he proposed a 'descriptive and analytical psychology' as opposed to the 'explanatory psychology' of the physicalists. He had high hopes that Husserl's phenomenology could aid him in his attempts to develop this new psychology.

Edmund Husserl (1859–1938) was a student of Franz Bretano (1838–1917). Bretano, a scientist and philosopher, sought a scientific foundation for a new philosophy. He also sought to devise a 'descriptive psychology'. One of his concepts was 'intentionality', a feature of such human acts as perceiving, imagining, judging and willing, and this became a major feature of Husserl's thinking.

When Husserl began, he thought of himself as a descriptive psychologist. In his philosophy the basic fact of pure psychology is consciousness. He took many ideas from Wilhelm Dilthey's book on *Psychology* of 1894, believing that this philosopher had properly paid attention to the concrete life of the spirit, to the individual, and to the socio-historical dimension in living concretions, its typical forms and purposeful structures. Both Dilthey and Husserl

---

[9] Michael Polanyi, *The Tacit Dimension*, Routledge, London, 1967.
[10] Michael Polanyi, *op. cit.*, p. 17.

reject naturalistic psychology and experimental psychology as being hopelessly inadequate for developing a scientific foundation for the study of man.

So, at the beginning of this development in the realm of 'reflective psychology', there is no anti-scientific impulse. There is an attempt to devise a descriptive psychology which begins in 'inner' lived experience, and in the intuition of the whole, the living context: 'natural-scientific *understanding*'. *Geisteswissenschaft*, which requires *Verstehen* (understanding) is different from *Naturwissenschaft*, which is based on *Eklarung* (explanation). Dilthey and Husserl sought understanding of *things alive*. This emphasis has led to the whole stream of thought analyzed by Marjorie Grene in *Approaches to a Philosophical Biology* in which she traces the attempt to find 'the category of life'. She emphasizes with Helmuth Plessner, that there can be no solution of the *Geisteswissenschaften* until we develop a philosophical anthropology and a philosophy of nature:

> Not ... in the Kantian sense of a set of principles for the inorganic world, leaving the life sciences to be quieted by a vague set of 'as ifs' or 'regulative principles', but in the sense of a philosophical examination of the question *what it means to be alive*.[11]

Other important figures are Max Scheler (1874–1928) and Martin Heidegger (1889–1975). Scheler was concerned to develop a philosophical anthropology along personalistic lines. He sought to develop a positive phenomenology of the emotions, as a basis for an ethic. One of his studies was of *sympathy* and he sought to make a case for the direct perception of other selves. He was an important influence on Helmuth Plessner, von Weizsäcker and F.J.J. Buytendijk. His works in English include *The Nature of Sympathy* and *Man's Place in Nature*.[12]

Heidegger began by charging psychology with neglect of its ontological foundations: it failed to explore the mode of being basic to psychological phenomena. He sought to unveil the meaning, often the hidden meaning, of the phenomenological, as distinguished from the vulgar phenomenon, and he sought to understand how it is related to Being. His concepts were large, and he raised questions of world, time and death—and *Dasein* 'being there'. Man and his psyche are placed against a vast background,

---

[11] Marjorie Grene, *Approaches to a Philosophical Biology*, Basic Books, New York, 1968, p. 65.

[12] Max Scheler, *The Nature of Sympathy*, Yale University Press, 1959; *Man's Place in Nature*, Beacon Press, U.S.A., 1961.

and then the questions are asked, how does man relate himself to Being? What is his world and his place in it? How does he experience time?

Dasein is being-in-the-world. Analysis of moods (*Stimmungen*) can be revealing clues to the modes of being (*Seineweissen*) of *Dasein*. In this connection he explored fear (*Furcht*). In our everyday life *Dasein* can 'fall away' (*Verfallen*). Other concepts offered by Heidegger include *Angst* (anxiety) and *Sorge* (concern), in relation to nothingness. Heidegger has had a considerable influence on psychotherapy, almost by accident, and according to Herbert Spiegelberg it was a misinterpretation of *Sein and Zeit* (*Being and Time*[13]) that contributed to the founding of French existentialism. Perhaps the most important influence has been on the *Daseinanalysis* of Ludwig Binswanger: this form of psychotherapy rests on a recognition of the patient's need to establish a sense of having meaningfully existed before he is swept into nothingness.

Apart from *Being and Time* Heidegger's next most important work is 'What is Metaphysics?' published in *Existence and Being*.[14] His influence in psychotherapy may be studied in Ludwig Binswanger's *Being-in-the-World*[15] and also in *Existence, a New Dimension in Psychiatry* edited by Rollo May and others.[16]

F.J.J. Buytendijk (b. 1887) a Dutch philosopher and biologist, was influenced both by Husserl and Heidegger. He is also interested in Jean-Paul Sartre, and Simone de Beauvoir, but rejects their view of human nature. Buytendijk is closer to Maurice Merleau-Ponty: in his book on *Woman*, for example, he quotes him frequently.

Buytendijk started out as a biologist, and was interested in the psychology of animals. 'Life is and remains a mystery', he said. His quest became that of understanding human existence in the context of animal life, in the great tradition of German philosophical anthropology which displays 'unconditional love for everything that bears the human name'. His major works include *The Mind of the Dog*, *Pain* and *Woman*.[17]

[13] Martin Heidegger, *Being and Time*, trans. J. Macquarrie and E. Robinson, Blackwell, Oxford, 1967.

[14] Martin Heidegger, *Existence and Being*, Regnery, U.S.A., 1969.

[15] Ludwig Binswanger, *Being-in-the-World*, Basic Books, U.S.A., 1963.

[16] Rollo May *et al.*, *Existence: a New Dimension in Psychiatry*, Basic Books, U.S.A., 1968.

[17] F.J.J. Buytendijk, *The Mind of the Dog*, Allen and Unwin, 1935; *Pain*, University of Chicago Press, 1962; *Woman*, Newman Press, 1965.

Another figure discussed in *Approaches to a Philosophical Biology* is Kurt Goldstein (1878–1965). In the work of psychotherapists like Rollo May and Paul Tillich we find the concept of self-actualization. This comes from Goldstein, and finds its expression in the work of Abraham Maslow. Goldstein's work on 'existence' was based on phenomenological observations. His philosophy sprang directly from his experience in medicine, especially in World War I. His work has been influential among existentialist psycho-therapists, and is highly honoured in France.[18] But Goldstein has been unheeded by English-speaking readers and his general theory of biological knowledge remains largely unknown.

Goldstein became aware from brain-damaged patients that what could be lost was the 'total capacity to handle an environment' by loss of 'the abstract attitude'. The brain-damaged patient, surprisingly, was unable to deal with the world because of impairment of his capacity to hold abstract concepts. He also found that in dealing with such impairment the person employed the whole of his organism to seek to overcome it. From this he went on to declare in his philosophy of biology that *each organism must always be studied as a whole.*

Goldstein's argument is that the 'pathways' organic model is inadequate. He asks 'Can it really teach us something about the functioning of the organism?' We must, he says, reject the assumption that in this way processes in the organism can be grasped directly. Some psychologists like Monakov and Pavlov believe that analysis of bodily phenomenon is the only firm foundation by which to obtain laws governing the processes in the organism: starting from physiological rather than psychological data. If we examine the paradigms of the physiological approach we find a belief in the capacity to come closer to an understanding of the processes of the organism through the physical than would be possible through a simple analysis of behaviour, be it somatic or psychic. It is this ghost that lies behind talk of 'processing' experience or 'competence' such as we find in the Bullock Report on the teaching of English in Britain.[19] Much linguistics is still based on 'reflex' theory and a reflex model.

---

[18] Goldstein's main work, *The Organism*, was included in translation in the Bibliothèque de Philosophie series of phenomenological works edited by Merleau-Ponty and Sartre.

[19] *The Bullock Report*, H.M.S.O., London, 1975.

According to the view underlying the reflex theory, the organism represents a bundle of isolable mechanisms which are constant in structure and which respond, in a constant way, to events in the environment (stimuli). The aim of research, according to this conception, is to discover those 'part processes' which can be considered as governed by mechanistic laws. To work out the laws, one exposes the organism to single stimuli, using various controls to make sure the response is as pure as possible. In this approach, 'analytical' experimentation has become the ideal foundation of knowledge.

It is this ideal foundation that is translated into the linguistic approach to language; only examine the part processes, and one will find laws—which can then be used to control 'competence'.

From this physiological knowledge we know a great deal about the difference between sensory and motor activity, and about the specific effects of glands, etc. But the implication is that individually disparate mechanisms are the constituents of behaviour. The life of the organism is considered to be composed of these disparate mechanisms. Is this true? Is it acceptable that, with complex life systems, the path to understanding is by microreduction and particulate analysis?

Goldstein questions the theory of a reflex: there are, he argues, a large number of diverse reactions to the same stimulus. Because of this, reflex phenomena cannot be properly understood in terms of the isolated mechanism alone. It is factually impossible, Goldstein shows, to reduce the processes in the organism to univocal relation between a single stimulus and a single response. Becoming aware of this, various authors have tried to introduce self-regulating processes—so that the organism becomes a system of regulation which compensate for the changes that arise by restoring the organism's 'equilibrium'. Everything seems to be made simply for the preservation of the organism's equilibrium. But how could any dynamics enter into this situation, to give *direction* to the behaviour, for *direction* is what we find to be the outstanding characteristic in the performances of an organism? Living things surely do not exist simply for 'equilibrium'?

Goldstein's work with brain-damaged patients led him to the conclusion that all such 'partial' theories were inadequate. A man whose seeing 'apparatus' was damaged so that, for instance, half his seeing nerves were lost in each eye, did not see the half-scenes, as it were. He saw everything as a whole, but imperfectly. When the organism is damaged in its perceptual 'machinery' it uses whatever is left *still* in a *whole* way. A holistic approach is necessary, which sees the whole directed at making use of its world, and its whole potentialities.

He emphasizes that even if we speak of 'the nervous system' (which undoubtedly exists) we must think of a whole, *which operates as a whole.*

> The nervous system, not only of invertebrates but also of vertebrates, including man, is a network in which ganglia are inserted at various places, and which is related to the outer-world by means of the sense organs and the moveable parts of the body. This network, in which the excitations take place, represents an apparatus *which always functions as a whole.*[20]

Goldstein insists that the system is never at rest, waiting to be 'stimulated': it is in a continual state of excitation. All a 'stimulus' does is to change the state of excitation. Moreover, besides 'outside' stimulation, there is 'inside' stimulation, which is constant.

When there is a 'stimulus', says Goldstein, it is not that there are impulses along 'pathways': because the system functions as a whole, 'a given stimulus must produce changes in the whole organism.' There may be a 'local near effect' but a proper understanding must take account of the *whole* response, and the impulse *to live.*

Goldstein knew from his work that neurological practice could not explain the phenomena he had observed in brain-damaged patients. Neurology is addicted to particular observation. The need was to consider *all* the phenomena presented, and thus try to establish a comprehensive understanding of the individual organism, studied as a whole. Despite the enormous importance of his argument, Goldstein's theory of biological knowledge is still largely unknown and unassimilated—except for his influence on Erwin Straus and on the existentialist psychotherapists. (He was understood by Merleau-Ponty and by George Canguilhem.[21]) In dealing with patients Goldstein insisted upon a holistic approach, *Ganzheit methode*, which Marjorie Grene suggests is translated as 'comprehensive'.

From this as a biological principle arising out of a methodology, the emphasis on the whole, many consequences follow. First, what

[20] Kurt Goldstein, *The Organism*, Beacon Press, Boston, 1963, p. 103, my italics.
[21] See M. Merleau-Ponty, *La Connaissance de la Vie*, Vrin, Paris, 1966; and George Canguilhem, *Le Normal et Le Pathologique*, Presses Universitaires de France, Paris, 1967.

is revealed is a *relative constancy* of the whole organism's achievements in its interaction with the environment. A constant pattern is maintained by a living organism, whatever happens to it partially or locally. This interaction of organism and environment geared to a constant mean Goldstein called the basic law of biology: *das biologische Grundgesez*.

The constancy of overall performance represents a *preferred* behaviour, either of the species or the individual. Some birds like to fly to South Africa for the winter. And as we know from our children and our pets, each living organism prefers to behave in such-and-such a way; 'the best expression of this organism's essential nature'. Obviously, this is a very different approach from behaviouristic psychology, and strict naturalistic biology. The smiling of an infant, as Goldstein sees it, is the expression of behaviour which is both 'species–specific' but also more personal, representing the first truly individual *encounter* of one human being with another, which will deepen into such richness of encounter as each person may attain.

Goldstein is thus one of those philosophical biologists whose work puts man back into the whole animal world, and sees his characteristics as evolving from those of animals. The albatross flies round and round the southern hemisphere; the eel and salmon swim thousands of miles and back, from ocean to stream—because they prefer to behave like that. Biology must study the best expression of *'this'* organism's essential nature. Preferred behaviour is that achievement *which best expresses the nature of the individual*.

From his work with brain-damaged behaviour, Goldstein came to relegate survival to a manifestation of damage or disease. Survival of course is a predominant concept in our biological thinking, as we stand so powerfully under the influence of Darwin (and Herbert Spencer). The essential picture in traditional evolutionary theory is of all living organisms just about coping with a dangerous world, rather passively. Even inexplicitly, the 'survival' view is nihilistic and depressing; could it not be that other factors are primary? Goldstein believes that this is so; perhaps self-maintenance is secondary to the *primary* criteria of *centricity* and *display*?

This is not a mere biological question, but raises the whole philosophical issue, of *how we know living things*. As Marjorie Grene points out, discussing Goldstein, 'a living thing—not a "type" but an individual, developing organism, looked at in itself, as figure against the background of its unique interaction with its environment—exhibits to the naturalist not only such a monotonous maintenance of indifferent particulars but comprehensive features of appearance and *achievement* which constitute the entity whose emergence and whose maintenance such devices as those of inheritance or homeostasis subserve.'[22]

Marjorie Grene invokes Adolf Portmann's concept of 'centricity'; Goldstein's 'preferred behaviour' is the visible expression of centricity—that autonomous unique operation from a centre through the boundaries to the world, which is 'the living principle' in all life. An organism does not so much 'adapt' itself to an environment, but strive to be adequate to its relationship to it: 'Preferred behaviour when achievable and achieved is the most adequate expression of this organism's nature in its on-going relation to the surrounding world.'[23]

We must think much more in our philosophical biology (of which philosophical anthropology is a branch) about *striving and achievement*. In terms of general philosophy we are dominated, (not least in English and the Humanities) often without knowing it, by a model of living creatures, including man, that conceives of 'life' as being a victim of circumstances, concerned with mere 'survival' rather than with creative autonomous creatures enjoying the world. As Polanyi points out, there is a radical difference between an elephant and a thunderstorm (a self-sustaining system): 'life strives'.

How Goldstein's thinking leads on to the work of Martin Buber and D.W. Winnicott should be evident. It should also be possible to work out its philosophical relevance to the Humanities, and such subjects as English. Strict naturalistic biology reduces the workings of organisms to the atomistic level: all one is aware of is the self-perpetuation of the constituent particulars ('the selfish gene'). In this view of living things, where is there a place for 'striving', for 'showing of the self on the surface' (*Selbstdarstellung*)? For *fulfilment* of the essential character of bird or man? A living thing, says Marjorie Grene, exhibits not only 'self maintenance', but 'comprehensive features of appearance and achievement ... which constitute the entity whose emergence and whose maintenance such devices as those of inheritance or homeostasis subserve'.[24]

Goldstein refutes the interpretation of behaviour in terms of reflexes: he argues that 'reflexes' belong to distorted and isolated

[22] Marjorie Grene, *Approaches to a Philosophical Biology*, p. 255.

[23] *Ibid.*, p. 235.

[24] *Ibid.*, p. 255.

parts of organisms, not the living whole. Moreover, reflexology is developed under highly artificial laboratory conditions; in nature a more spontaneous kind of behaviour is normally found. In these emphases Goldstein leads on to the work of Erwin Straus, who made a radical challenge to Pavlov and behavioural psychology in *The Primary World of Senses*.[25]

Another important biologist in this stream of thought is Adolf Portmann, the author of *Animals as Social Beings* and *New Paths in Biology*.[26] Portmann is opposed to reductionist biology, which seeks to reduce everything to the physico-chemical base. He urges a new philosophy of living things, to quote the biologist's understanding of his world. An important concept already noted is *centricity*— the autonomy of living creatures, and the way they relate from a centre to the world. Once centricity is recognized, together with the intrinsic value of the entities in the world of life, we must change our thinking about the universe. To 'find' centricity, we must relinquish one-level naturalism, and accept that there are other ways of knowing the world (of the kind biologists use when they observe lions). So, the world must cease to be that 'objective' matter-in-motion mechanism of the Galilean-Newtonian tradition; it becomes redeemed, by the 'category of life' that has that autonomous dimension, and culminates in man as the *knower* of nature.

It is in her chapter on Portmann that Marjorie Grene considers the whole problem of our concept of knowledge. Portmann urges us to bring together both aspects of our lives: the surface of experience, the colours, the sounds, the rhythms of movement that confront us on all sides—the world of primary experience—*and* 'our feelings, our desires, our dreams, the creative aspiration of artists, the vision of saints and prophets, even the delusions of the insane'.[27] Marjorie Grene discusses the traditional hostility of poetry found in Galileo: this hostility belongs to the perspective of modern objectivism. To seek the whole truth we must restore 'the whole work of the imagination: myth and metaphor, dream and prophecy'.

We must try, in other words, to achieve anew a whole vision of our nature.[28]

[25] Erwin Straus, *The Primary World of Senses*, Free Press of Glencoe, U.S.A., 1963.
[26] Adolf Portmann, *Animals as Social Beings*, Hutchinson, London, 1961; and *New Paths in Biology*, Harper, U.S.A., 1965.
[27] Marjorie Grene, *Approaches to a Philosophical Understanding*, p. 50.
[28] *Ibid.*, p. 51.

In this development one further important figure is Ludwig Binswanger (1881–1968). A proponent of phenomenology, he also devised *Daseins-analysis*, the approach to psychotherapy based on Heidegger's philosophy of being-unto-death, used in practice now in Europe and America. Binswanger was born into a German family which moved to Switzerland, and which had been involved in psychiatry. His grandfather had founded the Bellevue Sanatorium in Kreuzlingen. He studied medicine and served his internship with Eugene Bleuler at Burghölzli, Zurich. He worked with C.G. Jung, who introduced him to Freud. Max Scheler, Heidegger, Ernst Cassirer and Martin Buber all came to visit his sanitorium, which became an international meeting ground. Most of his important essays are published in *Being-in-the-World*.[29]

Martin Heidegger's *Sein und Zeit* was published in 1927, and its equivalent in psychopathology was the advent of the new *philosophical anthropology* of Binswanger, Viktor von Gebsattel and Erwin Straus. In 1930 a new journal was launched, *Nervenarzt*, which was an outlet for the new phenomenological anthropology.

Binswanger broke down the boundaries of Jasper's phenomenology. This had confined itself to describing isolated subjective phenomena characteristic of the psychotic patient. He extended this approach to make a study of the subjective life-history of a patient, and to describe the connections between successive elements of phenomenal experience. Jaspers thought schizophrenia unintelligible in principle. Binswanger tried to understand it, using Heidegger's analysis of human *Dasein*, 'being there'. Binswanger sought to develop a full-fledged philosophical anthropology (says Herbert Spiegelberg) based on Heidegger's conception of *Dasein* as being-in-the-world.

More easily accessible is the work of Viktor Frankl (1905–1975). Frankl became Professor of Neurology at the University of Vienna. He was the founder of 'logotherapy', a form of therapy based on meaning.

In *Psychotherapy and Existentialism*[30] he states his underlying philosophy of life in the form of three assumptions: (1) freedom of will, (2) the will to meaning, and (3) the meaning of life, for which

[29] Jacob Needleman, ed., *Being-in-the-World*, Basic Books, New York, 1963. Other essays by Ludwig Binswanger are in *Existence: A New Dimension in Psychiatry*, eds Rollo May *et al.*, Basic Books, New York, 1968. See also 'Existential Analysis and Psychotherapy', *Psychoanalytical Review*, xlv, 1958–9, 19–83.

[30] Viktor Frankl, *Psychotherapy and Existentialism*, Clarion Books, New York, 1958.

he claimed phenomenological support. His impulse was to find an alternative to Freud's psychology based on the will to pleasure and Adler's based on the will to power. He defined his approach as *Existenzanalyse* and *Logotherapie*, but Professor Spiegelberg believes his approach has little to do with Binswanger's *Daseins-analyse*, or Boss's *Daseinanalytic*. Frankl's aim was more therapeutic than theoretical, and concerned itself with psychological problems arising from the 'existential vacuum' or 'existential frustration', and the resultant spiritual or 'noogenic' neurosis.

Frankl's approach to psychotherapy was devised from his experiences during several years in Nazi concentration camps, where he lost his entire family but managed to construct a book which was taken from him and destroyed.[31]

As Spiegelberg says, Frankl is not one of the major practitioners of phenomenology, nor is phenomenology a major point of his work. But it has helped him to move beyond Freud and Adler, the two great proponents of individual psychology in Vienna. He has indicated how phenomenology could be applied more critically to work in psychotherapy.

A whole historical stream, of course, is represented by the transition of ideas from phenomenology to America, not least by the emigration of certain leading figures who were refugees from Nazism. Erwin Straus (1891–1975) was one of the most important figures here. Binswanger considers him the cleverest of the original circle of phenomenological anthropologists. He went to the United States in 1939 and from then on established an international reputation. He finally settled down at the Veterans Hospital, Lexington, Kentucky, and began to establish there an intellectual centre for phenomenology in the New World.

Straus started from and always returned to psychiatry. He believed, like Maslow, that in order to understand the abnormal it is necessary to study the norm, a task that required more than 'science' could supply. He sought an understanding of the *conditio humana* says Spiegelberg, the *Psychologie der menschlichen Welt*. This is the task of phenomenological psychology. Straus, too, attended one of Scheler's lectures. However, he was doubtful of

---

[31] See Viktor Frankl, *Man's Search for Meaning: From Death-camp to Existentialism*, trans. Ilse Lasch, Beacon Press, Boston, 1963; and *The Doctor and the Soul*, trans. Rand, Winston, New York, 1965. Frankl's books are now published in England by Souvenir Press and some are also in paperback, published by Penguin Books.

Husserl because, as an anti-Pavlovian psychologist, he felt that Husserl was too attached to Descartes. Straus's attack on Pavlov was itself condemned as anti-scientific, and this debate was the beginning of his first major work, *Vom Sinn der Sinne* (1935) translated as *The Primary World of Senses* (1963).

Later, Straus made contact with Binswanger; he had already been in touch with Minkowski and von Gebsattel. Binswanger and Straus disagreed over Straus's theories of *Erlebnis* (lived experience), and Straus felt fundamental disagreements with Binswanger over the concept from Heidegger of *Dasein*. At this moment the Nazi conquest disrupted Straus's work in Berlin as a neurologist and psychiatrist, and he fled to America, teaching psychology at first at Black Mountain College.

His work, which is discussed by Marjorie Grene in *Approaches*, may be summed up by his delineation of his project:

> In my own work I have tried to 'save' sensory experience from theoretical misinterpretation and then to apply the ingrained understanding of the norm to pathological manifestation.

Straus's major works, besides *The Primary World of Senses*, are *On Obsession: A Clinical and Methodological Study of Nervous and Mental Disease, Psychiatry and Philosophy* and *Phenomenological Psychology: Selected Papers*.[32]

Goldstein, Paul Tillich and Erwin Straus have been influential, as refugee scholars, on one of the most influential authorities on existential phenomenology in America, Rollo May (b. 1907). Straus asked May to speak on 'The Phenomenological Bases of Psychotherapy' at the first Lexington Conference on Phenomenology in 1964.[33]

May began his early adulthood as an artist in Europe and has never abandoned his interest in artistic creativity. In the 1930s he began his psychological work as a counsellor and wrote *The Meaning of Anxiety* (1950). His next work was *Man's Search for Himself* (1953), a pre-existentialist attempt to deal with problems of the loss of the sense of self in our time, the loss of the sense of tragedy.[34]

[32] Erwin Straus, *On Obsession: A Clinical and Methodological Study of Nervous and Mental Disease*, Monography, New York, 1948; *Psychiatry and Philosophy*, Springer, U.S.A., 1969; *Phenomenological Psychology: Selected Papers*, Tavistock, London, 1968.

[33] See *Phenomenology: Pure and Applied*, ed. Erwin Straus, Duquesne University Press, 1964.

[34] Rollo May, *The Meaning of Anxiety*, Norton, New York, 1950; and *Man's Search for Himself*, Norton, New York, 1953.

His solution is the rediscovery of self-hood, culminating in creative self-consciousness. From 1950 to 1954 he seems to have moved more deeply into European existentialist thought, and *Existence: a New Dimension in Psychiatry* was published in 1958, under a joint editorship with Ernest Angel and Henri F. Ellenberger.

In 1961 May published *Psychology and the Human Dilemma* and in 1969, *Love and Will*.[35] His work (especially *Existence*) generated a whole new movement in phenomenology and existentialism in America, and *Love and Will* has sold tens of thousands. The *Journal of Existential Psychiatry* was started in 1960 by Jordan Scher in Chicago. In 1964 it was converted into a more philosophical *Journal of Existentialism* under new editors, while Scher started another journal, *Existential Psychiatry*, in 1966. In 1959 was launched the American Association for Existential Psychology and Psychiatry, and in 1961 *The Review of Existential Psychology and Psychiatry*. In all these journals, Viktor Frankl, Minkowski, Binswanger, Medard Boss, Paul Tillich, F.J.J. Buytendijk, Marcel, Helmuth Plessner and Carl Rogers wrote articles.[36]

Abraham Maslow contributed to a new movement seeking an alternative to behaviourism and psychoanalysis, which he called 'Third Force Psychology', and he led a new movement called 'Humanistic Psychology' which published a journal called the *Journal of Humanistic Psychology*. In this, existentialist psychology was one stream, though in *Challenges of Humanistic Psychology* edited by J.F.T. Bugental, 1967, the only phenomenological contribution was by Colin Wilson on Husserl.

Bugental (who wrote *The Search for Authenticity*[37]) attempted to combine a humanistic psychology with existentialism. He, like Rollo May, stressed the tragic side of human existence, and emphasised the need for meaning and 'validation'. His central stress is on 'awareness' which seems to mean being-in-the-world in accord with the 'givenness' of man's nature and the world.

Maslow's *Towards a Psychology of Being* is important because he declares that too much in psychology and psychiatry has been developed from abnormal people who were incapable of joy, transcendence and meaning—what he calls 'peak experiences'.

---

[35] Rollo May, *Psychology and the Human Dilemma*, Van Nostrand Reinhold, Kentucky, 1967; and *Love and Will*, Norton, New York, 1969.
[36] The proceedings of a 1959 conference in New York were published as *Existential Psychology*, Random House, New York, 1961.
[37] J.F.T. Bugental, *The Search for Authenticity*, Holt, Reinhart, U.S.A., 1965.

Maslow also saw that in the more creative forms of existentialism and phenomenology there were emerging new models of man, and new concepts of value. Maslow's most important emphasis is on the moral implication of the rediscovery of the intentional, and of the primacy of man's pursuit of meaning. He speaks of

> ... a clear confrontation of one basic set of values by another newer system of values which claims to be not only more efficient but more true. It draws on some of the truly revolutionary consequences of the discovery that human nature has been sold short, that man has a higher nature which is just as 'instinctoid' as his lower nature and that this higher nature includes the need for meaningful work, for responsibility, for creativeness, for being fair and just, for doing what is worthwhile and for preferring to do it well ...[38]

'Reduction to the concrete is a loss of future', he says, speaking of the predicament of certain brain-damaged patients. But he is also evidently aware that this may be seen as a general statement about our kind of society, in its imprisonment in 'objective' or naturalistic concepts of man's make-up.

Other important recent figures in American existentialist and phenomenological thinking are Joseph Lyons[39] and Professor Spiegelberg.[40] Eugene Minkowski is another who began as a medical biologist, but became increasingly interested in psychology and philosophy, under the influence of Bergson and Husserl. His publications include La Schizophrénie, 1926, Le Temps Vécu, 1933, Vers un Cosmologie 1936, and he is a pioneer in phenomenological psychoanalysis.

To return to the English scene is to return to one in which, in blissful ignorance, intellectuals fiddle while Rome burns. It should be clear from the above brief survey how disastrous has been the failure of attention in Britain to this movement. R.D. Laing once had the links with Europe in his hands, for he edited studies in existentialism and phenomenology for the Tavistock Press (including the book by Straus). But here we encounter the danger of fanatical nihilistic movements which corrupt even the best growing points in thought. Laing fizzled out into subversiveness and the tail end of Sartrean nihilism, the Anti-University 'revolution' and

[38] Abraham H. Maslow, Towards a Psychology of Meaning, Van Nostrand, U.S.A., 1962, p. 122.

[39] See Joseph Lyons, Psychology and the Measure of Man, Free Press of Glencoe, U.S.A., 1963.

[40] See Herbert Spiegelberg's masterly Psychology and Psychiatry, Northwestern University Press, Chicago, 1972.

the drug-cult. A reviewer in the *Times Literary Supplement* now even calls Laing 'evil' because of his denial of all morality. Laing seriously failed to invoke the new movement in philosophical anthropology. Yet there are traditions in English thought that could have been linked with this movement—as manifest in the work of D.W. Winnicott, Peter Lomas, Harry Guntrip and W.R.D. Fairbairn. Marion Milner's work is essentially phenomenological[41] and there is also *Existential Neurosis* by E.K. Ledermann.[42] The relevance of these studies in psychotherapy does not, however, yet seem to be recognized by the British Society for Phenomenology: the work of drawing on this immense revolution has simply not yet begun in Britain.

This, then, is the history so far of an important revolution in thought about man and his nature. It leads towards an urgent concern with meaning and values, such as is seriously missing from much that has happened in philosophy in this century. Primary in this revolution (as in the work of Michael Polanyi) is the emphasis on the inevitable concern with meaning and values, which knowledge must bring. This may be linked into the whole question of *what we can believe in.* Here we should note the powerful hopefulness which emerges (for example) from *New Knowledge in Human Values.*[43] This is the record of a symposium held at M.I.T. in 1957. Those taking part included Maslow himself, Professors Sorokin, Robert S. Hartman, Jacob Bronowski, Theodosius Dobzhansky, Walter A. Weiskopf, Gordon Allport, Erich Fromm and Kurt Goldstein. Their discussion manifests an attempt to establish that in many disciplines, including psychology, anthropology, biology, and other subjects, there are reasons for believing that values are grounded in the human condition. A humanistic source of values may be discovered, not least in the fact that every human being strives to 'become himself' and to realize potentialities. The effects of a limited 'objective' positivist approach to knowledge have been to promote anomie, amorality, rootlessness, emptiness, hopelessness and the lack of something to believe in. All traditional value-systems have turned out to be failures. Can any new approach solve our problems of finding something to

---

[41] See especially Marion Milner's *In the Hand of the Living God*, Hogarth, London, 1969.

[42] E.K. Ledermann, *Existential Neurosis*, Butterworth, London, 1972.

[43] Abraham H. Maslow, ed., *New Knowledge in Human Values*, Harper and Row, New York, 1959.

believe in? Maslow offers a psychology in which the healthy capacity for 'peak-moments' is a primary reality, and he says that we all experience moments of transcendent being, which give us a sense of meaning in our lives, emerging from our creative acts, and the realization of our potentialities. Certainly, from reading these scientists and philosophers, there seems no reason to despair of establishing a new system of values: but as yet we have nothing achieved—all that we can do is to point in the new directions of thought that are necessary.

This takes us on to Maslow's *Towards a Psychology of Being*, and the general area of the search for a new ontology. Maslow cannot be said to be a phenomenologist, but he is related to this philosophical stream in the sense that he is trying to establish an existentialist psychology, capable of giving a whole account of human experience, including the recognition that the human being is both what he is and what he desires to be—an approach evidently related to Husserl's concept of 'intentionality'.

Maslow called the new area a 'Third Force Psychology' apart from behaviourism and traditional psychoanalysis. *Towards a Psychology of Being* has perhaps been the most influential publication in this whole area, and in it he declares that 'existentialism rests on phenomenology: i.e. it uses personal subjective experience as the foundation upon which abstract knowledge is built.'

So far, however, the record of phenomenology is a record of glorious failures. As Spielgelberg says 'not only did Husserl fail to give a complete outline of his phenomenological psychology, but one finds surprisingly few concrete traces of his specific psychological insights in the subsequent literature.' Thus, he goes on, 'it was not Husserl the phenomenological psychologist, who proved to be the major contributor to the development of psychology. It was the philosopher Husserl whose general conception of phenomenology as the science of intentional consciousness, to be described in its essential structures, provided the major impulse for the future.'[44] Husserl's most illuminating chapters are those at the beginning of *The Crisis of the European Sciences*.[45]

[44] Herbert Spiegelberg, *Psychology and Psychiatry*, p. 13.
[45] Edmund Husserl, *The Crisis of the European Sciences*, Northwestern University Press, 1978. See also, about Husserl, 'The Relevance of Phenomenological Philosophy for Psychology' by Herbert Spiegelberg, in *Phenomenology and Existentialism*, eds E.N. Lee and M. Mandlebaum, Johns Hopkins Press, Baltimore, 1967, pp. 219–41.

But it is also true to say that philosophical anthropology is a stream of thought by which the universe is redeemed, because it becomes no longer a universe of matter-in-motion merely, operating by chance and necessity, but a universe in which living things 'strive', whatever that may mean, and in which consciousness has a place. Science itself is matter become conscious of itself, and capable of knowing—a development in evolution which places an enormous burden upon us, and moral responsibilities (as 'objective' science often fails to do).

The scientific modes of thought I have examined also question established evolutionary theory. The concept of 'heritable advantageous variations' is not enough to explain evolution. Many scientists of repute have sought teleological explanations—not necessarily in terms of 'God's purpose', but in terms of forms and activities that seem to express a 'striving', a *potentia* in the universe, seeking to fulfil itself. This is not mysticism, but legitimate biology, as the work of Bergson, Whitehead, Alexander, Collingwood, Husserl, Merleau-Ponty, Polanyi, Buytendijk, Straus, Goldstein and others have shown.[46] There seems to be a dynamic of being drawn forward towards possible goals: whatever can this mean? It requires a new sense of time, and attention to yet unexplained leaps forward in evolution.

In all these developments, the object of the quest is for a more adequate way of knowing. Darwin himself said that he blushed when he saw a peacock's tail, because he could not offer an explanation. It now seems that certain forms of display like the peacock's are not merely functional mating displays. The hens, for example, perform a back-stage role, becoming excited, but also helping to put on the show. Adolf Portmann as we have seen uses the terms *Selbstdarstellung* (self-display through the surface) and *Weltbezeihung durch Innerlichkeit* (relation to the environment from inwardness). W.H. Thorpe finds that birds improve their song even long after the functional purpose is fulfilled. Goldstein speaks of the 'preferred activities' of species which exploit the world they evidently 'enjoy'. All these biological observations demand a re-examination of evolutionary theory, with its roots in strict utilitarian thinking from the last century. They are certainly of value to the cultural worker, who finds himself today so daunted by scientific theories, which have reduced everything to mere

[46] See Marjorie Grene, *The Knower and the Known*, p. 239.

chance, 'energy requirements', all running down by the laws of entropy.

Yet here science in many areas remains dogmatic and reactionary —obscurantist in the extreme. In a recent study of evolutionary theory Norman Macbeth[47] reveals many inconsistencies in scientific thought, and many howlers and logical errors. He has no axe to grind, but he shows one serious problem: scientists admit difficulties among themselves, but to the susceptible public, as in school text books, they maintain an untroubled front, and offer unproven dogma. This duplicity suggests that darkness and confusion reside now in some areas of science itself, rather than in the emerging assault on the question 'What is man?' in the newer philosophical anthropology.

As Gabriel Marcel declares in his *Tragic Wisdom and Beyond*, philosophy can be supported only if it involves an actual responsibility in the face of the unprecedented crisis confronting man at the moment. The deadness of present-day philosophy is disastrous. As Marcel says, 'When I was at the Lima conference in 1951 I spoke with A.J. Ayer about a "philosophy of reflection"'; these words, Marcel found, which in France designated an incontestably venerable tradition, were meaningless for Ayer.[48] At Harvard, Marcel found that many philosophy professors were discouraging students 'from looking for a relation between the most exclusive analytical thought in which they were being trained and life— the problems that life poses to each one of us but which seemed in the professors' eye to be merely matters for personal discretion.'[49] While philosophy remains in academic centres this kind of intellectual game, a limbering-up exercise for the mind, and while philosophy and psychology claim that kind of abstract detachment, they cannot be justified at a time when 'our life is threatened at every level.' Indeed, some forms of psychology would seem to contribute to those developments, which Marcel believes we must

---

[47] Norman Macbeth, *Darwin Retried*, Garnstone Press, London, 1976.

[48] Yet Ayer evidently believes that he has solved all the important philosophical questions! As Roger Poole said, reviewing *The Central Questions of Philosophy*, 'They are no longer the central questions ... *The Central Questions leaves too much out* ... Professor Ayer (has) stated that he has come more and more to regard philosophy as the study of *proof*. '... The study of philosophy in the English-speaking world is stagnant. It refuses the urgent historical tasks before it ...' *Books and Bookmen*, June 1974, p. 60.

[49] Gabriel Marcel, *Tragic Wisdom and Beyond*, trans. S. Jolin and P. McCormack, Northwestern University Press, Evanston, Ill., 1973, p. 17.

fight. He ends his book with these words:

> Though I shall certainly cause some dismay and scandal among philo-
> sophers and theologians, I would say that in this age of absolute insecurity
> we live in, true wisdom lies in setting out, with prudence to be sure, but
> also with a kind of joyful anticipation, on the paths leading not necessarily
> beyond time but beyond our time, to where the technocrats and the
> statistics worshippers on the one hand, and the tyrants and torturers on
> the other, not only lose their footing but vanish like mists at the dawn
> of a beautiful day.[50]

It is in this general direction of a larger liberation that we may
find the sources of hope.

Philosophical anthropology points to a new and creative relationship between ourselves and the world, in which, instead of falling
into pessimism and despair, we may reassert our creative powers,
and envisage a new future: one in which it may be possible not
only to survive, but to develop a more adequate relationship
between ourselves and the world.

Here an important distinction to grasp is that between *understanding* (*Verstehen*) and *explanation* (*Erklarung*). I take these
contrasting terms from an essay by Ludwig Binswanger, 'Systematic Explanation and the Science of Psychoanalysis.'[51] Objective
scientific thinking has been largely directed at *explanation*; the new
modes of thought emphasize *understanding*.

This difference is being emphasized especially by the new
existentialists. Any attempt to explain man and his experience by a
science or philosophy tends to deal with *essences*. As Binswanger
says, 'each philosophical system comes with its own pre-established
criterion, by which something is recognized as an entity, as something to be encompassed in the system or as something by reference
to which all other entities encompassed can be "explained".'[52]
This is the effect of the empirical kind of psychology taught at
universities and colleges of education: this 'objective' kind of
explanation tends to disable student teachers in their response to
children's creative energies, as by making values and meanings
symbolism, seem unreal. But, as Cassirer argues, the natural
sciences cannot give an adequate account of man, because he is
the *animal symbolicum: meanings* are the central realities of his
existence. So, there is a radical difference between objective and
subjective disciplines here:

[50] Gabriel Marcel, *op. cit.*, p. 213.
[51] In Jacob Needleman, ed., *Being-in-the-World*, Basic Books, New York, 1963.
[52] *Ibid.*, p. 33.

The radical difference between the subject matter of physics, biology, etc., and psychology, history, literary criticism, etc., is indicated in the following manner: whereas in physics each datum is meaningless until it is brought into connection with other data through a conceptual scheme and hypothesis, in psychology each datum, a human perception, thought, emotion, etc., itself has its own meaning to the perceiver, thinker, feeler—to the human being.[53]

Moreover, there is a phenomenological aspect: whereas the variation of a light-pattern (physical data) does not of itself point to, refer to, intend of itself something beyond itself, 'an act of consciousness is essentially intentional, essentially refers beyond itself.' (Bretano, Husserl) 'Meaning is an intention of the mind.' (Husserl)

When science approaches such inner realities in human experience it tends to *strip the world of consciousness* and *intentionality*, by denying their existence implicitly, because of its 'objective' ideal. It cannot find the live creature making sense of his world—so it tends to make the world (and the being in it) seem meaningless; by its implication that only the 'physical' is real, it is nihilistic. So, creativity is inhibited by science because it offers a world in which it has no place. What we now have to learn to do, in the Humanities, is to develop subjective disciplines that *understand*, rather than *explain*, because it is the impulse to explain that has the effect of stripping the world of meaning, by its implication that microanalysis is the only valid way of meaning. By contrast, *understanding* does not menace *the intentional*, but indeed requires attention to that creative element in our thought, as in phenomenology.

This new existentialist understanding of man has its basis in the conception that man is no longer understood in terms of some theory—be it a mechanistic, a biologic or a psychological one—but in terms of his whole existence in the here and now, and in terms of the meanings by which he is trying to make sense of his life. This is not to explain, but to understand the 'total structure' of the individual's 'being-in-the-world'. This is not to be less empirical, but more so. It is not subjective irrationality, but a combination of science and humanism, and an attempt to 'cut below the cleavage between subject and object.'

Moreover, we are not seeking to devise a psychology that lends itself 'to the degrees of control and analysis necessary for the formu-

[53] *Ibid.*, p. 44.

lation of abstract laws'.[54] We are trying to understand better the ways in which men (and children) employ symbolism in their *becoming*—recognizing that underlying all creative activity there is a dread of nothingness, against which we need to assert the *Dasein*. All symbolizing activity is engaged with the existence problem. So, it belongs to the 'distinctive character of human existence' which is *Dasein*.

> Composed of *sein* (being) plus *da* (there) *Dasein* indicates that man is the being who *is there* and implies also that he *has* a 'there' in the sense that he can know he is there and can take a stand with reference to that fact. The 'there' is moreover not just any place, but the particular 'there' that is mind, the particular point *in time* as well as space of my existence at this given moment. Man is the being who can be conscious of, and therefore responsible for, his existence.[55]

Man is a creature who is not only 'being-in-itself' but 'being-for-itself'. Binswanger and other authors speak of '*Dasein* choosing' meaning 'the person-who-is-responsible-for-his-existence choosing.' By this *Daseinsanalysis* approach in psychiatry these therapists avoid stripping the world of consciousness and intentionality. Such existentialist approaches to human reality thus avoid the radical split in Western thought, between subject and object, and avoid fragmentation. Existentialism is not a comprehensive philosophy, or a way of life, but an endeavour to grasp reality. So, in applying these modes of understanding we are trying to rediscover the living person, amid the compartmentalization and dehumanization of modern culture, and trying to restore the creative dynamic to man, as his primary reality. The first thing to do is to read Marjorie Grene and Polanyi. They demolish the edifice on which the erroneous certainty of 'objective' approaches is based. Since her work is influenced by that of Polanyi—an outstanding chemist—Professor Grene is not anti-scientific; she is only concerned to see 'what science is' in a new and more human way. The established 'facts' of science, she says, however unquestioned, are still held in being by the same intellectual passions that first discovered them: they are conjectures. They may be so amply and confidently attested that no one 'in his senses'—that is, no one who accepts the authority of competent scientific opinion—would call them in doubt. But science is either something that human beings called scientists are

---

[54] Kenneth W. Spence, *Behaviour Theory and Conditioning*, Yale University Press, New Haven, Conn., 1956.
[55] Rollo May, *Existence, a New Dimension in Psychiatry*, p. 4.

doing, or it is nothing at all. Nothing any human being does has the wholly assured, wholly self-evident character of Cartesian method.

This essential personal basis of scientific knowledge—the recognition that it is, after all, only *one* way of knowing—is the clue to our escape from the consequences of the extrapolation from scientific reductionism into a general philosophy of life. It is our way to resist the intrusion of science into the sphere of ethics for example, a sphere in which, by its own terms, science has no authority to impinge. This theme is made clear in Dr Paul Roubiczek's *Ethical Values in an Age of Science*.[56] Since science is only *one* way of knowing, ethical choices need to be based on many disciplines, not least because scientific data does not provide its own interpretation. Moreover, science itself depends upon continual revision, and only becomes obscurantist if regarded as dogma. But what is also required is a new general philosophy developed from biology. As Marjorie Grene argues,

> There can be no resolution of the problem of the *Geisteswissenschaften* 'study of how the spirit knows', Plessner declares, without a general philosophy of man: 'A philosophical anthropology'. But a philosophical anthropology is in turn impossible, he says, unless it is itself founded on a philosophy of Nature, not, indeed, in the Kantian sense of a set of principles for the inorganic world, leading the life sciences to be guided by a vague set of 'as-ifs' or 'regulative principles' but in the sense of a philosophical examination of the question *what it means to be alive*.[57]

The kind of philosophical biology Marjorie Grene is discussing has found culture to be primary in human existence, and finds that this arises out of 'encounter', that is, out of love.

Biology itself has thus found the primacy of love as the source of being and social life, while in the study of organic forms it finds our specifically human attributes and our cultural existence at one with our biological form.[58] Social life, culture and love are inextricable, and so a positivist biology could never find 'full human nature'.

> What is full human nature? Portmann has mentioned its three chief characters: upright posture, speech, and rational action. Now, all these have to be *learned* by the infant in its first months through contact with human adults or in particular with one adult, his mother or foster mother.

[56] Paul Roubiczek, *Ethical Values in an Age of Science*, Cambridge University Press, London, 1969.
[57] *Approaches to a Philosophical Biology*, p. 65.
[58] Such an approach would surely be nothing strange to Dr Richard Leakey, who speaks of 'corporation' man. See *Origins*, Macdonald and Janes, London, 1977.

Of course parental care, and life in general, are essential, in a host of intricate and marvellous ways, to a host of other species as well. But nowhere else in living nature on this planet does this pattern of premature sociality occur.[59]

This unique period of post–embryonic, yet still psychically embryonic, growth is called by Adolf Portmann the period of *social gestation*. It demands not only nine months in the uterus, but a further twelve months in the '*social uterus of maternal care*'. It is like that psychic parturition with which psychoanalysis concerns itself, not least because this is a dynamic that involves the creative imagination and other intuitive capacities on the mother's part, and in the emerging infant's capacity to become himself according to 'the formative principle' in his living processes. We get a parallel picture in Winnicott and in the work of F.J.J. Buytendijk.

As Marjorie Grene insists, following Portmann, this development of cultural dynamics in man is no 'afterthought'; it is a central reality of our very existence, the special quality of man.

We must be careful also, Portmann warns us, not to take this lately developed pattern in evolution as a mere addendum to an otherwise 'ordinary' mammalian ontogenesis: our unique pattern of development is not an 'afterthought' tacked on to a standard embryo-genesis. The human attitudes and endowments which we must acquire in infancy are prepared for very early in embryonic growth: thus the first preparation for the upright posture, in the development of the pelvis, occurs in the second month of the foetus's growth. The preparation for the acquisition of speech, moreover, involves glottal structure very strikingly and thoroughly different from those of any other species. And the huge size of our infants relatively to the young of apes—born more 'mature' but very much smaller—is probably related, Portmann conjectures, to the immense development which begins, again, very early indeed in ontogenesis. In short, the whole biological development of a typical mammal *has been rewritten in our case in a new key*: the whole rhythm of growth, is directed, from first to last, to the emergence of a culture-dwelling animal—an animal not bound within a predetermined ecological niche like the tern or the stag or the dragonfly or even the chimpanzee, but, in its very tissues and organs and aptitudes, born to be open to its world, to be able to accept responsibility to make its own the traditions of a historical past and to make them into an unforeseeable future.[60]

We may reconsider our approach to culture, and perception, therefore, from these scientific observations that in our very flesh and bones, our emergence in the womb and our psychic parturition in the mother's care and love, the creative power of human culture

[59] *Approaches to a Philosophical Biology*, p. 47.
[60] *Approaches to a Philosophical Biology*, p. 48, my italics.

is integral as a manifestation of our evolution, and our movement forward to more adequate relationships with the world: our *knowing*. To say this links both science and the arts as ways of trying to make sense of our lives, a way of finding *meaning* in life, which is continually engaged with the world. (In this we have something like F.R. Leavis's 'living principle'.):

> We are always, as human beings, being in the world, in advance of our data in the aspiration to knowledge, yet caught in the ambiguity of our finitude between the explicit surface of our knowledge, the formulable, impersonal aspect of it, and the tacit, often even unknown clues to it in reliance on which we attend to that explicit core. There is no absolute, once for all, knowing by human beings, neither in supernatural confrontation with really reals nor in a logical checking off of falsified not-knowns. There are only ourselves, using all the means at our disposal: bodily orientation, sensory images, verbal formulations with their over-and-under-tone, social taboos and imperatives—including all the lore and practice and procedure of any given discipline we have been trained to—and, finally, our deepest, widest vision of the world we dwell in: using all these as clues to the nature we are in a given instance trying to understand ... [61]

Knowing is bound up with the whole existence of the being. Moreover, knowledge is bound up with questions of values. Some further arguments of Helmuth Plessner as discussed by Marjorie Grene seem relevant here. This philosopher of biology puts forward some valuable existential concepts, and he sees the essential creativity of man in his engagement with his reality—an engagement which can never quite bring the fulfilment he seeks but, through aspiration to the good, *makes* and *reveals* his world.

First of all Plessner sees man as a being 'who makes demands on himself.' With the psychoanalysts, Plessner sees a man as primarily a *moral* being.

> He is moral by nature, an organism which tames itself by making demands on itself, which domesticates itself ... the essential fact of his positionality becomes what is called conscience, the source from which ethical life and concrete moral existence flow. [62]

In conscience man expresses both his otherness from nature and his second nature. 'He is both alienated from nature, from his own nature, and turned to a higher nature, contrived nature, in which he becomes himself, in which he is at home.' In culture, true, he

---

[61] Marjorie Grene, *The Knower and the Known*, p. 33.
[62] Helmuth Plessner, *Die Stufen des Organischen und der Mensch*, quoted in Marjorie Grene, *Approaches to a Philosophical Biology*, p. 111.

transcends 'the more pervasive teleology of animal needs.' This means that, under the exigencies of the new *biology*, the new *science*, we have revealed the *moral* responsibility with which to resist the pseudo-biological nihilism that predominates in our culture. With Maslow, we must insist that man has a higher nature which is just as 'instinctoid'. If we defer to truth, this new hopeful dynamic view of man must triumph.

Of course, man never quite achieves the goods he seeks. Our knowing always belongs to the tension between appearance and reality, and this paradox is nonetheless found in our artistic and other cultural efforts. There is always a discrepancy between what we aim at and what we achieve, and all cultural efforts involve some kind of 'compromise with reality'. In this Plessner finds what he calls our 'contingency', and our eccentricity: yet our freedom lies in living with all these.

Another aspect of this eccentricity is what Plessner calls 'the utopian position', in conflict with the actuality of being mortal and insignificant:

> Man stands outside himself; he can do so totally, in the realization of his own nothingness or of the nothingness of the world. In his social relations, for example, the very fact of community displays his nothingness; for he, the individual, is replaceable by his fellow. *One* stands for *all*. But that is to deny that one is oneself; and yet one is oneself. This paradox ... underlies our social institutions: are we not born into clear, viable relations with others: we have to make them ...[63]

The political and social implications of these new views are enormous. What we should be looking for, and trying to create, is a society in which *meaning* is at a premium—and in which meaning can be created, to act against nothingness and death: only in such a society can individuals realize their potentialities. Yet both Capitalist and Marxist systems deny meaning.

The new biologists like Plessner tell us that if we really find our human biological nature, we shall also find hope and intentionality. The future tense is restored: 'in order to understand how something happens', Plessner says, 'we must first understand what it is that is to happen.' As Marjorie Grene says:

[63] Helmuth Plessner, quoted in Marjorie Grene, *Approaches to a Philosophical Biology*, pp. 113–14.

The morphology of human behaviour, both active and expressive, both goal-directed and intrinsically significant, precedes, logically and philosophically, the analysis of its physical and biological conditions.[64]

The main tradition of modern Western thought has put the cart before the horse. We need now to pay attention to such emphases as those of Plessner, which display our continuity with organic nature and yet our intrinsic creative difference from it. We need to recognize that

> We cannot analyse successfully the means through which our nature is expressed until we first understand what that nature is.[65]

That sentence of Marjorie Grene's alone, if accepted, would alter our whole approach to the world. The explicitness and air of complete certainty sometimes to be found in 'objective' science (though perhaps less nowadays) is spurious:

> No such understanding, on the other hand, is ever final and complete: it belongs to the very ambiguity of personhood that this is so.[66]

This means that we must live in the half-light uncertainty in which those working in the arts and humanities have always lived: not least in psychology, sociology and other such disciplines.[67] To accept this is not to be 'irrational', but rather to seek a fuller rationality at last:

> Overcoming both the absurdities of reductivities and the emptiness of idealism, it (Plessner's theory of organic modals) can provide, at long last a firm rational basis both for the biological sciences, in the many levelled structure, and for the sciences of man.[68]

And, we would hope, for the arts and education of man, too. These remarks by Marjorie Grene show how this kind of phenomenological study in philosophical anthropology is of interest to both science and the arts. It also shows how difficult such studies are—

[64] *Approaches to a Philosophical Biology*, p. 117.
[65] *Ibid.*
[66] *Ibid.*
[67] Plessner's *Laughter and Tears* lies between science and the humanities. 'The character of both as *reactions to a crisis of human behaviour as such* ... is the source of the contrast. To be a person ... is to *be* a body, to *have* a body, *and* to take a stand over against both these and the relation between them'. To understand what this means requires us to read Marjorie Grene's chapter carefully in *Approaches to a Philosophical Biology* and her preface to *Laughter and Tears*—and, of course, the book itself. As Buber says in *Distance and Relation*, the animal lives in its sensations like a fruit in its skin; we have a distance from ourselves and things, and it is this that makes us human.
[68] *Approaches to a Philosophical Biology*, p. 117.

yet how creative they can be. The solution to our problems lies in exploring our real nature, in painful awareness that this is a dark, groping, taxing progress. Our reward, however, is the recognition that the mind's element is not eternity, but 'the future through which, and towards which it aspires.'[69] Because of this, philosophy and psychology must recognize and accept their responsibility to the future in the sense indicated by my quotations earlier from Gabriel Marcel. We need to have sufficient courage to see that the unfolding true scientific awareness of our 'contingency', our 'nothingness', our nakedness, is not to leave us sprawled in the rubbish of the world but faced with a new responsibility as the *animal symbolicum:*

> ... the essential fact of his positionality becomes what is called con-science, the source from which ethical life and concrete moral existence flow.
>
> Plessner

We are moral by nature, and this morality is bound up with our capacity to envisage the future and make choices towards it.

This is what the new philosophical anthropology comprising psychoanalysis, *Daseinsanalysis*, the new existentialism, phenome-nology, philosophical biology and post-critical philosophy, all assert: that man is 'both alienated from nature, from his own nature, and turned to a higher nature, a contrived nature, in which he becomes himself, in which he is at home.' Nor is this just a 'compen-sation' for his natural neediness. 'We seek the completion of ourselves ... not simply through the assuagement of desire but through aspiration to the good.'[70] As Maslow says, we now need an emphasis, in the name of realism, on man's higher nature: and this can be a humanistic, non-religious, emphasis, albeit profoundly concerned with the meaning of life, and human striving.

It might seem at first hopeless to make such an emphasis—but I don't think so. The reduction of man to his functions, implicit in much of today's psychology and philosophy menaces the future—at a time when the whole tendency of the system of our society (whether in affluence or crisis) is to drive the meaning out of life by reducing man to his functions in his everyday life. A new psychology of being, and a philosophy that takes ontology seriously,

---

[69] Marjorie Grene, summarizing Plessner, in *Approaches to a Philosophical Biology*, p. 114.
[70] Marjorie Grene, *op. cit.*, p. 111.

are both urgently needed, and are in development in philosophical anthropology. These disciplines offer us the most profound hope for the future of the world: but, it should be said, they require us to revise our attitudes to life from top to bottom. I believe many are ready for such a change.

Post-critical Belief

Richard Gelwick

I am hopeful, and I think that I know why I am. I have discovered and learned to write and say 'I believe' without embarrassment. I have come to understand that by belief I really know something important, something that can make intelligible everything I do. This courage to say 'I believe' is a breakthrough shared with many others who have suffered and slaved under the objective ideal of knowledge that always warned against the subjective 'I'. No longer do I live under a total cloud of doubt, feeling that what is true can only be what I can prove to others in a laboratory-like test. My power to believe something to be true, that might conceivably be false, is awake and opening up new vistas and understanding. I am now free to take a stand and in doing so see that I am really closer to other minds rather than farther away from them. The objectivist dogma that the only way I can be a part of respectable human understanding is to give up my individuality and subordinate myself to an external and impersonal ideal has been shattered. Surprisingly, my new sense of self is also a break with the subjectivity of existentialism. The 'I' that I have found is one with a background and heritage, not a self-made ego building up a life from absurdity. Therefore, I want to say in a personal way that one of the sources of hope is in the recovery of our capacity to believe that something is true, when it might conceivably turn out to be false, and that this is the way we make contact with reality. Through this power to believe, we reach out to continuing ranges of comprehension and service. My aim here will be to explain this connection between 'I believe' and 'I hope'.

Belief, hope and the future

To put this approach in a slightly more philosophical manner, there are several theses, premises or axioms that ought to be exposed. Whether they are theses, premises or axioms depends upon the reader's point of view, for they may be debatable problems or they may be truisms already known. For me, they are conclusions from the experience I want to convey:

1. To believe means to reach out, for the self to act in a way that transcends vegetative existence. Belief at its most comprehensive levels issues in science, art and religion, but at its rudimentary level belief is a characteristic of the way a human being behaves who knows anything.

2. Belief and hope are inseparable. Hope itself is a belief that what is desirable and good is also possible. Belief in something is the foundation upon which hope rests, yet hope is the future promise of truth and good that sustains present belief. Hope is nothing less than the expectation of a deeper fulfilment of those things we believe to be true.

3. Belief and hope together lead to a growing knowledge of reality. Hope takes seriously the potentialities with which our present beliefs are in contact. Hope is not content with reality as it has been known but seeks to know it more deeply.

When belief and hope are set forth in this way, I think it may already be clearer why the capacity to say 'I believe' may be essential to the future functioning of our civilization. As one contemporary theologian of hope has suggested, the great temptation for the modern person is not so much wanting to be God as either wanting to achieve too little or wanting to achieve without patience.[1] Weak belief leads to weak hope and consequently to timidity, weariness and relativisms. On the other hand, weak hope leads to weak belief and the presumption of instant utopias. Unable to endure, the utopians become desperate persons trying to force the future into the present.

---

[1] Jürgen Moltmann, *Theology of Hope*, Harper and Row, New York, 1965, pp. 22ff, 34ff.

In 1974, Robert Heilbroner, economist and social thinker, sum-marized well many of our global problems in his book *An Inquiry into the Human Prospect*.[2] Besides the moral and ecological problems connected with overpopulation, war, limits to growth, and famine, he also observed symptoms of our civilizational malaise. Our inability to plan effectively even with the advantages of social science and our failure to pass on values from one gener-ation to another have produced a feeling of gloom and of despair. Along with the mounting complexity of world problems, Heilbroner saw the loss of confidence and the failure of nerve occurring in our situation. This pessimism and hopelessness is the most serious problem. Without belief and hope, we become futile in our thinking and actions; the possibilities of doom become more likely. It is for this reason that our capacity to believe again becomes most crucial.

Basic to the human prospect in the material and the social dimensions is the human prospect for imagination and creativity. The ability to solve immensely difficult problems will depend upon the ability to believe in and see things that we have not yet dis-covered. Without belief and hope, we accept things as they are. A state of resignation becomes prevalent as it did for the Cynics, Epicureans and Stoics of the ancient world. Indeed, the future of humankind depends more upon our power to believe and to hope than it does upon the quantity of our science and of our technology. Once scientific and technological solutions are available for meeting problems, belief and hope are essential for the political process of translating these discoveries into social order. Unless nations too, have confidence in the possibilities of a better future, they will not commit their resources, discipline their freedom and support the social order necessary for overcoming the gigantic problems we face. The political dimension then points to belief and hope as a religious problem, that is, in the sense of 'religion' as *religare*, 'to bind' or 'to tie together'. Of course, the uniting function of religion is dependent upon its credibility, which leads to the philosophical and theological dimension. Once we see this network of connections, we can begin to grasp the importance of why we need to be able to believe in things as true that conceivably might be false. We are a civilization threatened and impaired by the difficulties of physical and spiritual existence. Not only is there a scarcity of usable material resources, but there is a scarcity of credible spiritual resources.

[2] W. W. Norton, New York, 1974.

An archaeological example

One summer, I was a volunteer digger in an archaeological excavation at Tell Gezer, Israel.[3] For a philosopher and theologian, this experience was a microcosm of key intellectual issues in our desperate world. Central to the project was the epistemological question of how one moves from ignorance to knowledge, from the seemingly ordinary surface to the significant mine of information lying beneath it. My participation in the project was actually for such philosophical reasons, although the directors probably thought it was for the more immediate cause of rediscovering the past cultures that were buried there. But as one whose life had been spent mainly at the 'second order' level of reflection upon abstract ideas, I wanted to experience the process of discovery as it begins with our bodies, our senses, as they are focally engaged in material observations. This enterprise was one I could contribute to, without further elaborate training, with my general humanistic education and my willingness to be a laborer. The outcome of the experience proved to be a confirmation of the most basic features of an adequate philosophy of science, and the experience of archaeology itself remains a metaphor for understanding our way from the present to the future, from belief and hope to their realization.[4]

The chief archaeologist described the work as an art instead of a science because it did not live up to the standards of precision and exactness in physics and chemistry.[5] In his description, he revealed a source of modern despair, for it assumed that there was a sharp division between the sciences and the arts. Furthermore, it attributed to science the quality of exactitude as its primary feature. Without being aware of it, our leader had conceded to the dominance of the objectivist model of knowledge. Yet in the field, I found archaeology to follow essentially the same methodical principles as the natural sciences, although its problems were in many ways more complex because they dealt with human beings and would normally be related to the social sciences.

One of the first problems a field archaeologist faces is the selection of a worthy site for excavation. Such a choice is fundamentally like any other scientist's selection of a worthy research problem.

---

[3] The first report so far published on this six-year project is W.G. Dever, H.D. Lance and G.E. Wright, *Gezer I*, Keter Publishing Company, Jerusalem, 1970.
[4] The problem of an adequate philosophy of science will be dealt with in a later section.
[5] W.G. Dever, staff lecture, Tell Gezer, Israel, June 1971.

The choice is an informed one, growing from skill trained by years of apprenticeship and of awareness of relevant knowledge. Nevertheless, this decision is finally one of belief and of hope, for it entails both trusting in present knowledge with the expectation that it will lead to even more interesting and fruitful results if it is pursued.

In this case, the choice of the site was less difficult than some others because there had been prior but limited excavations of the area more than thirty years earlier. It was known to have been continuously occupied from the Copper Age to the Iron Age and to be the location of the largest fort found so far. Even though this evidence was promising, it was a major investment and risk to undertake further digging there.

The choice of this site was instructive in another way, in the importance of trained imagination. An uneducated observer passing by this location would notice very little except a modest hill. This hill though is not entirely a natural geological formation; it is a mound or 'tell', the accumulation of debris from centuries of occupation. The secrets this rather barren hill contained would not be expected by the lay-person, but the archaeologists, acting from their background of information and of beliefs, could hope to find significant objects, structures and patterns from earlier cultures.

Another feature of the archaeological process was its organization and leadership. Standards of research were maintained by a series of authoritative relationships. First were the sponsoring institutions, which had considered it and appropriated monetary and scholarly resources. Second was the hierarchical arrangement of authority on the site, with directors, core staff, general staff and volunteers. While there was much teamwork and conviviality, there was also a clear line of supervision and accountability that was based upon experience and expertise. In this way, the work was both orderly and creative. The most junior member could ask questions and make suggestions, but the final decisions were made by the directors or in consultation with their staff. When digging is at about two centimetres deep within a square, one can be tempted to want to go faster, to bore, to tear out. By belief in the total strategy and in its competence, the results slowly emerge from the minute steps of removing the earth. In my particular area, we had to follow the rule of not moving some large rocks until we could determine their relationships and significance. The dig progressed until we could not see each other because of the large rocks that separated us. At last their meaning became clear, and when they were removed carefully, a small plaster-lined granary was revealed. The roles of belief and of hope in an organization for acquiring knowledge are seen here as they contributed to our patience and to the success of the method of working very gradually under strict controls and standards.

Most obvious and already suggested is the way archaeology shows how we move from the known to the unknown by belief and hope. The archaeological enterprise is guided from beginning to end by a sense of unfolding drama, by the excitement of moving from the recent to the ancient. This drama is always a risky one where the efforts may be unproductive. One can miss important finds by certimetres. Since digging is virtually blind, in our not knowing what is underneath the surface, mistakes and irreparable destruction may occur. Despite the risks and the discomforts of the field, archaeologists are an enthusiastic and passionate group of professionals. Their intensity and zeal, displayed in patience and restraint as they inch their way through the earth, shows a classic parallel to that of a scientist pursuing a hypothesis believed to be promising but that could turn out to be gainless.

The way archaeological clues are joined to form a pattern is also like the way evidence in natural science is grasped to give new knowledge of nature. Working from limited acquisitions, the archaeologist must try to put together a whole puzzle without all the parts. From a collection of broken shards, a vase is reconstructed. From a trench of destroyed stones, a wall is rebuilt. From partial remnants, complete artifacts are discovered. This recovery is made possible by the ability of the human imagination to compare many samples and to discern in them enough of an outline to guide in the remaking of the old. There is a difference here from natural science in that archaeology does not disclose something never seen before by human beings, but the integration of parts into a whole through a Gestalt synthesis is very much like the work of the natural scientist.

When these characteristics of the way archaeology moves from the seen to the unseen are combined, they form a parable of the relations of belief and of hope. Archaeology is a discipline and field of inquiry employing many scientific and humanistic skills in the singular purpose of studying antiquity. To succeed, archaeology has to cross the boundaries of the present and grope for knowledge where there is great risk of failure. It is in accepting this liability and lack of certainty that it has added so much to our understanding of history.

The tell and mass death

An archaeologist's child was asked 'What do tells do?' and the child answered 'They tell things.' In the case of the excavation at Tell Gezer, this description was certainly true. Standing alone about twenty-two kilometres from the very visible Mediterranean Sea, this fortified mound with its commanding view spoke well of the hopes and despair of many centuries.

First, there was the military history of the tell. As one dug down through the layers of previous cultures, one was confronted repeatedly with cultural changes precipitated by invasion and war. In fact, there seemed to be less evidence of gradual peaceful change than of abrupt and sudden alterations. There was evidence of hasty departures, with beautiful jewellery and vases left behind. There were the burned slices of earth still speaking of the fires that had destroyed. There were the 'robbed out' architectural structures with their valuable stones removed to build up an enemy's palace. As these signs of human behaviour appeared at this fortress, one thought about how many times people had prepared to protect and defend themselves, only to fail. Despite its strategic location and advantages and despite its double-walled enclosures, Tell Gezer though difficult to attack had not remained invincible. In our age of modern warfare, one was led to wonder all the more about the value of our expensive defence systems.

A second thing 'told' by the tell was in the contemporary context of the excavation. Overhead flew the interceptors and the reconnaissance planes of the Israeli Air Force. Lying about the recent surface were empty shell casings and bullets from the Six Day War. On weekend trips into the cities, one saw young men and women, strolling as lovers in mufti, yet armed with carbines and ready to fight in the army at a moment's notice. One excavation that summer was digging down from the time of the early kings of Israel, David and Solomon, back beyond the time of the patriarchs, such as Abraham, Isaac, Jacob and Joseph. Our 'dig' was standing in ancient Israel while a modern Israel was struggling to establish itself. Most striking was the fact that this new Israel was the result of a people who had escaped from a holocaust and were trying to have one place in the world where they would not be persecuted.

A third thing was spoken by our tell. We were an international and inter-faith group, tied together by a purpose that transcended political and religious distinctions. Besides a large number of Americans, there were persons from many other countries. There was an artist from Germany who drew sketches of artifacts *in situ*. There were sabras, native-born Israelis, who had grown up on kibbutzim. There were Bedouins who helped with the very heavy labour of hauling away the dirt and rock after its excavation. There were scholars from Holland, England and Australia, as well as postmen, housewives, students and faculty, who had made this their vacation. We were united by the pursuit of meaning through the recovery of the past. Although we did not talk about it, standing between the wars of the ancient past and the Israeli defences of the present, we must have believed and hoped that in some way our activity would make a difference to our future.

Here the tell asks a question: 'How can we hope in the face of the mass destruction and evil of the twentieth century?' Brutal and violent death is itself a horror, but it is virtually impossible to find standards of measurement or of comprehension for the mass murdering of this century. Conservative estimates make this century one of the most violent in the number of deaths from war.[6] But there is no basis of comparison for the death camps of the Nazis or for the atomic bombings of Hiroshima and Nagasaki. Elie Wiesel, himself an eyewitness to the torture and murder at Auschwitz, has keenly preserved the indictment toward humanity that this event produces.

> My forehead was bathed in cold sweat. But I told him that I did not believe that they could burn people in our age, that humanity would never tolerate . . .
> 'Humanity? Humanity is not concerned with us. Today anything is allowed. Anything is possible, even these crematories . . . '[7]

> The inhabitants of Sodom didn't kill children before their mothers' eyes. The citizens of Gomorrah went in for vice, not for death. Our generation is worse than theirs. It's the generation of the guilty. We all have to share in the crime, even if we combat it; there's no escape from the trap.[8]

> I feel ashamed as a human being living in this century. I am ashamed to think that I belong to a civilization which has done what it has done. And I do not speak of the Germans. I speak of everybody else.[9]

[6] Martin Gilbert, *Recent History Atlas*, Weidenfeld and Nicholson, London, 1967.
[7] *Night*, Avon Books, New York, 1969, p. 43.
[8] 'A Witness Speaks', *Conservative Judaism*, 21, 3, p. 42.
[9] *Ibid.*, p. 43.

The poignancy of Wiesel's memories tends to focus us on the Jewish experience. There is a compelling power in the survivor's narrative as he tells what he personally saw. Atomic destruction by bombing from on high has received much less review outside Japan. The distance of the bomber from the people below, who were incinerated in a metropolitan-size crematorium, prevents the sense of personal knowledge and responsibility. Nevertheless, these events are one, for they mark our century as a turning point, as the time when gross evil turned not against individuals and enemies, but against humanity itself. We have lived in what Sartre has called the 'rummage sale, the liquidation of the human species . . . by the cruel enemy who has sown from time immemorial . . . to destroy him, that hairless, evil, flesh-eating beast—man himself.'[10] As we inquire into the human prospect, it is this revelation of *Homo sapiens'* inhumanity to humanity that makes us wonder if humanity can prevail.

Skepticism and truth
The proposition that humanity can prevail is a belief held to be true that might turn out to be false. It is a glaring certainty that without such belief, there will be no hope. It is also distinctly manifest that there are substantial grounds for doubting the human capacity to meet the challenges it acutely faces. It is still more obvious that we cannot stir up belief and hope with integrity if we ultimately are not convinced. Camus and other existential philosophers have well taught us that it would be better to die with honesty than to die deceiving ourselves that everything will turn out all right.[11] In fact, this facing of the absurdity of life is attractive in its heroic realism. An existentialist can at least hope that as human beings in a pointless universe, we will recognize our tragic situation and face it.

The existential analysis, though finally inadequate, is valuable in driving one to examine the sources of hope. It thoroughly challenges any easy answer based upon the 'bad faith' that some unseen and greater power will take care of us. The uncertainty of life described in existentialism underlines the constant risk of existence. In the existential outlook, belief and hope are revived in their definition, if not in fact, because they both become impossible without inherent risk. To believe truly becomes reaching out further than we

[10] *The Condemned of Altona*, Alfred A. Knopf, 1961, p. 177.
[11] *The Plague*, Modern Library, New York, 1948.

can see. To hope is to hold on to a goodness in what we believe. Still, the question remains 'If our condition is absurd and tragic, what are the grounds on which we can believe that humanity can abide with confidence in its future?'

The answer begins with an understanding of how we have come to our frightful predicament. Looking back at the history of the race, we see a pattern of change from the particular to the universal to the superficial in human standards.[12] At the earliest stages, human existence is taken up with the surrounding world. Reality is an overwhelming force where the inner and outer world inter-penetrate each other. It is a world of fascination and of awe. Even a human being's own entrails are considered an extension of the vegetative realm around him. What we think of as an individual consciousness of reality today does not exist. Rather, the indi-vidual's reality is in the clan with its mysterious oneness with nature. In this situation, loyalties are dominated by kinship ties to the group instead of rational standards.

These larger and more rational standards are a second major type that emerges when the human makes a clearer distinction between inner and outer reality, subject and object. Then reality begins to change, and the analytical questioning starts that asks 'What is that?' This search for essences opens up a vast part of the history of civilization, ranging from putting the gods on Mount Olympus to God as the Supreme Being. The central issue in this type of thinking is rationality. By its power, loyalties shift from clan and tribe to more universal ones represented by cities and states. It is now possible to have a deep common bond with other persons based upon ideas instead of upon blood ties. This change, while immensely liberating, became problematic and skeptical. The reason within gradually decreased, and the rationality of the external world became the dominant form. Reason achieved the systems of theology, but the content of the theology became distant and remote. A chasm had widened between the thinking subject and the thought object. A major force in this movement was the impact of modern science and technology.

In the place of the former universal essences, a third type of standards appears represented by a new provincialism based upon the functioning of things. With the loss of the transcendence of the 'essentialist' period of thinking and the immanence of the 'mythical'

---

[12] Cornelis A. Van Peursen, 'Man and Reality—The History of Human Thought', *Student World*, 56, 1 (1963), pp. 13–21.

stage of thinking, human beings began to relate to reality mainly in terms of its technological operations. The central issue in the primitive stage was that reality is. In the second stage, the central issue is analysis of reality. In this last and current stage, the issue is not reality, but how things work. This development is an impoverishment of reality, a reduction to an 'operational' scale that avoids the ultimate questions of belief and of hope.

While this sketch outlines changes in our standards, it does not state why the rise to universal standards and then their decline to the finite and operational has occurred. In the first two stages, there is a sense in each that we are at home in reality. In the last, there is a sense of aliens standing upon a surface of limited intelligibility; hence, existentialism and positivism rise from a common outlook. Existentialism teaches the alien that you must make up the values that will work for you. Positivism teaches the alien that we can function if we stick to what we can observe and measure in the world around us. This outline, so far, is only a suggestive description without an adequate explanation. The description points out how we have risen to a belief in universal standards of reality and then moved to a relativism of the operational.

A related step in finding an answer to whether or not there are grounds for belief and hope for humanity is to remember the moral development of our civilization. It was a Jewish belief in an infinite God that in the sixth century B.C. began the ethical monotheism that led to the long struggle for universal justice and peace. Combined with Greek rationalism, this vision of human perfection became the Judaeo-Christian tradition that set forth messianic visions of a kingdom of God. Though there were factions and varieties of the messianic expectation, the dream persisted of a society where no one would need to have the laws of right written because they would be inscribed on the human heart. These beliefs worked like a leaven within the political organization of the ancient and medieval world until they burst forth in the modern period with the abolition of monarchy and the establishment of democratic states. Gradually our belief in the value and dignity of every person led to the idea of self-rule. We moved from a belief in the authority of special rulers to a belief in our own authority in general for governing our lives.

Accompanying this political revolution was an even deeper social one: the change from a static society, content with conditions as they are, to a dynamic one, dedicated to unlimited social improvement. Before this transformation, there had been ages of great reform, but never until the modern period had this social striving for human perfection for all people become a dominant principle. By the end of the eighteenth century, it had become a general belief that we could by enlightened reason liberate all persons from the darkness of ignorance and of oppression and build a society of free persons. The pursuit of such hopes achieved in the nineteenth and twentieth centuries the most humane and liberal societies the world had yet seen. It increased the education and wealth of the masses and seemed to move closer to the messianic dream of the abolition of ignorance, poverty and war.

Beneath the optimism and the ideal of progress in the eighteenth and nineteenth centuries, there was a contrary current of skepticism. This doubt, paradoxically, grew from one of the same forces that was serving to free human-kind—namely, the objectivist ideal of modern science. It was largely the objectivist method of the new science that had united with the moral zeal of the past to provide a way for the construction of a better life for humanity. It was not so much the technological advances made possible by the discoveries of science, but it was the ideal of impersonal reason applied to observed experience that inspired the confidence that we could reform the whole world. Thus, the method that controlled the vision of the French philosophers of progress was also the objectivist method that guided the thought of the new skeptics.

David Hume, one of the most influential of the British empiricists, is representative of this new current of skepticism that grew from the objectivist understanding of the method of natural science. Educated in the ideas of Newton and impressed that Newton had thrown so much light on the phenomena of nature by working with hypotheses that could be empirically tested, Hume tried to develop a similar philosophical system of understanding human nature. The consequence of Hume's investigations was a devastating skepticism. Hume found that while certainty can be attained within the formal relations of ideas, such as in mathematics, only probability ratios can be attained in dealing with matters of fact, such as in judgments about human nature. Although Hume was saved from the radicalness of his conclusions, by balancing the uncertainty of our knowledge with custom and habit, his observation that we would not follow the dangerous implications of his logic has not turned out to be true. In the long run, the uncertainty of knowledge, keenly set forth by Hume, has come to haunt the modern consciousness.

At this point, an interruption in our survey is justified. Seeking an answer to the question of human belief and hope in the future, we should acknowledge that the proposal that we can do an important action, for example excavation, only by being able to hold on to beliefs as true that might conceivably be false is the very opposite of Hume's skepticism. One is invited to say 'Yes, I see the risk in knowing, and I am prepared to accept it.' What is proposed is not that we ignore the presence of doubt or that we return to authoritarian dogmas but that we entertain belief with its risk as the only way we can approach the deeper truth that opens up reality to us. This alternative is to reverse the one left by Hume.

To understand how we got into the moral predicament of the twentieth century with its unparalleled atrocities, there is one more major step. The twin ideals of moral perfection and of objectivist study of science, joined in the eighteenth and nineteenth centuries, become transformed into a 'dynamo-objective' coupling producing a 'moral inversion.'[13] The dynamo in this coupling is the moral fervour stemming from the Judaeo-Christian heritage, the striving for perfection according to the standards of an infinite and righteous God. The mechanism is the objectivism of a scientific outlook that increasingly denied the grounds of belief by asserting that only what could be impersonally and empirically measured is true. This objectivist ideal of strict detachment undercut not only all religious beliefs but also all moral beliefs. Nevertheless, the moral passion of the centuries continued in disguised forms. Once religion and morality were denied on the objectivist grounds, they were covertly restored within the objectivist approach itself.

The way this covert restoration of values within an objectivist framework occurred can be seen in two major examples: romantic nihilism and Stalinist Marxism.[14] The nihilist is motivated by a radical sense of autonomy, refuses to bow to any authority and feels that only the destruction of traditional values and institutions can give genuine freedom. Portrayed by Turgenev, Dostoevsky and Nietzsche, this nihilist dissolves all restraints upon human beha-

---

[13] Michael Polanyi, *Personal Knowledge*, University of Chicago Press, 1958, pp. 222–39; Richard Gelwick, *The Way of Discovery*, Oxford University Press, 1977, pp. 6–14.

[14] Michael Polanyi, 'Science and Man', *Proceedings of the Royal Society of Medicine*, 63, September 1970, pp. 972–73.

viour. Traditional morality, contends nihilism, is guilty of hypocrisy because it does not live up to its ideals. Furthermore, it is in-authentic because it is based upon conventional standards. There-fore, even naked and brutal truth is higher than this morality. In Dostoevsky's character, Raskolnikov, we see the nihilist murdering an innocent old woman to prove his freedom from traditional values. Here morality is in one sense destroyed but in another preserved as it appears under the banner of the objectivity of scientific truth. Immoral morality is justified because of its honesty.

The second example of moral inversion is seen in the way Stalinist Marxism coupled the moral zeal for a better society with an objectivist scientific theory. According to Marxism, traditional morality is bourgeois ideology supporting the oppressive structure of a capitalist state. A better world can be formed only on the scientific principles of history in dialectical materialism. These scientific principles, oddly, both deny morality on the basis that it is the subjective interest of the ruling class and at the same time offer a new morality disguised as scientific fact. Once this inversion was established by the Communist Revolution, it was possible for Stalin to liquidate all opponents on the grounds that they were resisting the truth of science. The possibility of critical argument and moral accusation was taken away from all dissenters from Communism because traditional morality was untrustworthy bourgeois propaganda, and truth is Marxist fact based on science. The independence of truth, on which morality depends for its persuasiveness, has been assimilated into a totalitarian ideology.

From this investigation, it becomes clearer that one of the primary causes of our tragic and inhumane century was the loss of our belief in ideals as true that might conceivably be false. The capacity to say 'no' to an ideology, an opinion or a supposed fact depends upon the possibility that truth exceeds and is greater than anyone's interpretation. The willingness of others to listen to a minority or dissenting view depends upon the same possibility. We have seen that there has been an attrition of human standards from the universal to the operational and from the ideal of social progress to moral inversion. The power of belief in truth to chal-lenge and to question the distorted logic of nihilism and of totali-tarianism was eroded by the objectivist ideal of science. When belief in truth as a power independent of the control and the possession of any particular group or historical manifestation was forsaken, the violence of human conflicts was unleashed. The only effective way to deal with power was with brute force. Discussion and argument became impotent. From such a vantage point, the world appeared absurd, 'the rummage sale' of the human race.

Belief and truth

At this point, one more lesson from the archaeological excavation will help our discussion. On the final night, before the conclusion of the dig and the departure of the volunteers, a banquet was held under the roof of our dining shelter. This banquet 'hall' was really the multipurpose room used for lectures, meals, marking pottery, library tables, letter writing, and common room. Our last official gathering was a happy celebration with awards and skits high-lighting the foibles and the achievements of the summer's work. I was quite pleased and surprised when my supervisor presented me with an award.[15]

During that summer, I had the fortune to be assigned to the square that became known as 'the goodie corner' because so many significant small objects were being found there. One day, under the scrutiny of my supervisor, I came upon a small but very beautiful piece of cerulean-coloured glass. Within minutes, its exposure to the air began to tarnish its bright colour. My supervisor immediately called in the geologist, the photographer and the directors. Very careful records were made of the stratigraphic location and of the mode of this artifact's appearance. From all of the excitement and of the inrush of additional experts, I knew that we had found something important.

Upon analysis, the small fragment of glass proved to be Amarna glass, which helped to establish that our excavation had reached the period of the Amarna age. This period in the fourteenth century B.C. in Egypt was one of the dazzling but brief episodes in that history. It was the time of Akhenaten, the pharaoh whose religious reform to worship of the sun may be the first monotheism. It was the time of Nefertiti, Akhenaten's beautiful queen whose limestone bust is one of the artistic wonders of the ancient world. It was also the time of Tutankhamen, the boy-king whose recovered tomb has become a modern legend. This interesting period was also con-nected with Tell Gezer by the discovery in 1887 of more than three hundred and fifty cuneiform tablets, which were letters written to or from Amarna, the capital of Akhenaten. In these letters

---

[15] The supervisor was Janet MacLennan, M.A., University of Michigan.

that were found at Amarna, there is evidence of correspondence with three kings of Gezer.

The combination of our 'goodie corner' and the identification of our stratification as Amarna age established a strong belief and hope in me that we would find a cuneiform tablet from an Egyptian ruler, or an official, to one of the Gezer kings. On weekends at the Rockefeller Museum in Jerusalem, I studied carefully the size and shape of cuneiform tablets, preparing my eyes for the discovery of an Amarna age tablet in our square. Our general success was sufficient to make it seem possible that we might uncover one of the most valuable types of archaeological finds, written information. Every morning when I went to our square in Field Six, I went with the vision before me of a small pillow-shaped piece of clay inscribed with pictorial writing. Such a tablet was not found. Even though it was not, there is a possibility that one is there, awaiting the skill and the right guess to find it. It was probably my attachment to this expectation that caused my supervisor to award me a likeness of a clay tablet, a souvenir I still cherish.

Belief in the truth is a belief in an independent reality, not of our own making, which gives hope. It is like the field archaeologist's belief in the potentiality of his or her discoveries. It has reasonable grounds, but they are not absolutely certain. They require the taking of risks in order to find their reality. It is this deeper kind of objectivity that was eclipsed by the mistaken ideal of objectivist science. This objectivism limited our view of truth to the most tangible aspects of reality and gradually led to the destruction and absurdities of our century.

An alternative theory of knowledge

Despite the influence of the objectivist ideal of knowledge in our culture, a reform in our epistemological outlook has begun that contradicts this approach and establishes an alternative ideal. This alternative, most clearly set forth by Michael Polanyi, is what I have called 'the way of discovery' and 'heuristic philosophy.'[16] Polanyi, himself a distinguished physical chemist, shows that science in practice never did and never could attain knowledge by the method of objectivist science. Guided by the example and the traditions of its own community, science followed a different method deeply dependent upon the role of belief in knowing. The

[16] *The Way of Discovery*, pp. 84–85.

objectivist ideal of knowledge would have remained largely harmless if the attempt to purge all beliefs from knowledge had not been taken up as an ideal for the whole of society. The alternative presented by Polanyi is to begin with the way science actually achieves knowledge and from there to generalize to a common structure of knowing.

The first major step of Polanyi's thought is to show that knowing intrinsically involves a coefficient of belief. This belief component is decisive in the way knowing is able to gain new knowledge. His analysis of knowledge is original in articulating in more specific and less charged concepts the way belief functions in knowing. This analysis is set forth in what Polanyi calls 'tacit knowing.'[17]

Tacit knowing explains that in all knowing there are two types of awareness, 'subsidiary' and 'focal'. These terms indicate the perceptual model of Gestalt psychology, which first gave Polanyi the clue to the problem of belief and of knowledge. The subsidiary awareness is the background awareness including thousands of clues from previous experience as well as the stimuli of the immediate target of knowing. We dwell in these clues and assimilate them into our knowing without a direct awareness of them. Our subsidiary awareness guides us to what we focally know. It also contributes the particulars that are integrated into the focal knowledge. Central in this 'from–to' knowing is the person. The person is the agent for both subsidiary awareness and focal awareness, linking the two together.

To know anything or to say something is true, according to the evidence of Polanyi, entails the structure of tacit knowing. It is this structure which shows that belief as a fiduciary component is effective in all knowing. Polanyi shows this structure in the basic forms of knowing such as speech, performances and feats of imagination. In each there is subsidiarily a relying upon myriad clues in order to attend focally to a target. A typical example is the way we recognize a familiar countenance. We look for a characteristic pattern as a whole, which is our target for recognition. We do not look for the particulars or details of the face because they have to be seen in the whole to which they contribute. If we concentrate upon some feature of a countenance, the whole pattern dissolves and cannot be recognized. Another example is playing a piano where the performance depends upon the integration of many

17 *The Tacit Dimension*, Doubleday, Garden City, New York, 1966.

muscular movements and musical concepts into harmonious action. If the pianist tries to play by thinking about which finger to move and what note to strike, the performance will falter or even be paralyzed. All knowing is a skilful action tacitly combining the subsidiaries upon which we depend into a coherent pattern.

The discovery of new areas of truth in science is essentially the same as a skilful performance. The scientist is one who is prepared by a long education of immersion in the scientific community to look for patterns in nature. The scientist approaches a problem from a background awareness that guides her or him in the most promising direction. By relying upon this background, much of which may be described as 'hunch', the scientist senses focally an approaching coherence. This possibility is the hope for deeper truth discerned by reliance upon her or his beliefs. Scientific beliefs developed by schooling and experience are relied upon tacitly and subsidiarily in order to guide the scientist to the truer understanding of reality.

Such a view shows that knowledge of reality is attained by our indwelling a body of clues that constitute its coherence and pattern. The terms 'indwelling' and 'body' are important because they indicate the extent to which tacit knowing is counter to the objectivist ideal of detachment. The very careful and laborious control represented by objectivism is actually a passionate act of concentration in which the scientist subordinates and trains all of her faculties upon a worthy problem. The limitations and constraints under which a field archaeologist or a laboratory scientist places herself are done in order to pour herself into the project at hand.

At every level of our excavation of reality, new dimensions of hope appear. Truth is shown by tacit knowing to be a relation to an unfolding reality. We join in a search and give up other opportunities because we sense the prospect of a find. Reality speaks to us through promises. It invites and prompts us to a place where related but widening areas of intelligibility are present.

The objectivist ideal of knowledge is limited to one level of knowledge, the surface. It has no stratigraphy. Tacit knowing, however, points to a stratified view of the universe. The notions of subsidiary awareness and of focal awareness correspond to the structures of our evolutionary understanding. Matter evolves from the inorganic to the organic and from the organic to the conscious level by the principle of 'dual control.'[18] Each level of the organiza-

[18] *Ibid.*, p. 36.

tion of matter is both determinant and indeterminant. It has the distinctive characteristics that make it what it is. For example, an atom has a nucleus and orbiting electrons. It also has the potentialities for the combination with other atoms to form molecules. Higher and more complex forms of matter come into being because a lower level of conditions leaves open the possibility of being harnessed by a higher one. Far up the evolutionary scale, we can see this vividly in the way the appearance of a central nervous system leaves open to natural selection the possibility of a creature that knows.

This hierarchical picture of reality, disclosed by tacit knowing, is also seen in the way tradition and experiment are related. The advancement of knowledge is possible only by reliance upon a broad background. Without basic belief in the traditions and the lore of the scientific community, the researcher is not equipped with the skills and the interests that will enable her or him to make significant breakthroughs. Such a researcher would be blind to the prospects and pass by the mound of reality unaware of what it could tell. The objectivist attempt to establish values or knowledge by the rejection of all beliefs is an emptying of our subsidiary awareness culturally and personally, preventing us from being able to focus upon reality itself. It is by reliance upon the standards of the past that we have intimations of greater standards that lead us to challenge the old and seek the new. In this development, there is both continuity and discontinuity.

Polanyi's alternative theory of knowledge shows how belief and hope link the past, present and future. By relying upon what is present from past human experience as well as immediate experience, we are guided to the intimations of new aspects of reality. Belief in these intimations leads us to the investigations that establish new knowledge of reality. For this process to occur, belief and hope have to meet two conditions. First, belief in the possibility of finding the truth must be strong enough to initiate action. Secondly, the hope of finding the truer grasp of reality must be strong enough to sustain the action throughout long periods, even over centuries, as in the case of the Copernican revolution. From this it becomes apparent that in order to know truth in its growth in thought and in application, we are called to accept the risk of belief with the possibility that our beliefs may be false.

Credo ergo sum

After more than three centuries of critical doubts that have weakened confidence in religious knowledge and replaced it with the objectivist ideal, a new type of authority is appearing, the authority of 'I'. Previously to say 'I' in scholarship was tabu, an indication of subjectivity and lack of erudition. Increasingly it is a sign of the recovery of the role of belief in knowing.

When Descartes set out on his quest for certainty by the method of doubt, he thought he had ended it with his famous discovery of the *cogito*. But his thinker was imprisoned within the body and unable to establish contact with the external world. At that point, one of the influential separations of belief and of hope began that have led to our anxiety and despair.

It takes courage to say 'I', to take responsibility for the knowledge that I hold to be true. I have learned that the acknowledgment of my believing participation in knowing is the way I express universal intent. Instead of isolating me in idiosyncrasies, 'I believe' identifies the common ground that I share with all knowers. It is the common ground that makes it possible for me to indwell and to assimiliate the reality so far discerned by the human race. It is also the way I discover that reality is alluring, promising a range of indeterminate possibilities. In this respect, it is like, as Polanyi pointed out, a Christian worshipping God.[19]

[19] *Personal Knowledge*, p. 405.

Hope and Time:
Theory-Praxis in the Long Run

Ernst Bloch

INTRODUCTION
by Wayne Hudson

When man hopes, he hopes in time, but whereas a literature exists on the subject of hope, comparatively little has been written on the relationship between hope and time. The German Marxist philosopher Ernst Bloch (1885–1977) is one of the few who has taken up this problem and made it a central concern.

Bloch is known internationally as 'the philosopher of hope', and as the author of *The Principle of Hope (Das Prinzip Hoffnung)*[1], an eighteen-hundred page exploration of hope, which is sometimes regarded as one of the major philosophical works of the twentieth century. Nonetheless, what Bloch means by hope is easily misunderstood. Bloch is not a 'philosopher of hope' in a narrowly psychological sense. For Bloch, hope is not only psychological. It is a fundamental determination within reality in general.

---

[1] The title *Das Prinzip Hoffnung* is difficult to translate. Bloch uses the term *Prinzip* in a technical meaning common in philosophical German but rare in English: 'principle' in the sense of *principium* or *archē*. The standard translations, 'The Principle of Hope', 'Hope the Principle', 'The Hope Principle' are all somewhat misleading. 'The Principle-Hope' (suggested by George Steiner) is more accurate, but awkward in English and a little too ontological. *Das Prinzip Hoffnung* hints at the technical meaning without committing Bloch to it. On the whole, I prefer to retain 'The Principle of Hope', which already has a wide currency in English, and to correct any misunderstanding with a technical gloss.

Expectation, hope, intention to still unbecome possibility, is not only a fundamental characteristic of human consciousness. Concretely rectified and grasped, it is a fundamental determination within objective reality as a whole.[2]

Bloch does not mean that a human psychological state can be attributed to reality in general. He means that what appears in man as hope cannot be understood in terms of a Cartesian dualism which locates hope as a psychological state in man, considered as an ensouled spirit in an alien and fundamentally disparate world. For Bloch, human hope must be related to the world in which it occurs, and to the possibility content developing in that world. Bloch distinguishes between *subjective* or *psychological hope*: the hope that hopes (*spes, qua speratur*), and *objective hope*, the correlate of psychological hope in possibility: the hope that is hoped (*spes, quae speratur*).[3]

Bloch claims that subjective hope has a basis in objective hope or the possibility developing in the world. Obviously the relationship between subjective and objective hope is not a simple one. Some hopes turn out to be illusory, while other hopes may have an internal psychological function despite the fact that they can never be realized in the world. Again, it is not easy to determine which subjective hopes have a basis in developing possibility, since many hopes which seem to be impossible, later turn out to be possible. No doubt it is necessary to have a theory about which subjective hopes relate to objective possibilities and which do not, but beyond the most evident cases, such a theory can only be based on supposition. Ultimately, the only test is praxis. This means, however, that the problem of hope needs to be re-posed as a problem of the relationship between hope and time, since many hopes cannot be tested by praxis now, but may be able to be tested by praxis in the future.

Most traditional approaches to hope assume that the limits to hope are set by the nature of things and by what the nature of things makes possible. Bloch's contribution is to challenge this assumption, and to propose an entirely new conception of reality which introduces a radical time dimension into the understanding of ontology and possibility, in a way which transforms the traditional problem of the realizability of human hope. From his early

[2] *Das Prinzip Hoffnung, Gesamtausgabe* (hereafter *GA.*), published by Suhrkamp Verlag in sixteen volumes, Vol. 5, p. 5.
[3] *Ibid.*, pp. 1623–4.

masterpiece, *Spirit of Utopia* (*Geist der Utopie*) (1918), to his last work, *Between Worlds in the History of Philosophy* (*Zwischenwelten in der Philosophiegeschichte*) (1977), Bloch takes account of the fact that man hopes for more than can be realized in the world at hand, and seeks to understand the meaning of this for metaphysics and political praxis. Where other thinkers have concluded (1) that the existence of such meta-mundane hope means that man must ultimately base his hope on a transcendent order, or (2) that human utopianism must be controlled, because it is unrealistic and dangerous, Bloch takes the radical step of asking what the nature of reality must be, if men so habitually, universally and at every level of consciousness intend a higher level of being than is found in the world at hand and the possibilities which can be extrapolated from it. Confronted with the reality of anti-mundane human hope, in a world in which it is not and never has been realizable, Bloch concludes not that such hope is unrealistic, but that the nature of reality has been not been rightly understood, and has been prematurely fixated by the closed ontological systems elaborated in class society.[4]

Bloch denies that the nature of reality can be taken for granted as a matter of common sense, or as something already determined by the history of philosophical or scientific speculation. Bloch is a critic of the history of philosophy until now; he is also, though more implicitly, a critic of the degree to which the present or past state of scientific theory can be taken as a trustworthy guide to the question of the nature of reality in general.[5] Like Heidegger, Bloch attempts to break with the history of Western metaphysics. Western metaphysics since Thales, he argues, has been based on the assumption of a settled ontology, as though the world was *in being*, something given and settled from the start. It has tended to posit a *fixum* or concluded substratum, which contained the world contents *in potentia*. Whether this substratum was called 'substance', 'idea', 'matter' or 'spirit', it was assumed that the ontological structure and possibility content of the world were in being.[6] Bloch rejects this conception of reality. He rejects all *anamnesis*, in the sense of backward-looking epistemology and ontology, and

---

[4] *Subjekt-Objekt Erlaüterungen zu Hegel, GA.*, Vol. 8, pp. 361–65.
[5] See, for example, *Erbschaft dieser Zeit, GA.*, Vol. 4, pp. 279–95, and *Das Materialismusproblem, seine Geschichte und Substanz, GA.*, Vol. 7, pp. 316–58.
[6] *Subjekt-Objekt, GA.*, Vol. 8, pp. 362–65.

rebels against the ban against the future and the new which he claims has characterized Western metaphysics.

Bloch denies that the ontological structure and possibility content of the world are in being. Instead, he argues that the world is open to real future and to genuinely new possibilities. For Bloch, reality is an open system, which is not pre-given, settled or finished, but a process which can be shaped and decided by men.[7] Bloch bases this new conception of reality on the principle of hope. In traditional metaphysical systems 'the principle' (*principium* or *archē*) was the starting point or beginning out of which things arose. For Bloch, hope (and not some settled substratum of pre-given possibilities) is 'the principle' or *archē* of the process. This is another way of saying that for Bloch the world has no 'principle' in the traditional sense, that it is open and unfinished, and that hope functions as 'the principle', as the origin out of which and through which things arise, as long as the world is still unfinished and the actual ontological 'principle' is still not yet.[8] Bloch's position here is technical and involves a radicalization of Schelling's dynamicist process metaphysics, according to which reality is a process developing from a non-ground to Omega or Genesis.[9] Bloch is a process metaphysician, like Bergson or Whitehead, and his Open System is a new Marxist process metaphysics. Without entering into the details of his system, it is clear that Bloch gives hope an unprecedented role in determining what the world can become. He also changes the dimensions of the problem by providing a new conception of reality in which hope is not defeated *ab initio* by the prison house of a concluded and unchangeable ontological order.

Similarly, Bloch transforms the traditional understanding of possibility by providing a new delineation of the category possibility. In place of the traditional analysis into actual and potential possibility, Bloch argues that the most fundamental class of possibility is *objective-real possibility*: possibility which has not yet achieved all of its conditions, even theoretically, and is therefore objectively incomplete.[10] This is a conception of possibility which

---

[7] *Experimentum Mundi Frage, Kategorien des Herausbringens, Praxis*, GA., Vol. 15, pp. 24–31.

[8] *Ibid.*, pp. 178–81.

[9] For a discussion of Schelling's process metaphysics, see P.C. Hayner, *Reason and Existence, Schelling's Philosophy of History* E.J. Brill, Leiden, 1967, pp. 34–61, 92–124; and C. Wild, *Reflexion und Erfahrung Eine Interpretation der Früh— und Spätphilosophie Schellings* Alber Verlag, Munich, 1968.

[10] For a full discussion, see 'Die Schichten der Kategorie Möglichkeit', in *Das Prinzip Hoffnung*, GA., Vol. 5, pp. 258–88.

cannot be reconciled with traditional ontology, because it assumes that the ontological structure of the world is open to real future. Objective real possibilities are not fixed or settled: they are the possibilities of what things may become in the future through human intervention and praxis. Man, for example, is the objective-real possibility of what he may become in the future, not a wholly pre-determined being, who has only to realize his essentially pre-given potentialities. Granted this conception of possibility, the problem of hope becomes the problem of which subjective hopes correlate with dialectically developing, still open objective real possibilities, which can become fully objective possibilities in the future. This means that the problem of which hopes have a correlate in possibility cannot be foreclosed or decided dogmatically now, because possibility is itself historical, and can be decisively influenced by praxis, by the future intervention and labour of men.

This relationship between possibility and praxis means that what men take as the goals of praxis, both in the short and in the long run, has an effect on what comes to be possible. But this makes the traditional problem of which hopes can be realized the problem of which hopes can be realized *if they are hoped for and formulated as goals for praxis*. In other words, continuation in hope (despite disappointments and disparities) and attempts to formulate hopes as goals for praxis (despite difficulties or even the impossibility of achieving immediate concretion) may influence what becomes possible in the future. This awareness of *the causality of hope*, once it has been related to praxis, underlies Bloch's attempt to make hope central to a renewed Marxism.

Marxism, Bloch argues, must become the theory-praxis of hope. It must base itself on educated hope (*docta spes*).[11] That is, on hope which has been grasped and understood in a dialectical materialist manner: on hope which has been related to praxis, and then tested and reformulated as a result of mediation with process trends. This implies a revolutionary extension of the range and scope of Marxism, as well as a new emphasis on the historical causality of what is willed and experimented for as against purely naturalistic or automaticist conceptions of the future. Such a conception of Marxism requires a new understanding of the conventional Marxist concept of theory-praxis. It requires an understanding which takes account of hopes which will only find

[11] *Das Prinzip Hoffnung, GA.*, Vol. 5, pp. 5, 15–16.

a full correlation in possibility in the future, if men envisage them as theoretical possibilities now, before they become fully possible. For Bloch, the theory-praxis of hope is a causal *sine qua non*, which itself transforms the possibility of realizing the hopes which it attempts to bring to realization.

Bloch takes up this problem in 'Theory-Praxis in the Long Run'. Like many of Bloch's writings, it is a highly esoteric text, full of oblique references and difficult terminology. To make the text accessible to English-speaking readers, I have expanded the translation where necessary (with the permission of Karola Bloch), and provided explanatory footnotes. Since Bloch's article remains elliptical and indirect, it may be useful to briefly elucidate his argument in the light of his work in general.

Bloch holds that a more sophisticated understanding of the relationship between theory and praxis is needed in Marxism. Marxists, Bloch claims, have often misunderstood the relationship between theory and praxis, with disastrous practical consequences for the praxis of hope. They have demanded an immediate usefulness of theory, as if the goals of praxis could be divided into those which can be realized in the foreseeable future, and those which cannot, the latter being utopian and unrealistic. Bloch maintains that this view is short-sighted, that it assumes an ontology of a classical sort which is incompatible with the dialectical, future-oriented conception of reality inaugurated by Marx, that it premises a present availability of the possibility content of the world which is simply not the case.[12] Clearly there is a problem about the relationship between the goals of praxis and what can be achieved at any particular time. It is only too easy to fall into a facile optimism which ignores the objective lack of conditions in the world at hand, or into a premature pessimism which concludes that the more radical hopes of humanity will always remain unrealizable. To escape from this dilemma, Marxism, Bloch implies, must develop a concept of 'theory-praxis in the long run'.

Bloch presents his argument in quasi-Hegelian terminology (concept, content, essence, mediation, appearance, etc.). This terminology is difficult to understand because it has a technical meaning in Hegel's idealist philosophy which may not be what it means for Bloch. Nonetheless, the general thrust of Bloch's position is clear and very important. Bloch uses the term 'content'

[12] *Philosophische Aufsätze zur objektiven Phantasie*, *GA.*, Vol. 10, pp. 617–21, 621–27; and *Das Prinzip Hoffnung*, *GA.*, Vol. 5, pp. 288–334.

to refer to what is contained in the possibility structure of reality. Like Hegel, he uses a non-formal material logic which emphasizes the difference between the developing world contents (what is developing in the possibility structure of the world) and what is given in abstract appearance, in the foreground of so-called 'facts'. For Bloch, as for Hegel, the world contents only become 'concrete' when they are brought to realization in a fully mediated form, but they have a form of reality before their full mediation is achieved. This means that at any given time some world contents are 'still remote' and remain 'merely theoretical'. They are not at hand as already realized realities. Such world contents, Bloch argues, can only be grasped by thoughts which cannot be immediately cashed in practical terms. Moreover, they must remain 'theoretical' for longer than those world contents which are at hand as realized realities now; they are also less quickly understood and more difficult to survey than world contents which are at hand. They are partially present now as 'still remote', merely 'theoretical' contents, but they are not wholly present, because what they will be, if and when they are realized, is still 'inaccessible' and not at hand.

Bloch argues that such remote world contents must be raised to the level of theory now, even though they cannot yet be made the object of praxis. Marxist theory must not confine itself to immediate tasks and current contradictions: it must also extend to remote contents, the realization of which belongs to 'the long run'. According to Bloch, such remote contents pre-appear in cultural productions, especially in great works of art and great philosophy. Here he breaks with the vulgar Marxist view that the realm of cultural production or 'superstructure' is simply epiphenomenal and ideological. For Bloch, cultural productions can transcend the ideological forms in which they appear. They can be futuristic. The formations of the genuinely creative sphere contain 'a part of man', something which belongs to the not-yet-fully actualized human essence: a *utopian surplus*, which goes beyond the class-conditioned form in which they arise, and is capable of a late-ripening in the future. At present, this utopian surplus is merely pre-appearance (*Vor-Schein*), the coming before itself in a utopian manner of world contents which are still futuristic.[13]

---

[13] cf. 'Künstlerischer Schein als sichtbarer Vor-Schein' in *Das Prinzip Hoffnung*, GA., Vol. 5, pp. 242–250.

Bloch does not deny that such great cultural productions have a class character, that they contain ideology and illusion, or that they reflect the social relations existing in the societies in which they arise. Nor does he deny that such works can have, and traditionally have had, a reactionary political function as sources of illusory consolation which demand no transformation of the unjust and oppressive conditions in the world at hand. For this very reason, however, Bloch argues that Marxist theory needs to delineate the distant *practical* horizons present in such works, in 'a theory with a long breath' which looks not only to what is possible now, but also to what may become possible in the future, including what may become possible when the classless society has commenced. Theoretical configurations are needed in Marxist theory which take account of the presence of long term goals for praxis in great cultural productions, and give such long term goals *a transformed functionality* in a theory aiming at praxis in the long run. In other words, Bloch claims that great cultural productions, especially great art and philosophy, provide an indication now of remote world contents, which need to be made the object of a new Marxist concept of 'theory-praxis in the long run'.

According to Bloch, a differentiation or grading of the relationship between 'theory' and 'praxis' is necessary, based on the recognition that there are different incubation times of praxis and that different time scales are appropriate to different praxis contents. As well as a theory of what is possible now, based on the contradictions in the economy at hand, Marxism requires a theory of set times (*Terminlehre*) for what may theoretically become realizable in the future. It requires a hierarchy of different praxis contents, which takes account of when different praxis contents may become realizable.

Bloch's argument here is radical on two different levels. On a political level, his argument is directed at the distortions of Marxist praxis in our century. Bloch is concerned to challenge the abstract rationalism and half-enlightened 'tough mindedness' of those Marxists who take Marx's materialism to involve a sharp break with a preoccupation with superstructural phenomena, and who argue that the superiority of Marxism rests on the recognition that it is necessary to transform the existing mode of production and the social relations to which it gives rise. Bloch does not deny the need for such a transformation; he presupposes it. He insists that Marxists have been disastrously wrong to underestimate both the present political functionality of cultural productions and their practical relevance to any attempt to build a socialist society. Here Bloch's position has parallels with the thought of Gramsci and Mao Tse-tung.

Bloch argues that great cultural productions have a political functionality now, and that the only question is whether they will be used to promote or to impede social change. Great works, Bloch claims, have a quality of 'arousal', which is 'crypto-revolutionary' in the sense that they encourage men to want and hope for more than is available in the world at hand. If, however, Marxists ignore the crypto-revolutionary character of such 'arousal', if they fail to integrate it into their theory and propaganda, then the forces of reaction can locate such works in a realm of pure 'Spirit,' independent of the economy at hand. They can relieve such 'arousal' and turn it into a form of consolation, a 'song of solace,' which actually impedes social change. Here Bloch is thinking of the catastrophic effect of the adoption of such a policy by the German Communist party in the 1920s, which allowed the Nazis to utilize the 'arousal' present in great cultural productions for their own purposes.

On a second, more metaphysical level, Bloch's argument involves a new conception of reality as an open process in which there is real anticipation. According to Bloch, every great work of art contains the promise of a condition in which the non-illusory hopes of mankind will be realized. It contains an encapsulated anticipation of a really possible future. Here Bloch is not intent on a merely psychological observation. Rather, he relates the common experience of 'self encounter' in the presence of great works of art to a praxis-orientated theory of reality as *a process in which the non-illusory hopes of humanity could be realized*. Bloch is a political radical on the philosophical front. He relates the remote world contents which pre-appear in great cultural productions to the tendencies and latencies of the unfinished process, and advances the praxis-orientated supposition that great works contain the still theoretical 'pre-reality' of the last world content towards which the process is tending: utopia or self encounter.

Bloch's position here is a statement about how such remote contents can be used to provide images and outlines of a possible future in the 'theory' of Marxist theory-praxis. It is not a metaphysical assertion of a traditional type, but a metaphysical supposition to be tested and reformulated in praxis over a long historical period.

Hence, Bloch emphasizes that the theoretical 'surmisal' which we can make in response to the 'promise' of great works of art or the 'pre-light' of great philosophy is itself still 'encapsulated'. The praxis of hope depends on us daring to make such a surmisal, but we need to remember, as Bloch puts it in a poetic prelude to his argument, that what we have dared (to surmise) changes into something daring 'only in a very different form'.

THEORY-PRAXIS IN THE LONG RUN
by Ernst Bloch

What we have dared changes into something daring only in a very different form. A thought that is immediately useable will do its duty more easily and then disappear than one that is more remote. Because not everything can be done at once, the more remote, that is, the deeper lying contents, must remain theoretical longer than those that are suitable for immediate use. The more remote contents are less quickly understood for the same reason as they are less quickly useable. The not-yet-accessible part in them certainly does not render them difficult to see, like objects in close proximity, but it renders them difficult to survey because of the untried, at present still untestable distant content in the remote image. This property of being difficult to survey also characterizes actively engaged, goal-oriented thoughts, which are not exhausted on paper like unengaged thoughts, but which are also not immediately cashable: they are long term bills of exchange.

The surveyability which makes a speedy circulation possible does not always belong (in its subjective origin) to the pre-appearance (*Vor-Schein*)[1] of such goals, especially in important works. While smaller formations (especially those which are petty-bourgeois in format) are immediately negotiable because of their heart-felt emotional appeal, solitude, if not *l'expression pour l'expression*,[2] has been essential so far to great works (apart from any consideration of their ideology). Indeed, the supposition is not unjustified that all important production as such was simply 'evil', in the sense of 'demonic'.[3] There is a demonism of 'light' in contrast to the goodness of the 'soul' (cf. the relevant article in *Philosophische Aufsätze zur objectiven Phantasie, GA.*, vol. 10, p. 219ff.). This condition of solitude cannot yet be superseded. It will also accompany for a long time, in a still uncracked mythical manner, even the creations made by and for the proletariat (as soon as they are at hand in greatness and in depth). A preliminary insolubility in immediate intelligibility, and consequently in the ensuing praxis, belongs especially to the objective *content* of all great works, as a content which is barely objectively 'meaningful': that is, which is still symbolic.

In respect to intelligibility, growing theoretical difficulties of the central concrete concept arise precisely from the difficulty of making concrete such contents and giving them practical effect. But the active concept[4] does not become weakened in any way in the end because of this. It does not bow down before contemplation.[5] The merely contemplative nucleus receives no paradox contribution from the central difficulties of praxis. Rather until the end, praxis is considered as the proof, as the limiting boundary, as the purpose of all theory. Until the end, instruction for action predominates over the enjoyment of the play. But in order to prepare the end, theoretical configurations which border on the end and are occupied with it, take up elements of artistic and philosophical delay[6] and reorganize them (*umfunktionieren*)[7]. The work-like essence in formations of the genuinely 'creative' sphere[8] proves itself in the mine of for the time being unmined substance.

This is also so where no 'high rank', no 'theatre of minorities' continues to officiate, where the great works of the former ruling class are in no way any longer considered as ideologies of feudal splendour, or even as the profundity of the so-called intellectual elite. There is a part of man in the evident humanism of these works, in their late-ripening and surplus[9], which remains still colourful pre-appearance (*Vor-Schein*), and so does not yet enter into any changed real being (*Realsein*). The force and 'justification' of these works does not lie in their immediate, even less in their possible most general use. They themselves still stand outside their socialist application, in so far as this aims at cultural wealth of an educative kind and its circulation to everyone. While this remains so, one must especially pay attention to the fact that the distant practical horizons of a theory with a long breath (which have been kept in mind here) are incompatible with that demand for praxis which, in a reformist petty-bourgeois manner, only wants to know that the realities of the day are respected, without regard to further history.

'Praxis in the long run', however, is not incompatible with a day-to-day political struggle, which, in an expression of the young

Lukács, keeps the apocalyptical awake in every miners' strike. On the contrary, the day-to-day political struggle carries out the practical steps which are necessary for a radical reconstruction of the relations of man to man and of man of nature. Praxis in the long run also has nothing in common with a retreat into contemplative aesthetics and theory which wants to put revolutionary praxis on the shelf. On the contrary, it keeps awake the sensitivity in revolutionary praxis for those tasks which man can approach without narrow ideological confinements and with practical consistency only when the classless society has commenced. These tasks must not be lost, must not be forgotten on the way to the classless society. Hence, for the time being, the only 'praxis' to which the *C Sharp Minor Quartet*[10] is appropriate, is that praxis which takes place in a moving upward glance to the content which here deals with us, to the content which is enclosed in the work and lights up the path ahead—even though the pouring out of this content into the surrounding accessible reality has not yet occurred. The statue of the sculptor Pygmalion can come alive, but the statues of a Michelangelo cannot. Pygmalion chiselled a lover who can exist in the flesh of an already existing woman, but the statues of Michelangelo are a human *plus ultra*[11], for which no company has yet arrived. However, if praxis is attempted midway on work contents for which, for the time being, the 'top position'[12] is above all an essential and, as it were, actual (not social) aggregate state[13], then they become unrecognizable.

It follows that there are very different incubation times of praxis. What is common to them is the fruit itself, which prepares itself in the protective covering—even within the important protective covering. A work is only important in so far as it signifies germinating contents, even if for the time being these germinating contents are present in an encapsulated form. The important work is the one permeated by freedom contents of a very central sort. A work of explicit revolutionary content (above all *Fidelio*) accordingly stands in the first rank, but this trumpet signal[14] is not lacking even in static works, at least not in the long run. Its startling effect sounds out from every work of genius, even from one which was intended and arranged quite differently at its time and place of origin. Every important work speaks, *à la longue*, of Floristan incarcerated, holds the light of the messenger who descends and announces the arrival of liberation. The category 'arousal' (which is conceded without question to the effect of works of genius) is at

all times crypto-revolutionary, albeit in a time-bound manner—
that is, in a manner which is needful of and capable of a late-ripening.
Quite apart from any consideration of their unmediated ideological
content, the 'arousal', even the 'upward glance', which works of
genius evoke, always involves a promise, a more than merely
aesthetic self-encounter, an encapsulated anticipation of the
possible future.

It was only therefore because a practicism[15] which insisted on
immediate usefulness did not honour the far-away blue horizons,
or even the ultra-violet ones, that reaction could suppress arousal
and re-encapsulate its encapsulation. In this way, an alleged
independence of 'Spirit' (*Geist*) from the economy was raised to a
formal idealistic autarchy of a Spirit which only propagates from
itself. At best, the arousal was quietistically relieved, was made
shallow by theological 'depth', and the trumpet signal appeared
only as the 'song of solace' of the non-appearing Messiah. The
same reactionary defusing (which applies to the autarchy as well
as to the song of solace) also armed itself however with great
philosophy, with the closed 'systems' of philosophy. The equivalent
to what is reactionary in works of art (the beautiful as satisfying in
itself, as an elevated holiday realm, or as a 'door to the morning'
which remains eternally the same) was achieved in philosophy by
concluded knowledge, or by the defeatism of all kinds of finished
solutions. These absolutizations of theoretical long-term existence,
of seduction to eternal theory as an eternal lamp, could sometimes
gain a place again with Marxists, where a misunderstood praxis
relation demanded an immediate usefulness of theory. Instead of
this misunderstanding and for the sake of its causal expulsion, a
differentiation of the theory-praxis relation is necessary, a theory of
set times (*Terminlehre*) for what theoretically may become realizable, ultimately, a hierarchy of praxis contents.

Such more central, undoubtedly more difficult, realizable praxis
contents are always those of the 'tendency'[16] (in contrast to the
mere foreground of the so-called 'facts'). This especially applies to
the contents of the work-like, mediated, self-announcing tendency,
which announces itself first of all as aesthetic 'promise' or as
philosophical 'pre-light'. The tendencies of the process and their
latencies are not only effective in the immediate (so often regressive)
course of history. They are equally effective in its more than
ideological superstructure—that is, in inheritable art and philosophy. The works of genius of this superstructure are not only

the most brilliant false consciousness of their time. Nor are they only the height of consciousness which already permits a glance into the ensuing period. Rather there is in them, in their late-ripening and concurrent transformation, the theoretical pre-reality of the last tendency content in general: self encounter.[17] This content is certainly theoretically (and even more in terms of praxis, which is its proof), still unknown and undiscovered. Even the theoretical 'surmisal', as it is imparted by the aesthetic promise or the philosophical pre-light, is still encapsulated and very remote from what is surmised.

Translated by Wayne Hudson

NOTES

1 *pre-appearance (Vor-Schein)*
Pre-appearance is a fundamental category of Bloch's philosophy. The 'not yet' pre-appears (pre-semblance, fore-glow) in a way which signals to men, and rouses them to act to bring it into being.

2 *l'expression pour l'expression*
Expression for the sake of expression, 'art for art's sake'.

3 *demonic*
A reference to Bloch's reworking of Goethe's theory that great art is 'demonic' and not reducible to any Romantic 'goodness of the soul'.

4 *concrete concept*
Bloch's meaning here is obscure. The terminology is Hegelian, but Bloch rejects Hegel's theory of ontological concepts as 'idealist'. Bloch might mean that it is difficult to arrive at the fully mediated ('concrete') concept which would enable men to grasp such contents and actively work for their realization.

5 *contemplation*
Marxist term used to characterize an attitude or epistemology which leaves things as they are and does not attempt to change them.

6 *artistic and philosophical delay*
The contents present in great art and philosophy cannot be made the object of praxis now and are therefore 'delayed'.

7 *umfunktionieren*
A technical term meaning that the elements of an existing cultural production are reworked and given a transformed functionality in a different problematic.

8 *work-like essence, formations of the genuinely 'creative' sphere*
Here, the presence in cultural forms of 'essence' which is still to be achieved, but which has a work-like character which will enable it to be worked on in the future.

9 *late-ripening, surplus*
There is a utopian surplus in great works of art, which cannot be the object of praxis now, but which is capable of a further development in the future.

10 *C Sharp Minor Quartet*
Beethoven's famous String Quartet No. 14 in C Sharp Minor, Opus 131.

11 *plus ultra*
Word play on Latin *ne plus ultra*. Here, something in the present which points to something more still to come.

12 *top position*
Such remote contents occupy the 'top position' in the world at hand, in the sense that they are the most futuristic elements in it.

13 *actual (not social)*
This 'top position' is what might be called the 'actual' (*sachlich*) state of such contents considered 'in aggregate', but this 'aggregate state' is not yet a 'social' one because such contents have not yet been 'poured out' and so have not entered into contact with the reality around them.

14 *trumpet signal*
A reference to the trumpet signal in Beethoven's overture *Fidelio* which announces the liberation of Floristan, an imprisoned Spanish nobleman, by his wife Leonora.

15 *practicism*
A reference to the disastrous policies of the German Communist party in the 1920s and 1930s. Bloch believes that the German Communist party helped Hitler to come to power by ignoring quasi-irreal cultural contents ('blue horizons', 'ultra-violet ones'), in a way which allowed the Nazis ('reaction') to suppress their crypto-revolutionary potential and 're-encapsulate' it in reactionary ideology.

16 *tendency*
Technical term in Bloch's philosophy. Here, the active tendency of the process which underlies and is at work in the process forms.

17 *theoretical pre-reality, last tendency content, self encounter*
Utopia or self encounter, which is the last or final content towards which the process is tending, pre-appears as a 'pre-reality' in works of genius.

Apart from his significance as the greatest philosopher of hope in the history of the West, Bloch has had a major impact on contemporary Christian theology through his influence on the distinguished German Protestant theologian Jürgen Moltmann. Moltmann's *Theology of Hope* (German 1964, English 1967) transformed contemporary theology by asserting that Christianity was hope, and that God was a 'God of hope', with the future as his mode of being.[1]

Bloch's inspiration is also evident in Moltmann's later work available in English in such collections as *Religion, Revolution and the Future* (1969), *Hope and Planning* (1971) and *The Experiment Hope* (1975). In his later work Moltmann has stressed the need for theology to understand man and the world as 'experiments' grounded in the hope of God.[2] Moltmann's theology of hope does not derive exclusively from Bloch's philosophy[3], but an understanding of Bloch's philosophy will be crucial for any future development of the theology of hope which Moltmann has founded.

[1] J. Moltmann, *Theology of Hope*, transl. James W. Leitch, S.C.M. Press, London, 1967, p. 16.
[2] J. Moltmann, *The Experiment Hope*, transl. and ed. M. Douglas Meeks, Fortress Press, Philadelphia, 1975, p. 27.
[3] For a full discussion, see M. Douglas Meeks, *Origins of the Theology of Hope*, Fortress Press, Philadelphia, 1974.

Since Bloch's *The Principle of Hope* has not been translated into English (although selections are available[4]), it would be useful to have a short introduction which gives some idea of the book's arrangement, content and strategy, as well as its extraordinary range and symphonic texture. Moltmann himself has provided such an introduction in an influential review, part of which is translated here for the first time.

THE ARRANGEMENT, CHARACTER AND PURPOSE OF ERNST BLOCH'S 'THE PRINCIPLE OF HOPE'*
by Jürgen Moltmann

'The main thing', Bloch says in the foreword, 'is to learn to hope. Hope, being above fear, is not passive like fear, nor is it locked into a nothing. Hope as an affect is able to express itself. It gives men a wide perspective instead of narrowing their view. But it cannot know enough about what drives them inwardly and what may be allied with them in the external world. The work of this affect needs human beings who throw themselves actively into what is becoming, to which they themselves belong. It doesn't put up with the dog's life which feels itself only passively thrown into the existing reality, with the life which is not seen through, and lamentably is taken to be acceptable. The work against the fear of life and the machinations of fear is the work which is directed against the originators of fear— who are to a great extent very obvious. It is something which men can discover. How splendidly men have been dreaming in all periods of the better life which is possible. The life of all men is shot through with day dreams.' (DPH I) Bloch's design is to bring philosophy to hope as 'a place in the world which is the best culture

---

[4] See the selections in *Man On His Own: Essays in the Philosophy of Religion* by Ernst Bloch, transl. E.B. Ashton, Herder and Herder, New York, 1970 and *On Karl Marx* by Ernst Bloch, transl. John Maxwell, Herder and Herder, New York, 1971.

*The passages which follow are taken from Moltmann's review, 'Messianismus und Marxismus' (*Kirche in der Zeit* 15, 1960, No. 8), reprinted in J. Moltmann, *Im Gespräch mit Ernst Bloch Eine theologische Wegbegleitung*, Chr. Kaiser Verlag, Munich, 1976, pp. 18, 20–22.

land and which is as undiscovered as Antarctica.' It is to develop
a hermeneutics of hope . . .

The Principle of Hope begins (Part I: Report) with a fair of little
day dreams. It sounds like a stall at a fair: 'Step right in. It doesn't
cost much.' 'We begin empty. Many things taste of more. Develop
daily into the blue. Flight and return of the victor. Riper wishes
and their pictures. What there remains to wish for in old age—and
so forth.' Part II (The Anticipatory Consciousness) becomes more
demanding. Indeed, it is the foundation of the whole work. It
deals with the 'discovery and unmistakeable delineation of "the
Not-Yet-Conscious".' With that definition Bloch interprets the
psychological phenomena of the unconscious, repression, and so-
called 'archetypes' in contradiction to S. Freud and C.G. Jung
(whom he labels 'a raving fascist psychoanalyst'), not as hereditary
(as storage of the primeval past in the cellar of consciousness), or
as in any way biological, but rather historically: as the dawning new.
He goes from that to a comprehensive 'Ontology of the Not-Yet'
and demonstrates the outstanding fruitfulness of process thinking
in the concept of matter. The highpoint of chapter 19 is his interpretation of Marx's eleven theses on Feuerbach. Part III attempts
to effect a transition. This time one is led into the landscape of
trivial hopes, of window shopping, fashion and beauty queens on to
fairy tales, travel, film and the stage, to the idol of 'the happy
ending', of which he says: 'Seen through, but nonetheless
defended'.

Part IV, Construction—the Outlines of a Better World, deals
with the social utopias of the land of milk and honey, from Plato's
state utopia to science fiction. The medical utopias (of long life and
life force), the technical utopias (from alchemy to non-Euclidean
geometry), the geographical utopias (Eldorado and Eden) right up
to music and the muses, are interwoven with social utopias such as
Zionism and the women's movement.

Finally, Part V concentrates on eschatological identity. It begins
with wish pictures of the 'fulfilled moment' (*Don Quixote, Don
Giovanni* and *Faust*). Music is interpreted in its deepest meaning
as 'conjuring theurgy', as summons, and as the sounding of a not
yet at hand harmonious world. And then finally, the principle of
hope is tested by a trial of fire. The essence of the problem was set
out already in *Spirit of Utopia* in the triad: 'Karl Marx, Death and
the Apocalypse'. Now Bloch's hopes are confronted with the
strongest 'non-utopia': death. It is no accident that the chapter

dealing with the critique of religion follows: 'Man's Increasing Entry Into Religious Mystery, in Astral Mythology, Exodus, Kingdom, Atheism, and the Utopia of the Kingdom'. The conclusion takes the form of a finale on Karl Marx and Humanity: 'Man still lives everywhere in pre-history, everything is still before the creation of the world—as a right world. *The real genesis is not at the beginning, but at the end.* And it only starts to begin when society and existence become radical, that is, when they comprehend their own roots. But the root of history is the creative working man, who rebuilds and transforms the given. Once man has comprehended himself and established in real democracy existence without externalization and alienation, something arises in the world which all men have glimpsed in childhood, but where no one has yet been: homeland.' (DPH II, 1628)

Translated by Dieter Freundlieb

Bloch has also influenced contemporary Christian theology in other directions which are a source of hope. He has changed the quality and also the practical significance of the Christian-Marxist dialogue by outlining the possibility of a new Christian-Marxist alliance in which both Christianity and Marxism would undergo a transformation and experience a deepening. Bloch's *Atheism in Christianity* (1968) has exerted an influence on the emergence of a developed political theology and on its leading theologians, such as Metz, Bonino, and Gutiérrez.[1] The possibility that atheism and Christianity require each other if they are to emerge from credulity and to work for a social order which would be good, is one which no modern theologian can afford to ignore. It is this challenge and this contribution which Moltmann has in mind in the moving postscript which follows.

---

[1] See Johannes B. Metz, *Theology of the World*, transl. by William Glen-Doepel, Burns and Oates/Herder and Herder, London, 1969; José Míguez Bonino, *Christians and Marxists: The Mutual Challenge to Revolution*, Hodder and Stoughton, London, 1976; and Gustavo Gutiérrez, *A Theology of Liberation* transl. Sister Caridad Inda and John Eagleson, Orbis Books, Maryknoll, 1973.

IN GRATITUDE TO ERNST BLOCH
by Jürgen Moltmann

With Ernst Bloch the theologians have lost a philosopher, from whom they have much to be thankful. We have lost a friend in whose vicinity one could breathe freely, summon up courage and learn to question. How many theologians, young and old, from numerous countries in the last years have made the pilgrimage to his modest apartment on the Neckar, have sat opposite Ernst Bloch at his little table, questioned and been questioned (and how!), and then taken away something more hopeful than when they came onto the street. He was so free from vanity and pretensions that everyone who came close to him sensed the atmosphere of trust and brotherhood. He was at once so wholly preoccupied with his own central concern and with the questions of his time, that no one who came close to him could engage in non-committal conversation. He was a good neighbour to everyone who was of honest intention and good will. In his intellectual company theology also began to uncover its biblical horizon of hope again.

I first got to know Bloch when he was already seventy. What impressed me right up until our last conversation on the day before his death was the *originality of his thinking*, in the sense of its closeness to the source or origin, the, if one may so put it, *childlike quality about him*. He had preserved in himself something which he was able to develop, that others lose so quickly: the capacity to keep before him the simple question and the bottomless wonder. From *Spirit of Utopia* 1918 on, he called that 'the darkness of the lived moment'. Out of this mysterious presence he questioned, thought and talked. In it he was authentic. Things struck him which others carelessly passed over. He noticed changes where one only saw the same. He heard tones where others did not even find notes. His interest from early on in those phenomena which were too close by to notice stemmed from that. The world in which he lived was full of traces, indications and signals which he attempted to decipher. And he could open the eyes and ears of others to such things.

Almost every chapter in each of his books begins with the uttering of simple, very near, obvious things and with a deep astonishment about them. As he put it on the first page of *Traces*, 1930, 'I am. But I do not possess myself. And so at first we come to be.' Three sentences, which encompass his whole philosophy.

Three sentences, between which every man can relate his life, his hope, his suffering, his solitude and what he has in common with others. 'Who are we? Where do we come from? Where are we going?' *The Principle of Hope*, 1959, begins with these old metaphysical questions, and then goes further: 'What do we expect?' That is the question of hope. And 'What awaits us?' That is the question about what is to come, the eschatological question. Does anything at all await us in the world in the future, in death? Bloch went on questioning where others think it is better not to ask any more questions. Often the simple things strike us as the most difficult because we ourselves have not remained simple, that is, able to ask what we want to ask and to hope for what we wish for. When one was with Ernst Bloch, this difficult thing was made easy again. That was the liberating thing about him. 'Who thinks the deepest loves what is most full of life.' In that respect he was related to Hölderlin. The fact that his *The Principle of Hope* finally seeks fulfilment in the universally extended category 'homeland', points to that light of childhood which Bloch preserved for himself and for us. In his last months he enjoyed meditating on the concluding sentence of *The Principle of Hope*: 'Once man has comprehended himself and established in real democracy existence without externalization and alienation, something arises in the world which all men have glimpsed in childhood, but where no one has yet been: homeland.'

Ernst Bloch as a theologian—that is a provocative theme for us, for himself, for his friends and his enemies. Nonetheless it is a relevant theme that cannot be put aside. I well remember our first meeting. It was in the winter of 1959 after a lecture which Bloch gave in Wuppertal when he was still a Marxist from Leipzig. After that we sat together in a smoky pub. I asked him naïvely, 'Herr Bloch, you are an atheist, aren't you?' Whereupon he sparkled and hoarsley thrust back at me: 'I am an atheist for the sake of God.' This paradox contains a long history of struggle. It includes Prometheus and Job, the Mosaic prohibition of image-making and the cry of the crucified, mystical theology and Marxist critique of religion. Bloch has not accepted any theological system and still remains loyal to the piety based on 'revolutionary gnosis' of *Spirit of Utopia*. He wants to bring 'Marxism and religion united in a will to the kingdom' into the 'harvest festival of the Apocalypse'. By that he means the finally successful self-encounter of mankind. He quotes the passage 'but mirrored in us all is now the light of

the Lord, *with uncovered countenance* ...' in order to end his first
book with the sanctification of the name of God, which is laid into
the hands of 'our Godswearing philosophy and of truth as prayer'.

This Messianic passion can be traced as an impelling motive in
all his works. It is true that he later became more reserved in his
positive statements and ever more severe in his critique of the
church of the masters and religious resignation. But there were
political experiences which provided ample justification for that.
Nonetheless, in the book which he especially dedicated to Christians, *Atheism in Christianity*, 1968, the early desire for a finally
politically credible 'religion of the Exodus and of the Kingdom'
remains predominant. Marxism (as analysis and critique of the
existing alienation) and eschatological hope in the Apocalypse as
the power of overcoming every impoverishment, come together in
a harmonious association, in which neither side must abandon
itself but rather must come into its own likeness.

So in the 1960s Bloch came to the theologians and the theologians came to Bloch. Since then the Christians have come to the
socialists, and the socialists to the Christians. United in the will to
that Kingdom which is promised to the poor, they have left their
own camps to the annoyance of their crowd and drawn upon
themselves the anger of their respective leaders. And the more
they concern themselves with the real problem of alienation, the
more they experience that spirit of the Kingdom, which alone makes
one certain one is on the right path. Honest, reciprocal criticism is
a pre-condition for that. Bloch expressed it by saying: 'Only an
atheist can be a good Christian', because atheistic socialism
liberates the world from gods and idols. I answered him at the time
'Only a Christian can be a good atheist', because belief in the cross
also liberates man from ersatz religion and personality cults. Bloch
took up the offer at once and used both critical sentences in the
subtitle of *Atheism in Christianity* to indicate what he wanted to
achieve with that work. Indeed the personality and work of Ernst
Bloch have brought about more harmonious relations between
Christians and socialists—even between socialists and socialists—
than any contemporary party or ideology. This should not be
forgotten now that he is no longer with us. Rather in light of this
legacy, his name remains present as a summons and an opportunity.

Ernst Bloch—*the socialist with the raised fist*—has remained a
riddle to many contemporaries, for whom the word 'socialism' is
associated with negative personal experiences or is filled with only

private dreams of wish fulfilment. In a divided Germany discussions about socialism are almost always highly unpleasant, because of the repression and obsessions which come to expression in them. The fact that Ernst Bloch had himself passed through different forms of socialism, enthusiastic, disappointed, but still hopeful, made it much more difficult for other people to share his point of view. Nonetheless, no intricate ideological riddle is involved here, but something which is very simple and quite clear: 'Socialism, then Communism, is what was sought for so long under the name of morality.' (*Political Assessments*, 1970) For the sake of morality, with Kant's categorical imperative and the unpretentious will to self respect, Bloch became a socialist. He abandoned dictatorial socialism, struggled for democratic socialism, and hoped for communism which would bring men to self encounter and the world to homeland. *Bloch was a moralist* before he became active as a socialist. He remained this same moralist with integrity in anger and militant hope, who only seldom indulged in silence for the sake of love of peace and quiet. For the sake of morality, that is, for the sake of the troubled and the heavy laden, he depicted the social utopias. For the sake of morality, that is, for the sake of the humiliated and affronted, he developed a natural law with a future perspective. For the sake of morality, he drew attention to the valid contemporary symbols of 'upright carriage' and 'head uplifted'. Socialism, democracy and communism as questions of morality also raise in reverse the question of morality as a critical question in socialism, democracy and (possible) communism, namely as the question of their 'human countenance'.

Ernst Bloch was often asked about his understanding of *death, immortality and resurrection*. He responded to that in his writings and interviews with remarkable reserve. Death did not frighten him. He also laid no veil over it. For him death was an opponent—a radical anti-utopia—and also a secret—'unimaginable nothing, that still has not been illuminated'. Nonetheless, he knew of a connection with what lies beyond. He found the link with death as the 'absolute silence' in the 'resounding silence' of music. On the evening before his death he heard again the music which he loved most, Beethoven's *Fidelio* overture, with its trumpet signal at the end signifying the liberation of the imprisoned, which had always impressed him very much. As he once wrote, 'it announces in Beethoven a coming of the Messiah. Thus, freedom, utopian recollection, the presence of the great moment, the star of fulfilled hope in the here and now, sound down to the gaol below . . .'

Ernst Bloch's own work is one such overture for a future with that trumpet signal for the imprisoned in it, which Paul called 'suddenly, in a moment, at the sound of the last trumpet' (1 Cor. 15). He made those imprisoned in alienation into 'prisoners of hope'. Anyone who bears this hope in mind owes Ernst Bloch eternal gratitude.

Translated by Wayne Hudson

Hope: An Ontological Foundation?

Max Charlesworth

Despite the profound work of Ernst Bloch I think it true to say that contemporary thinkers are not comfortable with the idea of hope. For Bloch, as we know, hope was one of the primordial principles or categories of human existence; for him, indeed, a human being was precisely a being capable of hope, that is, one capable of transcending his present situation and projecting a future for himself. For Bloch also there was an ontological basis for hope, in that human hope in the future—that evil and disorder and meaninglessness will not prevail—is not merely 'a wishful projection into the void'.[1]

However, for most of Bloch's contemporaries the term 'hope' has been coloured by the failure of the historical optimism of the eighteenth and nineteenth centuries—the optimism in the future that pervaded religious and anti-religious thought (including scientific humanism and Marxism) alike. For many of the great symptomatic thinkers of our time (one thinks of Freud, for example) the concept of hope has been irremediably compromised by the bankruptcy of the utopianism that assumed that history had a

This essay is based in part upon an article by the author, 'Préalables anthropologiques à la question: la vie a-t-elle un sens?', in *Concilium*, 128, 1977.
[1] Harvey Cox, Foreword to Ernst Bloch, *Man on His Own*, New York, 1970, p. 14.

direction in favour of man and that human hope was thus guaranteed.

Even for a number of contemporary neo-Marxists the optimistic and hope-ful aspect of Marx's own thought has been something of an embarrassment. Marcuse's interpretation of Marx is, for example, a profoundly pessimistic one. In his hands Marxism is no longer a doctrine of human hope.[2]

If we are uncomfortable with the concept of hope we are, however, completely at ease with the idea of *meaning*. Instead of defining human beings in terms of a capacity for hope we define the human in terms of a capacity for introducing meanings into the world. What is distinctive about human beings is that they are able to discern meanings in the world and in human existence and able to create meanings (in art, social relationships, etc.). For us therefore the question of hope is translated into a question of meaning. Of course, the notions of meaning and hope are inextricably bound up with each other, for to say that human existence is meaningless is to say that it is hope-less. Again, if there is no ground of meaning—no ontological basis for the meaning with which we endow human existence—then equally human life will be hope-less, nothing more than 'a wishful projection into the void'. To discuss the meaning of existence is therefore also to discuss the basis or foundation of hope.

It would be ludicrous for me here to attempt even the beginning of an answer to the question 'What is the meaning of human existence?'. What I am concerned with rather is to discuss the meta-question whether and under what conditions that question can be intelligibly asked.

For many people today the question 'What is the meaning of life?' no longer has a clear and urgent meaning. It is not that such people are stupid and of bad faith, or that they are flippant and unthinking hedonists living only for the present moment. Rather, for such people questions about the meaning of human existence do not make sense any more since, so they claim, the conditions under which such questions make sense no longer obtain. Such

[2] It is interesting to compare Marcuse's early position where he criticises Hegel because his philosophy 'ends in doubt and resignation' (*Reason and Revolution*, p. 248), and his own later pessimism expressed in the preface to the 1960 edition of *Reason and Revolution* (p. xiv): 'Those social groups which dialectical theory identified as the forces of negation are either defeated or reconciled with the established system'. The same pessimism is forcefully expressed in *One Dimensional Man*.

questions, it is argued, can only arise within a certain cultural context or 'thought structure' or 'field of discourse' or (to use Michel Foucault's convenient term) *episteme*, and such a context or structure is no longer viable. In a culture shaped on the one hand by scientific naturalism, which abstracts from questions of value and meaning, and on the other hand by the various forms of 'idealism' or 'constructivism', which see value and meaning as human constructs imported by man into existence, questions about the meaning of life seem naive and pointless.

If human existence is seen as being part of the natural order, and if the natural order is seen within an empiricist perspective according to which nature is simply the sum total of the 'brute facts' (the 'value free' facts) of physics and chemistry, then human existence itself comes to be seen as a 'brute' and 'value free' fact. Within the context of scientific empiricism we cannot ask whether the world has a purpose or a meaning or whether it is good or bad, and equally we cannot ask whether human life has a meaning and value. Like the brute facts of physics human life simply *is*.

In the same way, if value and meaning are human constructs imposed by man upon reality and upon human existence, then it is simple-minded to ask 'What is the meaning of life?'. It is I who must make myself to be, I who must endow my life with a meaning, for life does not have any ready-made God-given meaning. Nietzsche has expressed this point perfectly in *The Genealogy of Morals*: 'To view nature as if it were a proof of the goodness and providence of a God; to interpret history to the glory of a divine reason, as the perpetual witness to a moral world order and moral intentions; to interpret one's own experiences, as pious men long interpreted them, as if everything were preordained, everything a sign, everything sent for the salvation of the soul—that now belongs to the *past*, that has the conscience *against* it, that seems to every more sensitive conscience indecent, dishonest, mendacious, feminism, weakness, cowardice . . .'[3]

If we look a little more carefully at the two great thought-structures or *epistemes* just mentioned, within which questions about the meaning of life become unintelligible, then we may perhaps be able, in an indirect way, to discern the anthropological presuppositions required for those questions to be *meaningful* to contemporary man.

[3] F. Nietzsche, *The Genealogy of Morals*, Third Essay, Section 27, trans. W. Kaufmann and R.J. Hollingdale, New York, 1969.

I cannot here analyze in any detail the various historical forces that brought about the emergence of the natural sciences in the sixteenth and seventeenth centuries and that caused those sciences to be allied with an empiricist epistemology and a naturalistic world-view. There is nothing in the intrinsic logic of the natural sciences that makes such an alliance with empiricism or naturalism either necessary or inevitable. Nevertheless, the scientific view of the world and of man, which has had such a powerful influence on the modern mind, has been for the most part radically empiricist and radically naturalistic.

Within the context of Humean empiricism the world is simple the totality of facts—facts that are simply *there* in spatio-temporal juxtaposition. It is a world in which the categories of possibility and necessity do not operate and a world in which there are no causal connexions between the 'loose and separate' atomic facts. It is also a world devoid of values. In themselves the empirical facts are neither good nor bad, neither valuable nor valueless.

Within the context of naturalism man is seen as part of nature, nature in turn being defined as that which is the object of classical physics and chemistry. Since, once again, the world of physics and chemistry is 'value free', values can only enter into this world through man. Values are born, so to speak, from the meeting of human needs and interests with the world of neutral physico-chemical facts. However, since man himself is part of nature his needs and interests and attitudes are themselves explicable in naturalistic, physico-chemical terms, so that ultimately, as in the work of B.F. Skinner[4], values simply denote the way in which the human organism—with its biological 'givens'—interacts with and adapts itself to its environment in order to survive. In the Skinnerian world the question 'What is the meaning of human existence?' is translated into 'How can that part of nature which we call the human organism interact with and adapt itself to other parts of nature in order to secure its survival?'.

It is not my purpose here to chart the history of this movement of thought and to show the alliances and 'marriages of convenience' it has entered into with other ideas and movements. There was, for instance, the fortuitous conjunction between scientific empiricism and naturalism and the movement of Liberalism.[5] Thus

---

[4] B.F. Skinner, *Beyond Freedom and Dignity*, New York, 1971.
[5] This alliance is expressed very clearly, for example, in the thought of nineteenth century English Liberal thinkers such as John Stuart Mill.

science was seen as the main agency of liberation from religious superstition and mythical ways of thinking, and the scientific spirit—supposedly experimental and non-dogmatic—was directly linked with the moral and political values of Liberalism. However, as I have suggested, the connection between scientific naturalism and liberal values, or any other kind of values, is purely accidental. Within the devalued world of naturalism man simply *is*; he exists with a given biological structure and given needs and interests; he interacts with his environment, and he survives. No doubt it is possible to formulate a kind of humanism within this framework—as Freud, Huxley, Monod and others have tried to do—but it is a humanism of a radically attenuated and impoverished kind and one with, so to speak, an extremely limited vocabulary.

Within the perspectives of what I have called idealism or 'constructivism', values and meaning are seen as constructs which we impose upon reality and human existence. In its purely epistemological form, constructivism is classically expressed in Kant's *The Critique of Pure Reason*, and in its moral and social form in the complex movement of Promethean humanism which runs from Hegel, through Feuerbach and Marx and Nietzsche to Sartre. Thus for Marx the world we know and live in is the world we ourselves have made—the world that is the product of *praxis*—and we know ourselves and 'make' ourselves in the process of our interchanges with the world. The world has no intrinsic meaning apart from human *praxis*, and equally man's existence has no ready-made or given meaning apart from his creative transformation of nature. As Marx puts it: 'The practical construction of an objective world, the manipulation of inorganic nature, is the confirmation of man as a conscious species-being ... He no longer reproduces himself merely intellectually, as in consciousness, but actually and in a real sense, and he sees his own reflection in a world which he has constructed.'[6]

From a rather different point of view, for Nietzsche also, meaning and value are human constructs. With the death of God man must become his own God, that is to say his own creator and law-giver. For Nietzsche the full implications of what this means becomes clear only when we have confronted the possibility of nihilism. So he writes in *The Will to Power*: 'Scepticism regarding morality is what is decisive. The end of the moral interpretation of the world,

---

[6] K. Marx, *Economic and Philosophical Mss*, trans. T.B. Bottomore, London, 1963, 1st Ms, xxiv.

which no longer has any sanction after it has tried to escape into some beyond, leads to nihilism. "All lacks meaning".[7] For Nietzsche there is a radical choice between belief in God on the one hand, and the acceptance and affirmation of human freedom and autonomy on the other. If there is a God then man cannot be fully free and autonomous; if we take man's freedom and autonomy *seriously* then there cannot be a God. No doubt Christianity has given value and meaning of a certain kind to human existence but it is a false kind of meaning which is incompatible with man's dignity and seriousness.

Sartre, in his pre-Marxist phase, expressed the same Nietzschean idea in his popular essay *Existentialism and Humanism*: 'The existentialist is strongly opposed to a certain type of secular moralism which seeks to suppress God at the least possible expense . . . In other words—and this is, I believe, the purport of all that we in France call radicalism—nothing will be changed if God does not exist; we shall rediscover the same norms of honesty, progress and humanity, and we shall have disposed of God as an out-of-date hypothesis which will die away quietly of itself.'[8] Sartre continues: 'The existentialist, on the contrary, finds it extremely embarrassing that God does not exist, for there disappears with Him all possibility of finding values in an intelligible heaven. There can no longer be any good *a priori* since there is no infinite and perfect consciousness to think it. It is nowhere written that "the good" exists, that one must be honest or must not lie, since we are now upon the plane where there are only men.'[9] Camus puts forward an even more radical version of this position in *The Myth of Sisyphus*.[10] Thus for Camus all reflection upon human existence must begin from the recognition that life is 'absurd' and has no intrinsic meaning. 'Suicide' is defined as any attempt to avoid the absurdity of life, any attempt to find a basis for hope. Religion is for Camus a form of suicide and there are many other forms of 'philosophical suicide', that is attempts to make sense of human existence and to provide a ground for hope. For Camus the sole appropriate attitude before the absurdity of existence is the stoicism of Sisyphus.

---

[7] F. Nietzsche, *The Will to Power*, trans. W. Kaufmann, New York, 1967, Book 1, section iii.

[8] Jean-Paul Sartre, *Existentialism and Humanism*, trans. P. Mairet, London, 1961, p. 10.

[9] *Ibid.*

[10] Albert Camus, *The Myth of Sisyphus*, trans. J. O'Brien, New York.

Another version of constructivism is to be found in the contemporary semiological and structuralist movement. For de Saussure, the founding father of semiology, language is wholly a human creation: sounds and other physical objects have no signifying power in themselves but are endowed with the status of signs by man. This model of language has been adopted by structuralists such as Lévi-Strauss and Foucault and applied to the whole of man's social existence. However, for the structuralists it is not the individual who creates systems of meaning but society. Just as the individual speaker of a language operates within a linguistic system that is already constituted (though it can be enlarged and modified), so also the individual finds himself in a social system—a tissue of social meanings and values—that is already given or determined for him. The semiologists also make the more radical point that, just as words have meaning and exist as signs wholly by virtue of their relationships (of opposition and difference) with other words ('in the linguistic system there are only differences with no positive terms'), so also in social existence it is differential relationships which are of primary importance. For de Saussure we must abandon the idea that words or linguistic phenomena have any 'substance' apart from the differential relationships that constitute them[11] and in the same way the semiologists argue that we must get away from the idea of the individual existing apart from the network of differential social relationships. From this point of view the individual member of society only has meaning as a kind of nodal point of a tissue of relationships. This had led some of these thinkers to radically anti-humanistic conclusions. For example, Michel Foucault has spoken of the 'death of man', meaning by this that the whole conception of man found in classical humanism is now past. The subject or self is a construct, the product of a system of social conventions; in other words, the constructor is itself constructed.[12] Thus, although for the semiologists meaning is a human creation—meaning comes into the world through man—this does not have the 'Promethean' and humanistic implications that it has for Marx or Nietzsche or Sartre.

So far we have seen in what contexts questions about the meaning of existence do *not* make sense. Within the 'value free' world of scientific naturalism it is no longer possible to ask 'What is the

[11] F. de Saussure, *Cours de linguistique générale*, Paris, 1963, p. 168–9.
[12] M. Foucault, *Les Mots et les choses*, Paris, 1966, J. Derrida, *De la grammatologie*, Paris, 1967.

meaning of life?'. And in the same way within the context of constructivism—represented variously by Kantianism, Promethean humanism, structuralism and semiology—since man is the creator of meaning we cannot ask whether man himself has a meaning.

It is easy enough to transpose what has been said above about the meaning of human existence into the language of hope. Thus within the world of scientific naturalism the concept of hope has no purchase. The brute fact world of empiricism is neither hope-ful nor hope-less: in a world denuded of values it is a 'category mistake' to ask whether reality is on the side of man and whether the category of hope is, as Bloch claims, fundamental to the human project. Similarly, for the various forms of constructivism existence is in itself neither hope-ful or hope-less. For Marx and Nietzsche and Sartre, if existence is hope-ful it is we who make it so; hope is a human projection and there is no ontological basis for it.

So far I have been discussing the conditions under which the concept of hope does *not* make sense. But now, more positively, how could it be shown that the concept does make sense and that there is an ontological basis or ground for human hope? Under what conditions could the concept of hope be used intelligibly? I can here merely indicate an answer to these questions.

First, a critique of both scientific naturalism and constructivism in its various forms is necessary in order to make a place, so to speak, for the category of hope. This is easy enough in the case of scientific naturalism which is now being critically assailed on all sides. It is, however, not so easy in the case of constructivism which enjoys an enormous vogue in the human sciences at the present time. I believe, nevertheless, that there are some signs of dis-enchantment with the position which sees meaning and value, and hope, as mere projections which we gratuitously introduce into human existence. In my view we are about to witness a pendulum swing against that position.

Second, we would need to show that the category of hope was basic and inescapable in much the same way as we demonstrate the basic character of other metaphysical categories. In other words, we would need to show that every attempt to do away with the category of hope in some sense presupposes its reality: that to deny hope we must in some way affirm it. It would be possible to show, for example, that Camus' apparently hope-less stoicism is only made to seem plausible because it smuggles in the category of hope in a disguised form. Thus, we are asked to admire Sisyphus because he keeps on with his absurd task and resists the temptation of suicide. No doubt the hope involved in Sisyphus' resolve to keep on with his task is of the most attenuated kind. Nevertheless it is a form of hope and it is true to say that ultimately Sisyphus is a hope-ful hero.

Again, in the grim world of Samuel Beckett, which at first sight appears to be denuded of any kind of human hope or expectation, his protagonists still exhibit a minimal kind of stoical persistence— a hoping against hope—which saves his view from utter nihilism. I believe that this kind of analysis of the work of symptomatic figures of the age such as Nietzsche, Freud, Sartre, Camus, Beckett, is a strictly philosophical task and one that could shed a great deal of light on the ontological basis of human hope. Properly carried out this analysis could show in an existential way that pure nihilism—the rejection of all meaning and value—is in a real sense a self-contradictory position in that one has to presuppose that life has a meaning and value in order to deny it.

Relational Metaphysics and the Human Future

Harold H. Oliver

The complexity of the question of the human future is such that all proposals for redirecting human energies towards the actualization of value seem utterly simplistic. Radical pessimism produces prophets of doom; extreme optimism produces preachers of utopia. Most of the world's sages fall somewhere between these extremes, convinced of the worth and dignity of life despite human evidence to the contrary, and fully expectant that humanity has the natural endowment necessary to redeem the tragic, at least partially.

There is very little triumphalism left in the West. Gone are the old religious and humanistic liberals who proclaimed the gospel of irreversible progress in late nineteenth century Europe and early twentieth century America. The harshness of defeat left a cultural crisis of the first magnitude in Germany after World War I; the ideological crises surrounding racism, terrorism, ecological deterioration, nuclear arms proliferation, and the morality and futility of war deeply eroded the vestiges of 'manifest destiny' still felt in the United States even after World War II. The ideal of 'One World' held out by some as an imminent *pax aeterna* turned out to be as morally and politically ambiguous as the idea of nationhood has proven to be in the modern world. The religious message of the Kingdom of God survived with considerable vitality through many of the radical and unexpected technological and

political novelties of modern society, but seems now to be completely immobilized, a victim of societal complexification. The great
ethical systems of the past, philosophical and religious, were
formulated in a simpler time and now seem to many to be adequate
only for simple times. Something of the mood of our times is
captured in a recent advertising line from a modern industrial
enterprise: 'There are no simple solutions. Only intelligent
choices.'[1]

National ideologies which for centuries have provided a cultural
womb of security and identity have been challenged by global
ideologies which promise a new trans-national security and identity.
But these global gospels have lost their credibility to the degree that
their means have proved to be sub-human. Even the phenomenon
of ideology has lost its revolutionary power, a victim of the re-
deeming human proclivity for dialogue. The truly resolute have
become very few, and the fewer they are, the more desperate they
become, especially when their resolve has ideological roots.

The international mood is ripe for cultural despair, a global-
ization of Spengler's *Kulturpessimismus*. It has assumed many
modern forms: resignation to cultural pluralism, rampant personal
and cultural disorientation, senseless acts of political and ideological terrorism and the frightening realization that human consumption is fast outstripping the known resources.

During the past decade a complete rethinking of individual,
cultural and global priorities was initiated with a view to providing
realistic alternatives to what has seemed to some to be a disaster
course for humankind. Massive quests for new energies, new food
sources and ecologically viable life-styles for nations and persons
have been undertaken. Masses of persons are turning to the occult,
the psychic and—in the West—to Oriental mysticism for a personal
and social wholeness not provided in established social institutions,
the lack of which has been the cause of much personal disorientation. Increased energies and fiscal resources are being poured into
the quest for contact with 'extra-terrestrial intelligence' in the hope
that some meaning may be restored to human existence in the face
of the current 'centreless cosmos' of modern cosmology and
astrophysics. There are today forms of hope never before imagined:
cryogenic resurrection, organ-transplant technology, the founding

---

[1] Caterpillar Tractor Company advertisement *National Geographic Magazine*, 150,
July 1976, 1.

of space communities, the discovery and elimination of the physiological causes of ageing, to name only a few. While the production
of global utopias has not been revived in the old classical style, the
quest for individual and societal salvation has come to dominate
the lives of many persons in the modern world. Whether that
salvation is sought in dietary experimentation, in vigorous exercise,
in meditation, in evangelical fervour or in technologically more
complex forms of leisure, it is sought with all the rigour and
abandon of the religious seekers of older times.

Since salvation has always proved to be more of a 'hope' than a
reality, it is appropriate in an essay on hope to probe the grounds
of this human preoccupation with the length and quality of life.
I should like to propose that a distinction be made between the
human conditions that generate the passion for future directed life,
on the one hand, and the dimensions of experience that supply the
form and content of convincing individual and social gospels,
on the other. The former, the situational conditions for refocusing
life towards the future, is best summed up in the word *despair*.
While etymologically it simply designates the lack of hope, socially
it designates a fundamental *not-having* that becomes a *not-being*.
While my reservations about Ernst Bloch's *Prinzip-Hoffnung* are a
matter of public record[2], I am the first to admit the impressiveness
of his insight that hope arises out of a lack, a *horror vacui*, that cries
for fulfilling. According to Bloch, driven philosophically by the
economic vision of the theories of Marx, the fundamental *horror
vacui* is *hunger*. Bloch develops a comprehensive social vision of
hope out of a systematic phenomenological analysis of this most
natural and threatening lack ... the lack of food. There is no
denying the ideological passion of Bloch's phenomenology of hope,
though most of us are aware that since he wrote his *opus classicus*
on hope in Cambridge, Massachusetts, in the 1940s, the problem
of meeting the world's physical needs is no longer the simple issue
of the means of production. There are the almost insurmountable
related issues of pollution of food-stuffs and air, the foretold end
of fossil fuels, and world inflation that always falls most heavily on
the truly poor. I realize that Bloch only uses hunger as a phenomenological instrument, and that his major focus is on the quality
of life in a larger sense. He is more concerned with the dehumanizing of life which the capitalistic solution to the meeting of human

---

[2] 'Hope and Knowledge: The Epistemic Status of Religious Language', *Cultural Hermeneutics*, 2, 1974, 75–78.

needs has produced, as for example in the Industrial Revolution, than he is with logistical problems of production and distribution, and this is appropriate for a social philosopher and theoretician.

Bloch is correct to point out that hope arises out of despair, that is, out of the desperation of persons who are experiencing some fundamental lack. When this lack is seen as the by-product of religious, economic or political conspiracy, it is rightly interpreted by the 'have-nots' as oppression, and the form hope then takes is some gospel of liberation. The apocalyptic texts produced by Jews and Christians living under Roman rule comprise such a gospel. The unwritten but passionately sung spirituals of American slaves announced liberation. And the new theologies of liberation reflect the cultural desperation of Afro-Americans, feminists, ethnic minorities and Third World peoples. The degree of passion with which any gospel is accepted is a measure of the depth of the despair to which it addresses itself. Moreover, gospels are iconoclastic; they denounce the present to bring about a better future.

In exploring aspects of the conditions that lead persons and societies to direct their lives to what is 'not-yet', I certainly do not wish to give the impression that what I shall have to say about the human future will measure up where others have fallen short. The complexity of the question of the human future, to which I referred in the opening sentence, should serve as a sober caveat to any social dreamer. The relational schema I shall set forth in the following pages is attended by the conviction that it may meet a deeply felt need in our times to which I have not yet given attention, namely, the feeling of despair arising from the inadequacy of prevailing theories of reality to account for what we experience. I should like to thematize this phenomenon of modern life under the heading:

I. Conceptual Origins of Modern Despair

The subdivision of world history into distinct periods often follows fundamental shifts in world-view, as for example, in the distinction of the Medieval from the Modern Period in the West. The emergence of any radically new way of conceiving reality has usually entailed both a new sense of what is the case, and an iconoclastic judgement upon a prevailing paradigm of reality. The Modern era in the West signalled the discovery of the modern subject and a negative evaluation of medieval introspection. With the subjectivity came *pari passu* the notion of 'objects' (*Gegenstände*), of an objective world 'over against the subject' which is at the subject's disposal.

Here lie the origins of modern scientific objectivity, as well as of modern psychology. The conceptual by-products are present at all levels of our modern Western culture: Idealism and Realism in philosophy, with their opposing claims of the reality of the subject and of the object-world, respectively; Transcendence and Behaviourism, with their opposing claims of the fundamentality of the spiritual and the psychophysical realms, respectively; and Theism and Naturalism, with their rival claims about which is ultimate, God or Nature.

These modern Western options may seem *prima facie* to be academic and removed from daily life, but further reflection should indicate that they have in fact pervaded our culture, determining the being and well-being of most of us as we make personal decisions, conduct our professions, decide what to do with our wealth and make commitments of time. I venture the judgement that these conceptual options are to a large degree responsible for our psychic moods, both good and ill. The modern asocial self—the extreme version of individual subjectivity—may well underlie the psychic disorders of our time which are signalled by the growing dependence upon mind-stabilizing drugs and psychotherapy. Modern psychotherapy is, like all modern sciences, a function of modern possibilities; but it can also be said that it came into being to deal with the modern subject, a truly new phenomenon in human history. The diagnosis of psychic ills follows the concept of the psyche current in a given culture. In societies where the psyche is conceived reciprocally, psychic disorder means the loss of social viability; in other societies where the psyche is conceived individualistically, psychic ills are diagnosed as derangement, that is, as loss of inner composure. In our modern Western society predominantly informed by modern subjectivism, the latter idea prevails. While it is the function of psychiatrists to effect personal diagnoses in accord with the prevailing paradigm by which psychic order is defined, it is the task of philosophers oriented to metaphysical questions to arbitrate the larger issue of the viability of prevailing paradigms of personal and societal well-being.

I have chosen to focus upon conceptual origins of despair because of my conviction that conceptual paradigms lie at the root of a culture's well-being or disorder. Since the notion of despair has been defined primarily as a lack or inadequacy of some kind, it is appropriate to assume that the conceptual categories selected for special mention below are ways of viewing reality which I have judged to be inadequate in some final sense. The conceptual categories I wish to discuss include the prevailing notions of ontology, ethics and religion.

(a) The inadequacy of prevailing options in ontology

An ontology is a systematic statement of what is fundamental. It selects from the infinite variety of experiences those features or components that are fundamental to any experience whatsoever. In everyday discourse we do not always make such distinctions, the result being that our first encounters with such rigorous statements are characterized by unbelief. Those who do make these distinctions out of ordinary 'everyday' experiences often find their judgements about what is fundamental to be inadequate for experiences that are 'below' (micro-) or 'above' (macro-) the physical and social dimensions of what I have called 'the middle range of the empirical'. Such persons often retain their 'everyday'-ontologies for the interpretation of the experiences from which they were derived, and turn to specialized ontologies for the interpretation of special experiences. For example, there are persons who use a special ontology for interpreting their quantum mechanical research, a different special ontology for their interpretation of macro-cosmic events and dimensions, and perhaps even a completely different special ontology to interpret their mystical experiences. While such persons may experience some discomfort due to the radical discontinuities of their separate ontologies, they are certainly likely to be less frustrated than others who try to extend *intact* their singular ontology based upon 'the middle range of the empirical' to experiences which are 'below' or 'above' that range. The desperate efforts of some physicists to defend a 'classical' interpretation of quantum phenomena illustrates the difficulty of the former, while John Wisdom's famous 'tale' of the Gardener[3] seriously threatens the propriety of the latter.

Prior cultural events have deeply affected the ways we think about reality in the West. The formation of all modern Western

---

[3] John Wisdom, 'Gods', originally published in *Proceedings of the Aristotelian Society*, 1944; reprinted in his *Philosophy and Psychoanalysis*, Philosophical Library, New York, 1953, pp. 149–68. The tale of the gardener is found in the latter publication on pp. 154f. Antony Flew developed this 'tale' into the so-called 'Parable of the Gardener' in his contribution to the university debate published as chapter VI in Antony Flew and Alasdair MacIntyre, eds, *New Essays in Philosophical Theology*, The Library of Philosophy and Theology, SCM Press, London, 1955, cf. esp. pp. 96f.

languages was such that it is virtually inevitable for Westerners to take their cues for what is fundamental from the linguistic structures of their language. Since these languages all embody a subject-predicate structure with the predication primarily announcing temporality, it was inevitable that persons who speak these languages should assign fundamentality to subjects, objects and time. These three notions, plus the related notion of space, have all been accorded the status of reality at various times in the West. The classical Newtonian theory of the world made time and space absolute, much to the regret of his contemporary, Leibniz, who regarded them as having only ideality. Newton's theory was operationally so successful that it was an impetus to the Age of Reason whose most representative ontology was that of Mechanistic Materialism. Newton has but one equal in terms of the role he played in shaping Western thought, and that was Descartes who laid the foundations for modern subjectivity. The long Augustinian tradition in the Western Church, not always determinative of Catholic thought, can be credited with having played a major role in creating the conditions for Descartes' instantaneous success. The establishing of the certainty of the *cogito* would, however, be costly; for the inevitable consequence would be uncertainty about the ontological status of the *cogitatum*. It was Immanuel Kant who would address this problem of the 'objectivity of the object'[4] in such a fundamental way that, as a consequence, subsequent Western philosophy would be dominated by the subject-object problematic wherever Kant's influence prevailed. The Cartesian-Kantian axis in Western philosophy determined that, thereafter, ontologies in the West would focus primarily upon the problem of certainty, and that means the problem of *knowing* with certainty. For anyone committed to Descartes as a starting point it was the reality of the 'known' rather than of the 'knower' that would be problematic. In this way the subjectivist bias of modern Western philosophy was established. Its most articulate expression appeared in the form of Modern Idealism according to which reality is mental. It reached its apex in Absolute Idealism with its notion of the Pure Ego composing its world. Once Descartes' assumptions were accepted as a point of departure, it was inevitable that the notion of the absolute subject would eventually arise. Modern

4 Martin Heidegger, *What is a Thing?*, transl. W.B. Barton, Jr, and Vera Deutsch, with an analysis by Eugene T. Gendlin, Gateway ed., Henry Regnery Co., Chicago, 1967, p. 55.

Western individualism and egoism owe their origins largely to these events. Although few persons bother to trace this legacy to its roots, Western values and life-styles are predominantly informed by the notions of subject and subjectivity that began with Descartes and received classical form at the hands of Kant. Idealism continues as one of the most respectable ontologies among Western metaphysicians.

Until rather recently, the only serious alternative to Idealism advocated in the West was Realism (or Materialism) which simply rejects the priority of the subject as a way of accommodating the objective reality of the world. Realism has its roots, oddly enough, in Medieval Nominalism which accorded ideas the status of abstractions, in contrast to the Realists of the time for whom the notions were judged to be fundamental. As would be imagined, for modern realists the problem of uncertainty surrounds the status of the subject, and various schools within the movement are distinguished by their diverse judgements on the reality of the subject-world.

My concern in relating these details is threefold: (1) to show that Western philosophy has made available only two major options, Idealism and Realism, which are polar opposites; (2) to establish for later consideration that these historic options are both variants of the same fundamental assumption, not always admitted, namely, that reality must be sought within a subject-object frame of reference. Idealism and Realism represent absolutizations of these polar aspects, respectively. (3) My final concern is more basic to the task I have set for myself in this essay: I want to suggest that modern Western life is so fundamentally interpenetrated with these options that few exercise the imagination needed to suggest radically new ways of conceiving reality. Moreover, the fact that so many psychological, social, economic and political ills of our culture are rooted in these one-sided options makes it all the more urgent that more holistic ontologies be proposed. Masses of people in the West are turning away from the traditional cultural options in search of more adequate ontologies; for the one common element underlying the current preoccupation with the occult, the psychic and Eastern spirituality is the desire for holistic alternatives to the predominantly analytic modes of Western thought. My conviction is that the Western cultural heritage has a tradition of holism which can and should be developed and made available to those in the West who are disaffected with current assumptions about reality.

(b) The inadequacy of prevailing options in ethics

However much professional philosophers and ethicists may question the propriety of deriving the *ought* from the *is*, it is a cultural fact that current Western notions of morality are grounded in accepted notions about what is real. I for one find this state of affairs fully justifiable, although my judgement stands that the historic onto-logical commitments in the West are woefully inadequate.

The absolutization of the subject in some forms of Modern Idealism has served to transcendentalize 'Good', that is, to make it into a mere regulative concept, '*the* Good'. Another way of stating this claim is to say that morality is *temporalized*, in that a temporal interval is established, conceptually, between Intention and Act. In other essays I have spoken of this distinctive feature of Western ethics as 'the temporalization of the will'.[5] Just as subjectivist ontology introduced a (spatial) interval between 'knower' and 'known', making the latter a transcendental object, so its notion of moral action makes 'Good' remote and inaccessible. For the intrusion of a temporal interval so isolates intention that it has become proverbial in the West to denigrate so-called 'good intentions'.

The personal and social by-products of this morality of 'the Good' are obsessive guilt on one hand, and an inordinate sense of subjective achievement on the other. In a society where indi-vidualism is the most determinate form of existence the 'subject-self' of its ontology becomes 'the Moral Ego' of its ethics.

Where Realism constitutes the ontology, the epistemic status of selfhood is made problematic. In certain political ideologies, which are variants of Realism or Materialism, the self is even trivialized by being reduced to the status of other 'objective things'. To the extent that modern forms of humanism presuppose a realistic ontology, the morality they advocate is grounded in pragmatic considerations. Even so, the pervasive power of Western sub-jectivism is such that realists generally assume with the idealists that Intention is temporally separate from Act. It is for this reason that one speaks justifiably of the subjectivist bias of modern Western culture. One has only to compare Asian and Oriental cultures to realize the extent of that subjectivist bias.

[5] 'Theses on the Relational Self and the Genesis of the Western Ego', *Theologische Zeitschrift*, 33, 1977, 326–35; and 'Western Introspection and the Temporalization of the Will', A paper for the Boston Theological Society, 1978.

(c) The inadequacy of prevailing religious options

The plasticity of ancient religious traditions has been demonstrated throughout world history. The vitality of religion within modern secular states is phenomenal, especially when one considers how vastly different the modern cultural matrix is from those ancient cultures in which religions were given traditional form. Rather than dying the death 'of a thousand qualifications' as predicted by analytic philosophers, Western theism seems more virulent than ever before, just at a time when non-Western religions are on the rise in the West.

Religion appears to be an ineradicable component in human identity, but is it always benign? The most cursory acquaintance with human history will convince one that religion has been a 'mixed blessing' in virtually all cultures, modern culture being no exception. Nevertheless, religious institutions, practices and beliefs perdure through cultural upheavals; one reason for this, socio-logically speaking, may be the almost universal willingness to cite human frailty rather than the inadequacy of current religious ideals when adherents of a religion malign or manipulate each other or 'outsiders' in the name of their deity (-ies).

While it would be presumptuous to speak of the West as 'Christian', it is certainly the case that Christianity is a Western religion. It arose in the West and has never made significant inroads in non-Western cultures. It is also the case that no other religion (Judaism and Islam are special cases) has had any significant success in the West. The fact that Western peoples and their cultures have never been at peace with themselves or with others was justified theologically by Luther who characterized a Christian as *simul justus et peccator*.

The apocalyptic origins of Christianity determined that this emergent out of Judaism would be a religion of hope of very specifiable content. The success of Christianity in originally pagan European cultures must be explained in part by the fact that it was equipped with the most powerful ideological weapon—the promise of everlasting life. In subsequent eras of depravity and deprivation Christian eschatological belief has surfaced with unusual power. An eschatological orientation is so fundamental to Christianity that the most universal of all negative evaluations placed upon that religion has been its 'otherworldliness'. As in other religions, so in Christianity the grounds of its strength have been the sources of its weakness.

Christianity is not a simple phenomenon; it is present in the West in a multiplex form. Its diversity follows cultural, geographic, linguistic and even regional divisions, and these overlap with other distinctions of intra- and inter-Church doctrine and practice. Even so, Western Christianity is unified through a doctrine of personhood that informs not only its confessed followers, but those 'without' as well (Eastern Orthodox Christianity represents a wholesome exception). Christian personhood as defined today has both informed and been informed by Western subjectivism. Radical individual*ism* has so thoroughly come to define Western Christian personhood that the latter's fundamental teaching of 'self-denial' is either trivialized by its followers or regarded as so paradoxical as to be irrelevant.

Its unholy alliance with subjectivism in its modern form has rendered Christian faith impotent to cope with the psychic and social ills arising from subjectivist ontology. Can the fact that Christians experience psychic disorientation and deterioration as fully as non-Christians also be laid at the door of human frailty? I should like to suggest, to the contrary, that it is Christianity *as presently conceived* that is at fault. There are many ways of conceiving the meaning of Christian faith, some of which have already proven their inadequacy in times past. What is it about the present conception that makes present-day Christianity more a part of the problem than of the solution? I hasten to venture the judgement that what plagues modern Christianity is a conceptual inadequacy. Its conceptual inadequacy is largely an ontological one, resulting from its alliance with subjectivism. The consequence is that Christians fall victim to all the ills accompanying subjectivist ontology, but— what is even more tragic—they fall victim as well to other anxieties uniquely endemic to any subjectivist version of theistic belief. A serious look at the dynamic of theism versus atheism in Western culture should suffice to illustrate this problem.

Within pre-reflective mythic awareness what we later call theism represents an affirmation of divine-human relatedness, that is, of the co-reality of the I and the Thou. It is the form through which the ancient religious imagination gave expression to its fundamental sense of reality. In the narrative world of myth this affirmation of relatedness is 'character-ized', that is, it is dramatically developed through characters-in-relation. Their independent reality, that is, their existence *outside* the drama, is of no concern to the text. My hermeneutical theory of myth is that myths—stories of the gods—

are most faithfully interpreted in a *relational* way, that is, as affirmations of the fundamentality of relatedness.

Since the rise of modern Rationalism a different hermeneutical paradigm has been in effect. The rationalists took the myths to be *'cognitively referential'*, but denied the reality of their 'referents'. Defenders of the faith responded by claiming the reality of those 'referents', that is, by insisting that the stories were true, little realizing that they, by becoming defenders, had undergone a hermeneutical transformation of the first magnitude. For they had succumbed to rationalistic *referential* hermeneutics; whatever had remained until that time of pre-reflective mythic awareness was exchanged—by the faithful—for a biblical literalism that owed its possibility to rationalism.

The importance of that development for the present problem of the inadequacy of modern Western religiosity should be readily apparent. Rationalism created both theism and atheism in the modern sense by the same gambit; for modern theism—the assertion of the existence of the Wholly Other—is understandable only as a counter-assertion to Modern Atheism. In the pre-differentiated world of mythic awareness neither claim makes any sense.

The Church became the cultural bastion of modern theism, while its members became potential victims of reasonable doubt about the external reality of the divine beings *referred to* in its doctrinal and liturgical heritage. The *cogitatum* methodically placed in doubt by Descartes, to whom it did not occur to include the Deity, became inexorably inclusive of all transcendent beings. Doubt became an obsessive way of life in the West, both 'within' and 'without' the community of the faithful. For those 'within', it adulterated the innocence of simple faith; for those 'without', it became the ultimate justification for their non-alliance. Those who are truly 'outside' have a measure of tranquillity not experienced by those whose faith is complicated by its uneasy contract with an alien hermeneutic. For these persons the original substance of the Christian hope is transformed into what in modern times has been called 'the eschatological argument', that is, into the expectation that the certainty of what is believed will come at the end of the journey. Belief is exhaustively transfigured into hope, but the 'object' of hope becomes the eschatological verification of the 'external referents' of belief. Hope becomes a form of despair. Only those who have experienced the anxiety attendant upon this debilitating state of affairs can appreciate its ultimate inadequacy. Later I shall outline an ontology developed as an alternative to the current subjectivist and objectivist ontologies, and will then indicate its significance for the residual role of religion in modern culture.

What sources of hope are available to Western folk who experience anxiety and disorientation due to inadequate conceptual options in ontology, morality and religion? Hope by its very nature is a protest against a lack, a deficiency, a non-fulfilment. Eschatological inversion is its classic Christian content; conceptual inversion is the needed modern response to despair arising from conceptual inadequacies.

II. Modern Sources of Hope: Radically New Reconceptualizations of Reality, Temporality, Morality and Religion

It should be apparent by this point that ontology, temporality, morality and religion are not separate issues, but are conceptually interwoven in the deepest way imaginable. Though the topics must appear *seriatim*, every effort will be made to show their theoretical and practical interconnection.

(a) A relational theory of reality: reality is *relatedness*

Idealism and Realism represent aspectual absolutizations of the subject-predicate paradigm, respectively. While the viability of this paradigm was not questioned seriously until the rise of phenomenology, the grounds for choice within its limits were routinely discussed under the topic of internal versus external relations. The three major modern positions taken in this debate were: (1) that all relations are external; (2) that all relations are internal; and (3) that some relations are external, some internal. Using the formula, aRb, we may say that position (1) takes the *relata* as fundamental, the relation as contingent. Position (2) takes the *relata* as ontologically defined by the relation. The final theory holds (1) to be the case for certain relations, (2) for others. Few modern philosophers have agreed with Bertrand Russell in holding all relations to be external, in that the unity of experience seems inexplicable on these terms. Bradley and his colleagues, including Brand Blanshard, have based their monism on the doctrine of the fundamentality of relations, a position its opponent, Charles Hartshorne, appropriately labels 'The Thesis of Universal Internality'. G.E. Moore, Hartshorne and his mentor, Whitehead, are the names usually thought of in connection with the view that some relations are external, some internal. It is certainly beyond dispute that any ontology that claims the fundamentality of process would necessarily support this latter position on relations.[6]

Relational metaphysics assumes the thesis of universal internality and rigorously carries through its implications with a view to effecting a generalization of experience. Absolute rigour in the application of this assumption leads to the conclusion that a and b represent 'functional dependencies'[7] (Cassirer's term) of the re-lating, R. Idealism is grounded in the assumption of the funda-mentality of a, the 'subject'; Realism, in the assumption of the fundamentality of some bs, that is, of those 'objects' that have a physical reference. Relationalism is based on the thesis that *all* and *only* relations are fundamental. It further argues that any and all ontologies based on the fundamentality of the *relata* commit the 'fallacy of misplaced concreteness' (Whitehead's term).[8] The extreme relational thesis could be falsely interpreted to mean that the *relata* are unreal, that is, illusory. According to my relational metaphysical scheme, the *relata* are purely abstractions; they are derivatives of fundamentals whose emergence is explained by the instrument I call *biperspectivism* (a term I learned from Ervin

---

[6] Bertrand Russell's view was set forth in his *Principles of Mathematics*, first pub-lished in 1903 and reprinted in a second edition by W.W. Norton Co., p. 100; he reiterated his position in 'The Monistic Theory of Truth', available in his *Philosophical Essays*, Simon and Schuster, New York, 1966 (repr. of 1910 ed.), pp. 131–46. G.E. Moore's historic essay on relations is available in his *Philo-sophical Studies*, Littlefield, Adams and Co., Totowa, N.J., 1968, cf. esp. pp. 276–308. Charles Hartshorne's defence of the asymmetry of relations is a principal feature of many of his publications, including *Man's Vision of God and The Logic of Theism*, Harper and Row, New York, 1964 (orig. pub. 1941), p. 326; *The Divine Relativity: A Social Conception of God*, Yale University Press, New Haven, 1948, esp. pp. 62–67, 103–14; and *Creative Synthesis and Philosophic Method*, SCM Press, London, 1970, esp. pp. 52ff, 84ff, 99–119, 210–23. F.H. Bradley's classic statement in favour of internality was set forth in the Appendix to his *Appearance and Reality*, Clarendon Press, Oxford, 1893, esp. in pp. 512–22. His view was defended and expanded by Brand Blanshard, *The Nature of Thought*, Macmillan Co., New York, 1940, pp. 449–91, and more recently in his article 'Internal Relations and their Importance to Philosophy', *Review of Metaphysics* 21, 1967, pp. 227–36. Since Alfred North Whitehead gives no extensive treatment of relations *per se*, I shall here simply concede to the 'scholastics'' view that Hartshorne faithfully represents his mentor's position.

[7] Ernst Cassirer, 'Einstein's Theory of Relativity', in his *Substance and Function in Einstein's Theory of Relativity*, Dover Publications, New York, 1953 (orig. publ. 1921), p. 379.

[8] This characteristic Whiteheadian phrase appeared in his *Science and the Modern World*, Lowell Lectures, 1925, The Free Press, New York, 1967 (orig. publ. 1925), cf. e.g. pp. 51 and 58; and in his *Process and Reality: An Essay in Cosmology*, Harper and Brothers, New York, 1960 (orig. publ. 1929), cf. pp. 11 and 27.

Laszlo).[9] As applied to relations, it means that when any relation is viewed *ingressively*, the notion of the subject emerges; when viewed *effectively*, the notion of the object appears.[10] Thus any action (R) has the possibility of such co-derivatives. Since all Western languages are structured in the subject-predicate form, it is in the West that there has been the greatest tendency to reify these relata. Since it is somewhat easier to show how these two idioms (that is, relational and subject-object) emerged by appeal to the philosophical notion of Pure Experience, I shall now turn to this latter idiom. I should say in advance that I judge the theory of Pure Experience to be a variant version of the relational scheme already set forth.

The adjective 'pure' in the notion, 'Pure Experience', means 'prior to reflection'. In Pure Experience, there is only Immediacy, Pure Activity. There is no 'subject', no 'object', no 'prior' and no 'posterior'. There is only the Now-Moment, lacking differentiations of time, 'actors' and 'acted upon' (to use terms met earlier in the discussion of relations). These differentiations emerge through reflection upon Pure Experience, which being mediated by re-flection is not longer Immediate. Thus on the model of Pure Experience, subject-selves, objects and object-selves, past and future are abstractions, rather than concrete entities. The grounds for their appearance lie not in Pure Experience but in the nature of reflection. Philosophers and theologians of 'consciousness' argue that thinking always implies 'thinking subject' and 'object thought'; Jaspers, for example, spoke of the 'subject-object schema of consciousness'. But as even these thinkers have indicated, not all experience is 'cognitive', that is, reflective. The thesis of Pure Experience entails the rejection of the entitivity of consciousness, holding it too to be an abstraction. 'Consciousness', as cognitively understood, is merely a product of reflection, nothing more.

Drawing upon both of these idioms, relational metaphysics and Pure Experience, I venture the following ontological conclusions which are radically significant for modern life. Reality consists

---

[9] Ervin Laszlo, *Introduction to Systems Philosophy* Harper Torchbook ed., Harper and Row, New York, 1972, p. 154.

[10] The terms 'ingressively' and 'effectively' are borrowed from Greek grammatical usage where they function to distinguish nuances of the aorist tense. The fact that the 'aorist' expressed 'undefined action' gave rise to the grammatical theory that one using it may have, under certain circumstances, intended to stress either the incipient character of the act (hence 'ingressive') or the act viewed in terms of its result (hence 'effectively').

not of 'things-in-relation' (that is, *relata*) but of *relations*. By extension, reality is *relatedness*. And relating is Immediacy, Pure Activity. Neither subject- nor object-selves, nor object-things, are fundamental. It is appropriate, however, to use the term selfhood, but only in the form, 'the (or a) Relational Self'. As I tried to indicate in an earlier essay[11] the relational self is not the subject-self, is not 'located in space and time' and does not calculate its moral worth. It is the self of Pure Experience, of the I-Thou. Those who want to read the purest statements on the notion of the relational self should turn to Zen texts, for there one will find a purity of expression that can only come from centuries of refinement of the notion. Two excerpts from Suzuki's phenomenal article, 'The Zen Doctrine of No-Mind', should suffice to illustrate the insight from that tradition:

> When thus the seeing of self-nature has no reference to a specific state of consciousness, which can be logically or relatively defined as a something, the Zen masters designate it in negative terms and call it 'no-thought' or 'no-mind', *wu-nien* or *wu-hsin*. As it is 'no-thought' or 'no-mind', the seeing is really the seeing.[12]

and

> The state of no-mind-ness refers to the time prior to the separation of mind and world, when there is yet no mind standing against an external world and receiving its impressions through the various sense-channels. Not only a mind, but a world, has not yet come into existence.[13]

While such ontological notions may seem utterly strange and inscrutable to the Western mind, I have tried to indicate that there are Western options which are isomorphic with them, such as Pure Experience. It would seem to follow that Eastern and Western conceptual interchange is not just some passing fad, but is absolutely crucial to the *bene esse* of Western self-perception.

(b) A relational theory of temporality: towards a phenomenology of 'futurity'

Ontological, ethical and eschatological considerations make it imperative that I treat the problem of temporality and experience in some detail. Classical physics strongly influenced Western philosophy to accept the fundamentality of linear time; considerable

---

[11] cf. reference 5, 1977 article.
[12] D.T. Suzuki, *Zen Buddhism: Selected Writings*, ed. William Barrett, Doubleday, Anchor Books, New York, 1956, p. 163.
[13] *Ibid.*, p. 219.

incentives towards that move had long been provided by the
temporalization of history and eschatology in Western theology
from the time of Augustine. Peoples who are ideologically non-
Western, such as Orientals and Native Americans, commonly view
Western culture as distinguished by its linear sense of history. It
should have come as no shock when I located the distinctive
problematic of Western morality in its temporalization of the Will.
The 'phenomenology of futurity' soon to be explicated will result
in an alternative interpretation of moral existence. As for eschatology, the third consideration mentioned above, the relational theory
of reality and temporality should issue in a recovery of the reality of
hope.

From the perspective of relational metaphysics time and space
as treated as derivatives—that is, abstractions—which are characterized as belonging exhaustively to the language and logic of measurement. This relational claim is fully commensurate with the theory
of space-time events advanced in the Special Theory of Relativity.
In Pure Experience there are no spatio-temporal differentiations,
no 'prior' or 'posterior' to separate 'knower' from 'known', or
Intention from Act. While these spatio-temporal distinctions appear
only through reflection, it is faithful to the notion of Pure Experience to speak of Immediacy as having a texture—a texture that
includes temporality, but not time in a physical sense. A phenomenology of this temporality will now be undertaken with a view
to indicating (1) in what ways it is appropriate to speak temporally
of experience, and (2) the experiential conditions out of which
Western metaphysics developed its questionable claim for the
fundamentality of time.

1. A phenomenology of temporality

Pure Experience is a Now-Moment, but its texture may include a
sense of pastness and a *sense* of futurity. There is a 'pastness' of the
present (Immediacy) which upon reflection is called '*the* Past';
there is a 'futurity' of the present (Immediacy) which upon reflection becomes '*the* Future'. We experience neither the 'Past' nor
the 'Future'; rather, the reality of the Past is only the experiential
'pastness' of the Present, the reality of the 'Future' is only the
experiential 'futurity' of the present. Ontologically speaking: to
the extent 'the Past' is not 'present to us', it *is* not; to the extent
'the Future' is not 'present to us', it *is* not. 'The Past' is but the
symbolic representation of that aspect of Immediacy we call

'pastness'; 'The Future' is but the symbolic representation of that aspect of Immediacy we call 'futurity'. It is only the present (= Immediacy) that gives the Past; it is only the present that gives the Future.

Even in ordinary language 'the Past' means 'what *was*, but *is* no longer *present*'; 'the Future' means 'what *is* not (yet) *present*'. The necessary negations in these statements signal the non-Immediacy, non-presence—hence non-fundamentality—of Past and Future. The word 'present' in both formulations is a clue of some importance: the pastness of Immediacy, which gives rise upon reflection to the notion of 'the Past', is the experienced 'non-presence of what *was* present'; 'the futurity of Immediacy, which gives rise to the notion of 'the Future', is the experienced 'non-presence of what *will be* present'. Thus in a fundamental way both the sense of pastness and the sense of futurity affirm the Immediacy of Presentness.

Put in another idiom: Pure Experience may include memory and anticipation. Memory is the sense of pastness, the recall of the no longer present; anticipation is the sense of futurity, the present 'leaning forward of the present'. The reflective reification of memory produces the notion of 'the Past'; the reflective reification of anticipation produces the notion of 'the Future'. Thus 'the Past' and 'the Future' are mere abstractions, that is, derivatives of what is fundamental. They are not fundamental themselves, for they arise only upon reflection and hence are 'mediated' (that is, non-Immediate). And what is non-Immediate is not fundamental.

It follows that there *is* no 'Past' and there *is* no 'Future'. There *is* only pastness; there *is* only futurity. Since the primary concern of this essay is to re-establish legitimate grounds for hope, I shall now attempt to relate hope to the notion of 'futurity' rather than of 'the Future'.

2. Hope as present anticipation

The reality of hope lies in the fact that it is Immediate. An anticipated hope is not yet hope. Hope's reality lies in the fact that it is the *present* anticipation *of something*; it is the *present* negation of a lack in one of the two forms in which a negation of what is present can be real. The other form is memory. Therefore, hope is the actualization of the Not-Yet, the only actuality it *has*. 'The Future' has no reality except the reality of 'futurity'. So far I have spoken of hope from the perspective of a phenomenology of futurity. Now it is imperative to speak phenomenologically about *hope* itself.

Hope is, ontologically speaking, present anticipation, which has both formal and material aspects. Formally, hope is always hope 'in something'. Bloch has taught us that hope is a formal protest against a *lack*, a deficiency. But hope never appears purely formally; materially considered, hope is always specific. Cultural factors account for this specificity; for persons whose experience has been truly trans-cultural, the cultural particularism of expectations becomes generalized into no less specific, but less particularistic content.

The relational reconceptualization of reality and of temporality proposed in this essay is intended as an option to existing problematic notions of entities, including subject-selves, objects and object-selves, as well as 'the Past' and 'the Future'. So far I have only been able to speak formally about hope in the light of these relational statements. Toward the end of this essay I shall attempt to indicate what may be learned from this relational approach about the material content of hope. For the present I must refocus attention on the 'phenomenology of futurity' in order to indicate the implications of relational ontology for morality.

(c) A relational theory of morality: reassessing 'Good'

Western morality reaches its highest expression in the notion of 'the Good'. I indicated earlier that this notion is a reification of 'Good'; it is the *mediated* form of the latter. When the ethical focuses on 'the Good', it commits itself to what *is not Immediate*, hence *is* not. 'Good' is transformed into an ideal, that is, into what has only ideality; it becomes an abstraction, lacking actuality. The temporalizing of the will, that is, the separation of Intention from Act, is the great de-realizer of 'Good'. When 'Good' is conceptually de-realized, that is, made non-Immediate, there *is* no moral action; for 'the moral' either *is*, or it *is* not. 'The Good' may be a moral idea, but it has no actuality. 'The Good' is no substitute for 'Good'.

Against the background of Western morality such claims may appear inscrutable. Actually the claim being made is a simple one: the enactment of the ethical is not future, but now, for enactment that is not *being enacted* is not yet (*is not*) enactment. It is not a moral act only to intend the Good, for good intention—separated from Act—does not constitute 'Good'. Moral prophets have known this throughout human history. They do not urge consideration of "the Good'; rather they warn: 'Enact "Good" Now'. They characteristically have no patience with 'later', for reality *is now*, or it *is* not. Those who are culturally conditioned by Western notions of morality alone may find this relational notion of the Immediacy of 'Good' morally suspect, for that is the general attitude of Westerners toward Zen religiosity which I find commensurate with morality relationally understood. I for one, however, see no other conceptual alternative to the particular moral problems of Western society than the one I have set forth. In my mind it is the only resolution of the problematic of the 'plagued conscience' of the West. The separation of 'Moral Subject' from the 'Moral Act' is fatal to morality; the interval becomes a cosmic abyss, like the Western theoretical distinction in, say, archery between the 'hitter' and the 'hit'. In Zen archery, on the contrary, since the bowstring must go through the archer's thumb, no such distinction exists.[14] The Western theoretical distinction referred to is as fatal to its ontological concepts as to its moral, for the former determines the latter. A relational ontology, which—like Zen—admits of no such distinction, provides for a reassessing of 'Good' in the Western context.

(d) A relational theory of religion: beyond belief and unbelief

It was claimed earlier that inadequate Western concepts of the function of religious affirmation often create an 'anxiety of faith' that can be as disorienting as that anxiety to which faith intends to respond. The *referential* interpretation of the great religious myths shifts the focus away from the stories to some supposed transcendent realm, with its transcendent beings, and for this reason alone fails to respect the narrative limits of the stories. Two consequences fatal to religious tranquillity regularly ensue: (1) the dynamic of the religious life becomes the quest for certainty about the reality of these transcendent entities; and (2) an intra-cultural debate develops primarily around this question of 'certainty' which divides the religious from the non-religious. In both instances the fundamental affirmation of religion can easily be lost.

Since it was essential to introduce my relational theory of religion earlier to support the thesis of the inadequacy of the

---

[14] Eugen Herrigel, *Zen in the Art of Archery*, with an Introduction by D.T. Suzuki, trans. R.F.C. Hull, Vintage Books eds, New York, 1971, p. 31f.

prevailing referential theory, I must now reiterate and then expand that statement.

Contrary to the reductionist claims of analytic philosophers and those theologians who tried to make sense of religious discourse by assuming those claims, the relational hermeneutics of such discourse holds it to be *ontological* affirmation. Religious discourse in its originative form is a mythical announcement about reality. The reality of which it speaks is the reality of experience; it is only when a *referential* theory of myth prevails that the claim arises that religious discourse is about some *trans*-empirical reality. Since from a relational perspective, experience is all there is, religious discourse is interpreted *relationally* as a statement about experience. Since its ontological claim is available apart from myth, as for example through metaphysics or even physics, it follows that the uniqueness of mythical affirmation lies not in its content, but in its particularized form. Such a statement about myth does not denigrate the religious affirmation, since it is made with the accompanying realization that the cultural appeal of a religion lies in its particularity.

Religion is the affirmation of *relatedness*, for myth images the insight that what is fundamental about experience is not that there *exist* fundamental entities who enjoy the occasional adventure of relationship, but that there *is* only *relatedness*. In the great religious epics the story does not exist to establish the reality of the trans-experiential; it exists rather to affirm the co-relational character of experience. The *referential* theory of myth assumes that mutuality is a contingent dimension of divine and human entities; the relational theory, that *mutuality* is what is fundamental. It would be a gross misunderstanding of the relational theory to interpret it as a denial of the transcendent dimension of the mythical; for myth *qua* myth does not reify the transcendent, but employs it to affirm the reality of relatedness. Thus the truly transcendent dimension of myth is its affirmation that experiential reality is relatedness. No other claim about the transcendent is commensurate with the relational theory of religious discourse. In Judaism the affirmation of relatedness takes the form of the I-Thou paradigm of prayer; in Christianity it takes the form of the God-Man paradigm culturally informed by Hellenistic-Oriental piety. Metaphysically considered, these religious paradigms are but culturally different versions of the same ontological affirmation.

III. Conclusion: The Reality of Hope

From the wisdom of the past we learn that 'hope that is seen is not hope'. Relationally rephrased, it is the insight that hope is not the reality of 'the Future', since the latter has no reality. Rather, hope is the reality of futurity; it is present anticipation. Today one hears a great deal about global planning, but from a relational perspective the caveat comes that *planning* is not the actualization of 'the Future'; it is rather only the reality of planning. Planning is not thereby discouraged; what is discouraged is the *allzumenschlich* human proclivity for ontologizing what *is* not present.

While the analytic of hope advanced in this essay has the potential for relieving some of the anxiety associated with illusory notions of time and reality, the relational metaphysical schema which informs this analytic has the power to speak materially of the content of world hope. That 'the Future' is uncertain follows not from some human weakness but from the abstract nature of 'the Future'. The emptiness of 'the Future' is compensated for in experience by the fullness of futurity, that is, of hope. To the degree that cultural despair is a function of inadequate conceptions of reality, the positive value of improved conceptions should be apparent. Since relational metaphysics does not subscribe to the ontologies of either Idealism or Realism, it undermines the extremes of subjectivism and objectivism which account for much of the cultural disorder of our times. Personal and social wholeness, desperately sought by so many in fragmented ways, must receive universal priority. But not simply as an ideal, for ideas have only ideality. A goal has only the reality of the means, hence the proverbial wisdom about means and ends. Let me illustrate this wisdom.

During the late 1960s a friend sent me a greeting card, on the face of which was printed:

> Peace is not the goal,
> Peace is the way.

By analogy it may be said: Hope is the actual form of the Not Yet, the only actuality it has. Therefore, hope is the generic form in which the goal of the human future becomes the way.

Marxism and Hope

Wayne Hudson

Marxism will occupy a central place in any future history of human hope. It has provided the most influential paradigm for world improvement to emerge in the last hundred years. It has also been the source of a rhetoric of social explanation, which has contributed to the social sciences as well as to the formulation of left-wing political ideologies in countries as diverse as France, Ethiopia, Korea, Jamaica, Cambodia and Afghanistan. Yet the question of what Marxism is remains disputed.

Students of Marxism are divided in their methods and objects of study. There is little effective integration of the study of: (1) 'Marxism' in the sense of a body of historically influential ideas allegedly derived from Karl Marx; (2) 'Marxism' in the sense of a scientific method of analysis; and (3) 'Marxism' in the sense of the functional ideologies articulated by Communist parties. Even the study of Marx's own ideas is often still locked in disciplinarian internments, as if *Capital* was a work dealing with economic questions or *The Eighteenth Brumaire* was a piece of historical writing. Indeed, Marx's ideas operate as the legitimating origin for one of the most interdisciplinary modes of current discourse, despite the fact that little interdisciplinary work has been done on them. There are few adequate translations, scarcely any dual texts supported by fully scholarly apparatus, and only a relatively small number of studies that observe minimum standards of historical exactitude and philosophical rigour. Historians of Marxist thought are emerging, but there are few sustained attempts to integrate the technical study of Marxist ideas with social and economic perspectives that rise above the level of mechanical assertion.

Granted that it is difficult to speak of 'Marxism' *simpliciter* without presuming critical delineations that have not yet been made, it may be more useful to think of Marxism as a matrix associated with identifiable texts, from which a variety of different doctrines can be extracted, rather than as a body of doctrine which would amount to only one 'Marxism'. Such a construction has its dangers. But it has the advantage of recognizing that the scientific study of Marxism is in its infancy; that the plurality of intellectual constellations seeking strength from the label call for a discerning taxonomy; and that the interpretation of the contents of the matrix may depend on current politico-economic history and paradigm shifts as much as on the growing legibility of what is there. In this paper the term 'Marxism' will be used to refer to such a matrix, and not to any one particular account of what Marxism is. The strategy of the paper is to attempt to suggest how Marxism could provide indications for new and hopeful initiatives *within capitalist society*—and so be a source of hope.

Firstly, Marxism may be able to provide indications for an initiative aimed at formulating a science of political economy that would not be a regurgitation of 'Marxist economics'. Such a science of political economy would not be bound by Marx's *dicta*, or by the structure of his problematic. It would be a science of modes of production and their internal dynamics, which would seek to account for the transition from one mode of production to another and for the fate of specific social classes within determinate social formations. There is already a vast and rapidly growing literature that aims to develop a science of political economy on Marxist principles.[1] So far its results have had only limited explanatory power; but they have the advantage of being contenders

---

[1] For a general survey, see A. Bose, *Marxian and Post-Marxian Political Economy, An Introduction*, Penguin, Harmondsworth, 1975; and, more specialized, P. Sraffa, *Production of Commodities by Means of Commodities*, Cambridge University Press, 1960; M. Morishima, *Marx's Economics, A Dual Theory of Value*, Cambridge University Press, 1973; M. Desai, *Marxian Economic Theory*, Gray-Mills, London, 1974; and I. Steedman, *Marx After Sraffa*, NLB, London, 1977. For a treatment of Marx's own position, see M.C. Howard and J.E. King, *The Political Economy of Marx*, Longman, London, 1975.

for scientific status which actively seek refutation, instead of hiding behind a barrage of scholasticism and a pretence to class partisanship, which allows rational criteria to confirm but never to refute its claims. Unfortunately, much of this literature has been vitiated, at least in part, by a tendency to remain locked in Marxian schemes and by a tendency to confuse a genuine science of political economy with a revamping of an ideologically conceived 'historical materialism'.[2] Instead, a science of political economy is needed that does not repeat Marx's schema for confessional reasons or prejudge central issues in a way designed to ensure its outcomes will be compatible with Marx's projections.

Such a science of political economy would be free of any automatic commitment to the demise of capitalism or to the saving role of the proletariat. It would seek to test Marx's assertions and to produce results at odds with the political commitments of its practitioners. Such a science would be incompatible, by definition, with 'historical materialism' in the sense of epistemological or ontological dogma. But it would not necessarily exclude 'historical materialism' in the sense of a set of tightly defined, testable assertions. On the contrary, a genuine science of political economy might well begin with a set of such doctrines, at least as a source of initial hypotheses. What would go would be the attempt to absolutize soteriological predictions about the inner logic and likely future development of capitalism, and the related tendency to regard the most fundamental methodological questions as settled. Such a science of political economy would no longer be 'Marxist' in the sectarian sense, but it would build on Marxist insights and find indications in Marxism itself for the decision to break with classical Marxian formulations. For example, it might apply Marx's claim that the mode of production of material life conditions the general process of social, political and intellectual life[3] to his own

[2] These tendencies are also apparent in much of the neo-Althusserian literature. See G. Therborn, *Science, Class and Society*, NLB, London, 1976; P. Anderson, *Lineages of the Absolutist State*, NLB, London, 1974, and *Passages from Antiquity to Feudalism*, NLB, London, 1974; C. Bettelheim, *The Transition to Socialist Economy*, transl. B. Pearce, Harvester, London, 1975, and *Economic Calculation* and *Forms of Property*, transl. I. Taylor, Routledge and Kegan Paul, London, 1976. For important semi-critical works, see B. Hindness and P.Q. Hirst, *Pre-Capitalist Modes of Production*, Routledge and Kegan Paul, London, 1975, and E. Mandel, *Late Capitalism*, transl. J. De Bres, NLB, London, 1975.
[3] Karl Marx, *A Contribution to the Critique of Political Economy* (1859), Russian translation, Progress Publishers, Moscow, 1970, pp. 20–1.

work and, in particular, to his theories about 'the natural laws of capitalist production'.[4]

Such a development would be hopeful because if such a science of political economy could be formulated, it could open up the possibility of understanding how and why traditional hopes have been rendered substantially unrealizable by a situation in which economic forces operate outside the conscious knowledge and rational control of men and women. Such a science might provide: (1) a rational basis for analyzing, classifying and correlating social formations; (2) a basis for predicting the contradictions likely to arise within the present mode of production; and (3) indications of structural changes that might enable men and women to control the world economy in ways that would keep its tendencies and contradictions from working to frustrate human purposes. Of course, such a science might turn out to be utopian. It might prove impossible to formulate. It could also be misconceived in principle. Certainly, such a science would be open to attack as 'pre-Marxist', as one more pretence to neutrality which fails to confront the problem of class standpoints. It could be argued that there can be no neutral class-free knowledge in class society, and that the pretence to neutrality and objectivity only serves as a defence of existing structures of hegemony and domination. Doubtless, there would be a problem about the knowledge interest operative in such a science, and also a problem about its critical character. Such a science could easily lapse into positivism. It would be likely to remain a 'proto-science' (a science still in the outline stage) for some time. Such a science would also probably take diverse or even contradictory forms, depending on the explanatory, predictive or critical goals set for it by different practitioners. But this impurity and conflict could itself prove creative. It would also be consistent with the diverse and pluralistic conditions for theoretical production found in, and to some extent sustained by, modern capitalism.

Secondly, Marxism could provide indications for a new initiative in psychology, based on an attempt to develop a praxis of self-constitution. Marx himself provided no systematic philosophical anthropology, and only the barest outlines of how a psychology that would be consistent with his principles could be developed. As a result, Marxist writers have developed a variety of distinct

---

[4] Karl Marx, *Capital*, Vol. I (1867), transl. S. Moore and E. Aveling, Lawrence and Wishart, London, 1970, Preface to the first German edition, p. 8.

and contradictory approaches to psychological questions. These have included: (1) attempts to develop speculative forms of philosophical anthropology; (2) attempts to combine Marxism with psychoanalysis; (3) attempts to develop a strictly behaviourist or explicitly Pavlovian psychology; (4) attempts to develop an 'historical materialist' approach to psychological problems, which stresses the socio-economic determination of the psychologies of individuals rather than the autonomy of the allegedly psychological; (5) attempts to rethink the significance of psychological data in the light of the opening up of traditional ontology which Marxism makes possible; and (6) attempts to develop a materialist theory of the emergence of the subject, based on a Lacanian renovation of Freud's theory of the unconscious.[5] There is also a vast technical Soviet literature, which attempts to explore the relationship between 'the spiritual world of the individual' and the socio-economic determinations of 'socialist' society.[6] Again, Marxist writers have contributed to the contemporary critique of psychoanalysis, psychiatry, male heteronomy and the nuclear family.

Nonetheless, it is fair to say that most Marxist writing on psychological questions suffers from scriptural fundamentalism and from one or another version of sociological reductionism. There is also a widespread evasion of an honest confrontation with genetic determinism and socio-biology, while many of the most radical implications of classical Marxist doctrines have never been developed in a psychological context, especially in the countries that call themselves 'socialist'. Marxists have been better at criticizing the alleged mystifications of 'bourgeois psychology', and at idealizing the psychological characteristics of people living in the 'socialist' countries, than at developing concrete proposals for

[5] Among a vast literature, see A. Schaff, *Marxism and the Human Individual*, transl. O. Wojtasiewicz, McGraw-Hill, New York, 1970; L. Sève, *Marxism and the Theory of Human Personality*, English transl., Lawrence and Wishart, London, 1975; P. Brown, *Towards a Marxist Psychology*, Harper, New York, 1974, and bibliography; W. Reich, *The Mass Psychology of Fascism*, transl. V. Carfagno, Farrar, Straus and Giroux, New York, 1970; E. Bloch, *Das Prinzip Hoffnung, Gesamtausgabe*, Vol. 5 (Suhrkamp), pt. II 'Das antizipierende Bewusstsein'; A. Lemaire, *Jacques Lacan*, transl. David Macey, Routledge and Kegan Paul, London, 1977; and R. Coward and J. Ellis *Language and Materialism* Routledge and Kegan Paul, London, 1977, chapter 6.

[6] For accessible examples, see M. Petrosyan, *Humanism: Its Philosophical, Ethical and Sociological Aspects*, transl. B. Bean and R. Daglish, Progress Publishers, Moscow, 1972, which includes bibliographical references to works in Russian; and G. Smirnov, *Soviet Man: The Making of a Socialist Type of Personality*, transl. R. Daglish, Progress Publishers, Moscow, 1973.

actualizing specific human potentialities repressed or impeded in class society.

However, Marxism could provide indications for a new initiative in psychology if the radical implications of classical Marxist doctrines could be drawn out and set to work in a new context. The classical Marxist doctrine of the historical-social character of human personality, with its implication that at least some existing manifestations of human personality may be transient and capable of change, leads to a series of radical postulates of openness. These postulates include: (1) that there is no *Homo psychologicus*, and no fixed or unchangeable human nature; (2) that there are no natural phases or divisions of human life, such as 'childhood', 'adolescence' or 'old age'; (3) that there are no 'natural' needs, drives or affections; (4) that there are no 'natural' human groupings, such as 'race', 'family' or 'divisions between the sexes'; and (5) that the existing limitations on human personality, such as disease, the need to sleep, and death, may be defeasible. Such postulates may be in conflict with existing scientific (especially genetic) theory. They are also open to a maximalist interpretation that confuses the fact that one or more of them might be partly true, with the quite ungrounded implication that such postulates, if true, support a strong form of historical optimism. Clearly the mutability of human personality does not of itself imply that further mutations, if they were achieved, would necessarily be improvements or would not involve new anti-utopian consequences. However, such postulates do raise the possibility that the self is not given once and for all, but may be a potentiality that can be made the object of an historical praxis of self-constitution.

Granted this perspective, Marxism could indicate ways in which a praxis of self-constitution could be developed under the capitalist mode of production and subject to the constraints of capitalist accumulation. Classical Marxist doctrine suggests that life under capitalism becomes reified and abstract, that human personality only tends to manifest under capitalism in thwarted and contradictory forms, and that individuals tend to become personifications of economic relationships in important respects.[7] A new initiative aiming at a praxis of self-constitution might seek to discover how these tendencies can be actively countered, and also their positive

---

[7] See, for example, Karl Marx, *Capital*, Vol. 1 (1867), *op. cit.*, Preface to the first German edition, p. 10, and text p. 71ff; and *Grundrisse* (written 1857–8) transl. M. Nicolaus, Penguin, Harmondsworth, 1973, pp. 409–10, 488, 496.

meaning for attempts to break with the concept of an immutable self. Such an initiative would seek to discover new, but still latent, dimensions of human personality that are emerging in capitalist society as a result of technological change, or even the presence of the elements of a new mode of production within capitalism itself. It would interpret the classical Marxist doctrines that consciousness (1) is determined by social being, and (2) is objectively limited by the stage of development of the forces of production, in a positive sense.[8] It would interpret these doctrines to mean that a praxis of self-constitution would require detailed changes and modifications of existing socio-economic determinations, without which any purely psychological radicalism would be naïve. Equally, however, such an initiative would investigate the possibility that the limits to consciousness alleged to be set by the stage of development of the existing forces of production have not been reached—or are actually expanding.

Such an initiative would also emphasize the importance of investigating the possibility of new forms of psychological praxis, including a possible inheritance of forms of psychological praxis (for example, memory techniques and imagination training systems) which prevailed in the past. It would investigate the question of whether different articulations of human personality, or even articulations of different human potentialities, prevailed in 'historical psychologies' that differed from our own, or may still exist in extant societies that embody earlier 'times', grounded in older modes of production. It would then seek to discover whether new forms of such articulations might be becoming possible under capitalism. Such an initiative would not be utopian. It would accept that class interests and existing structures might operate to frustrate the full realization of its goals. But it would be hopeful because it would not accept the present limitations on human personality passively, but would seek to change them in ways that were in accordance with developing socio-economic conditions.

Thirdly, it is possible that Marxism could provide indications for a new initiative in jurisprudence and the philosophy of law. Such an initiative would go beyond the standard Marxist attempts to expose the class-bound and mystified character of theories of law and justice, the class conflict and class interests behind specific judicial decisions and legislation, and the oppressive character of

[8] Karl Marx and Frederick Engels, *The German Ideology* (written 1845–6), Russian translation, Progress Publishers, Moscow, 1968, pp. 31–2, 37–8, 50, 89.

the existing criminal law and penal system.[9] It would go beyond every form of negative critique in the direction of an active jurisprudence. It would not be enough to operate at an ameliorative level: for example, to propose ways of decentralizing legislative procedures, of democratizing the judicial system, of reworking the common law, of transforming the legal profession into a caste with an objective economic interest in the realization of economic justice rather than in the protection and extension of its opposite. Nor would it be enough to attempt to implement the unfulfilled *telos* of liberalism, recognizable in such ideals as 'free enterprise', 'the freedom of the individual', 'freedom of speech', 'freedom of the press', 'the right to privacy', 'freedom of information', 'freedom of religion' and so on.

A new initiative in jurisprudence would seek to show that the classical Marxist doctrine of the socio-economic determination of law can be interpreted normatively. It would seek to show that a jurisprudence is possible, even under capitalism, that relates law to political economy *consciously* and in a *positive* way. It might then seek to show that existing legal arrangements are inadequate to the needs and imminent tendencies of the capitalist mode of production; that capitalism itself already contains the elements of a future mode of production; and that this mode of production will require new legal arrangements and procedures, which need to be prepared and initiated now.

Such an initiative would seek to analyze the tendencies of the capitalist mode of production, and to detail ways in which the positive possibilities for further human emancipation implicit in such tendencies can be assisted by anticipatory juristic postulates and new legal procedures. At the same time, it would take full account of the possible negative consequences of such tendencies, and seek to provide individuals with legal and institutional protection against the more heinous consequences of such tendencies operating unjustly. Such an initiative would not imagine that ideals of justice or moral ends can be guaranteed by the tendencies of a mode of production. It would not imagine that class interests would not operate to distort and partially defeat anything that might be

[9] See, for example, I. Taylor, P. Walton and J. Young, *The New Criminology*, Routledge and Kegan Paul, London, 1973, especially chapter 7 and bibliography; and V.A. Tumanov, *Contemporary Bourgeois Legal Thought, A Marxist Evaluation of the Basic Concepts*, transl. J. Gibbons, Progress Publishers, Moscow, 1974. For a contrast, see E. Bloch, *Naturrecht und menschliche Würde, Gesamtausgabe*, Vol. 6 (Suhrkamp), pp. 206–99.

achieved. But it would seek to provide a body of constructive legal and institutional innovation, based on the actual tendencies of the capitalist mode of production, which could also enter into a process of transmission to a future classless society, if and when it occurred. In view of the known consequences of attempting to build advanced societies with only primitive legal institutions and procedural systems, such an initiative could serve to emphasize the importance of purely legal change—and so be a source of hope.

Fourthly, Marxism could provide indications for a new initiative in aesthetics. It is true that the record so far is not wholly encouraging. Marxist dogma has been used in country after country to repress the cultural avant-garde and to legitimize the most sterile cultural Popery and aesthetic totalitarianism. The very term 'socialist realism' has come to be associated with servility and a politically submissive art that offers only the most regimented expressions of social criticism. On the other hand, there have been Marxist initiatives in almost every art: from the non-Aristotelian theatre of Bertolt Brecht to peasant painting from China. There is also a substantial body of Marxist literary and art criticism of high quality.[10] If the really creative application of Marxist insights to aesthetics is still lacking, it may be in part because: (1) Marxists have tended to absolutize the sociological criticism implicit in a Marxist approach, as though the problem of the ontological status of art were reducible to questions of socio-economic or political explanation; and because (2) Marxists have tended to accept a characterization of aesthetic objects as 'epiphenomenal', that is, as 'subjective' or 'ornamental'. Without an adequate ontology of art, Marxists have been unable to establish the specificity of the aesthetic (despite the attempts by Lukács[11] and others to do so) in a way that does justice to the potentially hopeful meaning of art. Indeed, the characterization of aesthetic objects as 'epiphenomenal' has made it difficult for Marxist writers to explain what aesthetic objects are, without reducing their functionality to hedonism, propaganda, the accumulation of public or private cultural wealth, or a celebration of individual and collective creativity.

[10] For a useful anthology, see B. Lang and F. Williams, *Marxism and Art*, David McKay, New York, 1972; and for a bibliographical guide, L. Baxandall, *Marxism and Aesthetics, A Selective Annotated Bibliography*, Humanities Press, New York, 1973.

[11] See G. Lukács, *Über die Besonderheit als Kategorie der Ästhetik*, Luchterhand, Neuwied, 1967 and *Die Eigenart des Ästhetischen*, Vols 11 and 12, in *Werke*, Luchterhand, Neuwied, 1963.

A new initiative in aesthetics would need to confront this problem. It would need to go beyond the standard Marxist attempts to expose the class character of existing art, the commodity character of aesthetic production under capitalism, and the way in which traditional aesthetic categories reflect hierarchical methods of social organization. A new initiative in aesthetics would need to rethink the problem of the ontological status of art in a historical and socio-economic perspective. Here Marxism can provide important indications. In particular, the classical Marxist critique of pre-Marxist philosophy, in terms of the class interests and the levels of economic development it reflects, could be radicalized and used to explain how the understanding of ontological problems generally has come to be mystified under capitalism—and so, paradoxically, in Marxism.

A new initiative in aesthetics would seek to expose such mystifications and to reopen the question of the ontological status of art in the context of 'a political metaphysics', for which 'what there is' (ontology) would be understood as the problem of what is projected as possible. The concept of 'a political metaphysics' is a difficult one. Here it must suffice to say that 'what there is' is not given or settled for human consciousness, but is always a theory of what there is, elaborated at a particular time in history and under a given mode of production. It may be possible therefore to formulate a theory of 'what there is' that recognizes its own conditioning and seeks to consciously explore the causal influence such theory acquires, in terms of what men and women project as possible and therefore seek to achieve. If so, a new initiative in aesthetics might seek to use such a 'political metaphysics' to ground a new confidence in the aesthetic, designed to counter the nihilism and dehumanization of avant-gardism and post-modernism. This confidence would be based on the postulate that aesthetic objects can acquire a new social functionality under capitalism, provided that 'what there is' is not taken as settled or given. In such a functionality, an attempt would be made to add to 'what there is', extending the range and content of aesthetic objects to include attempts to anticipate new positive possibilities (including new moral values and new social relationships)[12] that are emerging.

Finally, Marxism may be able to provide indications for a new initiative aiming at a radical renegotiation of the contemporary

[12] cf. Ernst Bloch's approach (to which I am indebted) in Ernst Bloch, *Ästhetik des Vor-Scheins*, 2 Vols, ed. G. Ueding, Suhrkamp Frankfurt am Main, 1974.

meaning and function of religion. The need for a more positive Marxist critique of religion has been a suppressed but constant theme in the Marxist tradition, just as neglect of the antinomies in Marx's own critique of religion and the vulgar anti-religion of the Marxist tradition have gone hand in hand. Indications for a new approach to religion (more strictly, *religions*) could, however, be developed from the antinomies of Marx's own critique. The classical Marxist doctrine, that religion is a form of false consciousness and a social activity distorted and voided by its complicity in the mystifications and oppressions of class society, can be interpreted positively to mean that it is necessary to distinguish the false forms religion takes in class society from the potentially legitimate area of concern, of which religion is the inauthentic expression.[13]

A new initiative in the area of religion might accept the bulk of the Marxist critique of religion but attempt to interpret this potentially legitimate area of concern as an historically conditioned projectivism, aiming at a praxis of relations with non-existent entities. Such an initiative would emphasize that religions project entities that have no existence into a heavenly or transcendent realm, and that such entities are reflections, to a greater or lesser degree, of the social relationships in the society in which religion is found. It would also recognize that such a projectivism, in so far as it aims at a praxis of relations with non-existent entities, seeks to operate a causal connection with such non-existent entities and may indeed, in both a psychological and a sociological sense, succeed in doing so. That is, a new initiative in the area of religion might recognize that the non-existent entities that are projected have a certain reality for believers, and that causal consequences follow from this. Assuming a perspective no longer backdated by a passive and credulous relationship to Marx's *dicta*, this projectivism would not necessarily be regarded as illusory. Similarly, the term 'non-existent entities' could be understood as a reference to the non-factual, imaginary character of the referents posited by religious activity, rather than as a premature closure of the possibly genuine question of the need not to reduce the final possibility

[13] For a discussion of the antinomies of Marx's own critique, see my article, 'Towards A Positive Marxist Critique of Religion' in *Australian Essays in World Religions*, ed. V. Hayes, The Australian Association for the Study of Religion, 1977, pp. 96–105; and, more generally, D.B. McKown, *The Classical Marxist Critiques of Religion: Marx, Engels, Lenin, Kautsky*, Martin Nijhoff, The Hague, 1975.

content of reality to regnant, and largely instrumental, scientific cosmology.

Such a new initiative in the area of religion would go on to investigate whether such projectivism might not be capable of acquiring a new functionality under capitalism. It may be that the rate of technological and social change under capitalism, the multiplication of knowledge and the emergence of a plurality of critiques of inherited conceptions of knowledge themselves open the way for a more conscious attempt to assume responsibility for how we imagine the universe to be, and how we seek to change it. In an increasingly critical or even post-theistic perspective, the problem of the alleged objectivity of non-existent entities is a declining one. But the problem of the need for such a projectivism may only be beginning to emerge, in part as a reaction against attempts to take current scientific theories about the physical universe as exhaustive or final.

A new approach to religion might seek to integrate a reinterpretation of the nature of religion with a critical philosophy of science that emphasizes the role of human labour in building theoretical models of what there is. It would investigate the need for a category of 'non-existence' (related to, but distinct from, the attempts to delineate such a category in Indian metaphysics[14]) able to give projective postulatory status to dimensions of reality, which it may be productive to postulate in the context of human self constitution —even though they cannot be shown to 'exist'. Once again, this proposal is not a simple one, just as the problem of religion itself is not simple. It is possible that no agreement could be reached about which non-existent entities, if any, should be projected into such dimensions of reality with the status of 'non-existence'. There would also be a problem about whether such an approach could be illusion-free. Such an initiative would be hopeful, however, because it would attempt to reconstitute the legitimate area of concern with which religion deals, in contrast to the tendency for modern theologians to substitute individualistic depth psychology, psychotherapy, philosophy of language or a Messianic secular humanism for it.

All these initiatives are little more than outlines, and would need to be developed more fully elsewhere. Clearly, each of them is

---

[14] For treatments of 'non-existence' in Indian metaphysics, see, for example, C. Sharma, *A Critical Survey of Indian Philosophy*, Motilal Banarsidass, Delhi, 1964, second edition, pp. 182–3, 223–40.

open to serious and cogent objection, not least to the objection that it involves an attempt to prostitute Marxism in a reformist manner. Here much depends on the crucial premise of the continuing viability and indeed creativity of capitalism in the short run. Such initiatives would remain intra-capitalist and not 'socialist' or 'Marxist' initiatives. They would depend on what might be called an intra-capitalist application of Marxist doctrines for essentially intra-capitalist purposes. From a strictly Marxist perspective, such initiatives might be 'erroneous'. Nonetheless, the fact that these initiatives are not wholly remote from perceptions of contemporary problems already current in capitalist society means that they might have a chance of influencing future perceptions of such problems. If Marxism could indeed provide indications for such 'errors', it would not be an unimportant source of hope.

Beyond the Illusions of the Left

Greg George and Brian Laver*

Throughout this discussion the questions of how a genuinely liberatory social change can occur and of what individuals and groups wishing to promote such change can do, remain entangled. What people do depends on what they think might happen. On the whole Marxism provides a practical example of what not to think and, consequently, what not to do.

Our theme can be summed up in the words of the anarchist Gustav Landauer, who pointed out that the State is not an institution which can be destroyed by revolution. 'The State is a condition, a certain relationship between human beings; we destroy it by contracting other relationships, by behaving differently.'[1] Similarly, Kropotkin corrected Bakunin's flaming words 'by destroying we create' with 'by creating we destroy' as a truer expression of a liberatory movement.

---

* Written substantially by G. George in association with B. Laver after a long mutual learning process with other comrades in the Brisbane libertarian socialist movement.

[1] Quoted in M. Buber, *Paths in Utopia*, Routledge and Kegan Paul, London, 1949, p. 46.

Cornelius Castoriadis[2], writing of the 1956 workers' council movement in Hungary, gives reality to this thought.

> The intellectuals (and students) had begun months before the outburst to play an important, positive role by demolishing the political, ideological and theoretical nonsense with which the Stalinist bureaucracy had (presented itself as socialism). They played this role not by bringing people to a new, ready-made truth, but by courageously exposing the old lies. New positive truths were created by the people themselves during and by means of their autonomous activity (not just against bureaucracy), but also as new forms for the organization of collective life on the basis of new principles. This, in turn, overthrew the traditional relationship between theory and practice, as well as that between theoreticians and plain people.[3]

'Is organization the opposite of spontaneity?' Castoriadis suggests that the question is precisely what organization, and whose organization? The spontaneous action of the Hungarian people was, he argues, action toward organization; and even more, their spontaneity was exactly that, their self-organization. Castoriadis points out that such organization simultaneously involves new consciousness:

> By the same token it obviously presupposes having become conscious of the essential characteristics and mechanisms of the established system and of the desire and the will to invent a new solution to the problem posed. (It is clear, for instance, that the understanding possessed by the Hungarian workers in their activity of the social character of the bureaucracy as an exploitative and oppressive class, and of the conditions for its existence, was from a theoretical viewpoint infinitely superior to all ... Trotskyist and most Marxist writings.) Self-organization is here self-organizing, and conscious is becoming-conscious; both are processes, not states. It is not that people have finally found the appropriate form of social organization, but that they realize that this form is their activity of organizing themselves in accordance with their understanding of the situation and the ends they set for themselves.[4]

Castoriadis draws a further lesson from the Hungarian events:

> History is creation; i.e. the emergence of that which is not already contained in its causes, conditions, etc., that which is not repetition ... The aims and the demands formulated by these Councils are in line with

---

[2] Castoriadis was a member of the group around the journal *Socialisme ou Barbarie*, which developed libertarian thought from 1944 to 1965 and has had a continuing influence, especially through the publication of pamphlets by the British group Solidarity.

[3] C. Castoriadis, 'The Hungarian Source', *Telos*, 29, Fall 1976, p. 82.

[4] *Ibid.*, pp. 12–13.

the aims and demands implied by the whole history of the working class movement, even if on certain basic points (e.g. self-management, abolition of work norms) they are more explicit and more radical. Thus, in the modern world, there is a unity of the revolutionary project. This unity can be rendered more intelligible by pointing to its historical inheritance and continuity; the similarity of the conditions in which the working class is placed ... But, even though these factors are relevant and important, they can never give us the sum of necessary and sufficient conditions for the production of the specific content of responses in 1871, 1905, 1917, 1936–37, 1956, or indeed, for the failure to produce such responses in other instances. For what we have here is not an objective unity—not a unity as in the identity of a class of effects stemming from a class of identical causes—but a unity in the making.[5]

The libertarian espousal of such creative self-activity will be reviewed later, but first Marxism will be examined from this perspective.

In the oft-quoted passage from the 'Preface to a Contribution to the Critique of Political Economy'[6] Marx describes the 'guiding thread' of his studies from 1844 onwards. The economic structure is the foundation of the social, political and intellectual life process. The economic structure is transformed because the material productive forces conflict with the existing relations of production when those relations come to restrain their development. In consequence the ideological (legal, political, religious, aesthetic, philosophic) forms express this conflict. This is an epoch of social revolution.

When Marx wrote this in 1859 he had already written the *Grundrisse* which was the foundation for the planned work of which *Capital* was only a part. Basic to his thought is a dichotomy in which one element is 'in the final analysis' primary: that is, social being determines consciousness. Passages show that class struggle is a subsidiary reflection of the economic base; that its course is determined by changes in the forces of production; and that its result in revolution and the society thereby created is an inevitable product of the level of development of these productive forces, for example, 'process of natural history', 'inexorable', 'analogous to the history of evolution', etc. The aims and consciousness of the proletariat do not determine the result but are determined. Marx approvingly quotes a Russian reviewer of *Capital*:

[5] *Ibid.*, p. 13.
[6] K. Marx and F. Engels, *Selected Works*, Progress Publishers, Moscow, 1968, pp. 182–83.

Marx only troubles himself about one thing, to show, by rigid scientific investigation, the necessity of successive determinate orders of social conditions, and to establish, as impartially as possible, the facts that serve him for fundamental starting-points. For this it is quite enough if he proves, at the same time, both the necessity of the present order of things, and the necessity of another order into which the first must inevitably pass over, and this all the same whether men believe or do not believe it, whether they are conscious or unconscious of it.[7]

What is the practical result of this theory of inevitability? In this view 'revolution becomes the mere question of more or less expenses on the bill of history—since the end result of history is already settled'.[8] There is no need to define or to create socialism in order to act in the way most likely to produce it. If the basis for revolutionary consciousness is the preordained developments of capitalism, no demand need be made for consistency of means and ends, since the end is so to speak 'value free'. This great brooding future did serve as the source of teleological ethics—the deferred future of communism as a justifying goal. Later adherents found solutions for the gaps and ambiguities left by Marx from within the logic of his system. In the absence of ethics, referral to the absolute inevitability of communism became the basis for the quite obvious conclusion that whatever assists this inevitable result can only be thoroughly right.

Wellmer has detected a gap between Marx's philosophy of history and his criticism—this criticism being designed to further the need for liberatory activity. Where this gap is revealed Marx's argument would, he asserts, seem through some tacit compulsion to be dually grounded, because only thus can the utopian goal be read in the lines of technical-economic necessity: 'In reality, the historico-philosophical scheme of interpretation, which is dominated by the logic of production, no longer admits of a formulation of problems of the social system in which questions of survival also appear as questions of the "good life".'[9] This is because the existentially necessary (that is, historically inevitable) new order of production is made equivalent to the commonwealth of freedom. Further, Wellmer argues that the objective possibility and the practical necessity of enlightening the proletariat about its social

---

[7] K. Marx, *Capital*, Vol. 1, Progress Publishers, Moscow, 1954, p. 27.
[8] A. Wellmer, *Critical Theory of Society*, Herder and Herder, New York, 1971, p. 75. See especially the second essay, 'The Latent Positivism of Marx's Philosophy of History'.
[9] *Ibid.*, pp. 105–6.

situation become the historical (existential) necessity that 'the proletariat comprehends its own situation, which in the end turns into the necessity that the proletariat will actually achieve the revolutionary goal—the building of the classless society—already "irrevocably ordained" in its present situation.'[10]

The belief that the coming of classless society is inevitable destroys the activity of actually building the classless society now. The idea that *a process* must produce the alternative, including the consciousness necessary for that alternative, leads to an abandonment of the centrality of the notion that personal change, active comprehension and collective effort around defined aims and applying recognized values are the basis for attaining classless society.

It is not denied that there is a stream of thought running through Marxism which could have avoided scientism and objectivism. Though this presence is maintained, it is conquered by a historical materialism which traces the dialectics of morality back to the dialectics of production and has been shown historically to have certain manifest consequences for revolutionary activity, chiefly the suppression of the view that liberating practice depends on a transformation of attitudes and modes of behaviour. This view is the major lesson provided by the women's movement for contemporary revolutionaries. The distinguishing feature of libertarian activity is the tendency to align with the creative activity of the masses which involved such a transformatory practice, while other leftists served to actively oppose or manipulate such tendencies. The anarcho-syndicalist abandonment of this principle, with the creation of organization which recruited without challenging attitudes and modes of behaviour, had the eventual result that anarchists stood in opposition to the self-activity of the people. Historical materialism neither allows the revolutionary process to be seriously comprehended as a process of enlightenment on which the success of the revolution is ultimately dependent, nor does it permit an appropriate materialistic explication and criticism of the bourgeois concept of political freedom from which practical norms for revolutionary political freedom can be deduced. As Wellmer demonstrates, the two are closely connected:

> Processes of collective enlightenment can be anticipated only on the premise of a normative concept of autonomy and 'undistorted' communication. Understood as a process of enlightenment, the revolutionary

[10] *Ibid.*, p. 70.

process is subject to norms the explication of which is at one and the same time an explication of the political freedom to be realized, and the fulfilment of which, moreover, no historic destiny can guarantee.[11]

The blind forces that supposedly guarantee the final collapse of capitalist society are also blind to the result and here they offer no guarantees. Marx's allegiance to the crisis theory was based on his overwhelming concern to be scientific. To the nineteenth century philosopher this meant to discover absolute laws. An unpredictable phenomenon like the class struggle, involving as it does so many unverifiable phenomena, could find no place in this science and had to be subsumed under other factors. For us, an understanding of capitalist crisis is neither restricted to economic phenomena (since economic phenomena are not restricted to economic factors) nor concerned to prove the inevitability of the exercise of laws. The significant crisis for us, the crisis that lays the basis for a challenge to capitalism, is a crisis of values, meanings, motivations, responsibility, beliefs, attitudes, socialization—in other words a cultural crisis. The challenge that such a crisis allows is based on the construction of alternative forms of interaction embodying socialist values. That there can be such a crisis is obviously the result of 'objective factors'. These can be summed up as the increasing bureaucratization of society—the phenomena of apathy, privatization, consumerism, alienation, etc. But a cultural crisis itself is an 'objective' factor. Indeed the possibility of an alternative is also dependent on 'objective' factors. But the realization of this possibility is dependent on personal change (on a mass scale), the spread of ideas and the expression of the self-activity of the majority in the form of democratic organization which sees itself as the total base for the management of society, in other words autonomy in organization and ideas.

This is the *only* objective factor that promises a communist future. Marx says (and there are many similar passages):

> Communism for us is not a state of things that ought to be made to exist, an ideal by which reality has to orient itself. We call communism the real movement which transcends the existing state of things. The determining factors of this movement are obtained from the premise existing now.[12]

After the factors that make a revolution a possibility are considered, the only premise existing now that can determine communism is

[11] *Ibid.*, p. 89.
[12] Quoted in A. Wellmer, *op. cit.*, p. 101.

that the revolution be a conscious attempt to bring a state of affairs that ought to exist into existence.

It seems quite likely that the determination of Marx and Engels to resist the proposing of ideals, ethics and a socialist vision was given a strong impetus by Max Stirner's denunciation of these elements in socialism.[13] In their defence they felt the need to remove all such elements from their socialism. The defeats of 1848 must also have added to a tendency to see socialism as a gift of historical forces rather than as a result of human will and the power of utopian thinking to activate people. In a market-dominated capitalism, in a positivistic scientific climate, in a post-idealist but pre-Freudian intellectual climate, it is not surprising that Marx's thought took a particular direction. But because of the tendency to accept Marx as a whole, it has taken the most terrible historical experiences and the most abject theoretical failure to bring some Marxists back to a consideration of the meaning of socialism and the nature of socialist values.

Despite his historical faith Marx did not abjure political action. But there is an implacable contradiction between the slogan 'the emancipation of the working class must be the act of the working class itself' and the idea that objective conditions would make the proletariat bring socialism about. How do you get to a situation where people determine the direction of society toward agreed goals, where there are no quasi-natural forces acting behind the backs of people, through the operation of a determinist causality in which awareness itself is determined? Scientific understanding of the laws operating assumes that people are totally controlled by processes. All this had powerful results in Marx's own political activity.

Marx stresses the direct self-emancipation of the proletariat by a process of enlightenment on a number of occasions. In 1852, 'What we say to the worker is: You will have 15, 20, 32 years of civil war and national struggle and that not merely to bring about a change in society but also to change yourselves and prepare yourselves for the exercise of political power.'[14] In his 1888 Preface to The Communist Manifesto Engels says Marx 'entirely trusted to the intellectual development of the working class, which was sure

---

[13] See 'Editor's Introduction' to K. Marx and F. Engels, The German Ideology, International, New York, 1970, p. 23ff.

[14] K. Marx, The Cologne Communist Trial, International, New York, 1971, p. 62.

to result from combined actions and mutual discussions.'[15] In *The German Ideology* they said 'In revolutionary activity the changing of oneself coincides with the changing of circumstances.'[16]

But in the objectivist framework the substitution for the change of people by the change of objective circumstance remained basic. A liberatory revolution should express the self-activity of people, not their victimization by *History* (or by a vanguard). They must create self-awareness and self-organization in order to make revolution, even if they do so in weeks or even days. But this is the reverse of what Marx requires. 'The alteration of men on a mass scale is necessary, an alteration which can only take place in a practical movement, a revolution; this revolution is necessary, therefore, not only because the ruling class cannot be overthrown in any other way, but also because the class overthrowing it can only in a revolution succeed in ridding itself of all the muck of ages and become fitted to found society anew.'[17]

Here Marx is saying 'You need a revolution to create revolutionary consciousness.' This statement and its reverse portray a mechanistic view of the interrelation between activity and thought which has its basis in the being and consciousness dichotomy. The Hungarians overthrew the traditional relationship between theory and practice. Their self-organization presupposed and expressed an understanding of the bureaucratic system and the will and ideas to invent libertarian relationships. In Marx's view, revolution is the last political act. It is followed by the introduction of a social form that supersedes political rulership.

Buber summarizes Marx's view:

> First the political act of social revolution will annihilate not merely the class state, but, the State as a power-formation altogether, whereas the political revolution was the very thing that 'constituted the state as a public concern, that, as the real State'. On the other hand, 'the organizing activity' will begin, i.e. the reconstruction of society, only after the complete overthrow of existing power—whatever organizing activity preceded the Revolution was only organization for the struggle.[18]

He argues that from this we can see with the greatest clarity what it is that connects Marx with 'utopian' socialism: the will to super-

[15] L. Feuer, ed., *Marx and Engel's Basic Writing on Politics and Philosophy*, Anchor, New York, 1959, p. 2.
[16] *The German Ideology*, p. 29.
[17] *Ibid.*, p. 95.
[18] M. Buber, *op. cit.*, p. 82.

sede the political principle by the social principle, and what divides him from it:

> His opinion that this supercession can be effected by exclusively political means—hence by way of sheer suicide, so to speak, on the part of the political principle. This opinion is rooted deep in Marx's dialectical view of history.[19]

The concept of the dictatorship of the proletariat gave Marx's attitude its permanent and historically disastrous form. Even with the post-Paris Commune correction that the bourgeois state must be smashed not seized, the commitment to political action amounted to the denial of the advocacy of the emancipation of the working class through a social movement which constructs alternative forms. Thus Marx says in 'On the Jewish Question'

> Revolution in general—the overthrow of the existing power and dissolution of previous relationships—is a political act. Socialism cannot be realized without a revolution. But when its organizing activity begins, when its peculiarities, its soul, comes forward, then socialism casts aside its political cloak.[20]

Only to reveal its political dagger! This dagger was first used by Lenin and Trotsky, and by Ebert and Noske. In each case it was used to violently suppress working class and peasant self-activity.

In the words of Erich Fromm (whose contribution will be discussed later) Marx and Engels 'could not free themselves from the traditional view of the importance of the state and political power, from the idea of the primary significance of mere political change, an idea which had been the guiding principle of the great middle-class revolutions of the seventeenth and eighteenth centuries. In this respect [they] were much more "bourgeois" thinkers than were men like Proudhon, Bakunin, Kropotkin and Landauer.'[21] In order to find out how this attitude is, as Buber claims, 'rooted deep in Marx's dialectical view of history', it is necessary to look further at Marx's political statements. In *The Civil War in France* Marx announced that the Paris Commune of 1871 was 'the political form, at last discovered under which to work out the economic emancipation of labour.'[22] The Commune was the positive abolition of the state and Marx's acceptance of this connects him with

[19] *Ibid.*, p. 83.
[20] D. McLellan, *The Thought of Karl Marx*, Macmillan, London, 1971, p. 27.
[21] E. Fromm, *The Sane Society*, Routledge and Kegan Paul, London, 1963, p. 259.
[22] *Selected Works*, p. 294.

a federation of co-operatives and communes under a common plan as 'Communism, "possible" Communism'.[23]

Yet it is unfortunately true that Marx's statements were prompted largely by respect for the dead and, along with them, he buried the lessons of the Commune. Marx was against the rising in the first place, but this could be accepted as realism. In 1881 Marx wrote that the Commune's policies 'were not socialist, nor in the circumstances could they have been'.[24] This might appear as initially necessary criticism of the Commune's failings. Kropotkin's criticism was chiefly designed to show that what the Commune required was more of the same—more democratization and more co-operative control. Kropotkin saw that, despite the right of recall, the Commune was a parliament. People sent delegates to the Commune without a clear mandate on given issues but with the right to represent them, to discuss and decide on whatever came up on behalf of their arrondissements, which remained merely constituencies rather than organized bodies for decision-making. The result was a loss of initiative and drive on the part of the populace and the incapability of the representatives on the Commune to deal with the manifold issues. The inchoate tendency, for both those reasons, to establish a dictatorial Committee of Public Safety is hardly surprising. Was this the nature of Marx's criticism? It seems unlikely. Before the Commune's defeat he wrote 'The Central Committee (of the National Guard) surrendered its power too soon, to make way for the Commune.'[25] In 1873 he wrote 'The workers must . . . influence the most decisive centralization of force in the hands of state power. They should not allow themselves to be confused by democratic talk of communes and self-government.'[26]

Marx often attacked co-operatives (and trade unions) because they did not change the system. He sometimes praised them as proving that wage-labour is destined to give way to associated labour. In these statements he ascribes a central significance to co-operation. But he still does not see the co-operatives as the basis for revolution. Russian revolutionaries were debating whether they should work amongst the peasants to end constraints on the already existing village co-operatives. Some thought the co-

[23] *Ibid.*, p. 294.
[24] D. McLellan, *op. cit.*, p. 185.
[25] *Selected Works*, p. 680.
[26] Quoted in H. Arendt, *On Revolution*, Penguin, Harmondsworth, 1973, p. 325.

operatives could be the basis of a socialist federation. Others were using *Capital* to argue that the co-operatives were doomed. They asked Marx to solve the dilemma, and after much thought he 'in theory affirmed the possibility of a pre-revolutionary development of the commune in the direction desired, but in practice he made its "salvation" dependent on the timely appearance of the revolution. Here as elsewhere the determining factor is clearly the political element.'[27] This question for the Russian socialists was a 'life and death' question. Whether they tried to free the communities or whether, in this peasant country, they stayed with urban workers was to be decided. Buber says Marx feared 'lest the constructive work should sap the strength of the revolutionary impetus'.[28]

In 1850 'The workers ... must not only strive for a single and indivisible German republic, but also within this republic for the most determined centralization of power in the hands of the state authority.'[29] McLellan remarks that such comments are usually associated with the problem of what aspects of the bourgeois revolution the proletariat should support. This is the clue to what ties all these statements together in the context of Marx's view of history. Because Marx identified the ultimate hope of revolution most essentially with the development of the productive forces, he wished to actively support the bourgeoisie's efforts. It is not that he did not want to see workers' or peasants' co-operatives. He was not being misanthropic. He believed they did not have a chance against the laws of capitalist development, so he sometimes called them 'reactionary'. They could only hold up the inevitable and it would bring with it revolution. It is with the same reasoning that he so often supported imperialism (U.S. vs. Mexicans, Britain vs. Indians, Anyone vs. Slavs), and why he took sides in the Crimean War and undertook his peculiar study of Russian diplomacy (he believed Russia would hold up development[30]). It is thus that the political principle and historical materialism are linked.

But if people are not to prepare themselves and their organizations for a new society, then there must be a transitional stage in which communism would not be applied but in which people would learn how to establish these personal and organizational

---

[27] M. Buber, *op. cit.*, p. 93 and p. 85.
[28] *Ibid.*, p. 93.
[29] Quoted in D. McLellan, *op. cit.*, p. 185.
[30] D. Fernbach, Introduction to K. Marx, *Surveys from Exile*, Penguin, Harmondsworth, 1973.

changes. Marx discusses this in *Critique of Gotha Programme*: 'Between capitalism and communist society lies the period of revolutionary transformation of the one into the other. Corresponding to this is also a political transition period in which the state can be nothing but the revolutionary dictatorship of the proletariat.'[31] 'Freedom consists in converting the state from an organization superimposed upon society into one completely subordinated to it.'[32] But then Marx goes on to speak of a state in communist society itself: 'What social functions will remain in existence there that are analogous to the present state functions? This question can only be answered scientifically.'[33] Libertarians accept that society requires a centre. If such a centre is not organized democratically then it will emerge in an authoritarian form. This problem requires explicit consideration. The Hungarian workers' council movement began to recognize itself as the total basis for management in society. Such a recognition allows the application of that ideal. This has nothing to do with 'science'. A conclusion that can be tentatively reached is that Marx remained ambiguous on the question. But the deeper problem here is the contrast between a transitional and a communist society.

The idea of a transitional society itself originates because people, even in revolution, have insufficiently removed the 'muck of ages'. Such a situation comes about because they did not institute the ideational, characterological and organizational changes to make revolution. It will become clear later how much this inability depends on the totally open, 'over-socialized' view of human nature that Marx has. Human alienation is 'practically complete'. This was necessary scientifically because laws can only be inevitable if people are totally conditioned. Totally conditioned people are dependent on change in circumstances to such a degree that, while they can develop needs that exceed the bounds of capitalism, and while they can (must) make revolution, they cannot construct true communism without an intervening period of new conditioning.

But just because of the belief in the total openness of humanity, the idea of the human in communist society becomes one of a remote otherness. As the gap grows between practically complete alienation of humanity and the human 'in the absolute movement

[31] *Selected Works*, p. 331.
[32] *Ibid.*, p. 330.
[33] *Ibid.*, p. 131.

of becoming'[34], the transitional period becomes more mundane and compromised. Vague injunctions to total human change actually become justifications for authoritarian and capitalist organization.

Self-activity and social change

Scientific Marxism has failed to explain the defeat of revolutions in the advanced countries and their repeated success in backward countries, the rise of fascism, the growth of Stalinism and its counter-revolutionary role, rising material standards in capitalist nations, the integration of the working class, capitalism's continuing development of the productive forces, the militancy of non-proletarian strata, the importance and independence of the State, the limitation of economic crises, bureaucracy and changes in class structure, etc. Many of the theoretical issues centre on exactly the questions of being and consciousness, of conditions and behaviour, of society and human nature, of class and class consciousness, of self-activity and social change.

The contemporary trend is the subsumption of humaneness under the constricting and obliterating growth of division and hierarchy. Human satisfaction is to be derived from increasingly partial and divided activity in all areas of life, including relatedness, in which the privatised nuclear unit is the model. The 'capitalist pimp' mediates for a shallow passion of consumption. Hence we seek to delineate the limits of this process and to find an explanation for the forces of resistance and revolt which daily place such palpable limitations on this process, so that the level of control never achieves its ideal state as in *Brave New World*[35] or the ideal bureaucratic type described by Castoriadis in *Modern Capitalism and Revolution*.[36]

It is certainly true that scientific and technological developments have expanded the realm of satisfaction of human needs. It is equally true that they have provided the basis of an ecologically unsound and consumerist society in which it becomes important to differentiate between needs, wants or desires in order to portray any alternative.

If certain benefits of technological progress are to become rights, then it makes sense to say that there are new and necessary needs,

[34] K. Marx, *Grundrisse*, Penguin, Harmondsworth, 1973, p. 488.

[35] A. Huxley, *Brave New World*, Harper Bros., New York, 1946.

[36] C. Castoriadis, *Modern Capitalism and Revolution*, Solidarity, London, 1967.

not needs that reside in the existential conditions of humanity, but needs that embody the demand of all people to take full advantage of what combined human effort can offer them. However, an analysis of consumer society, of conspicuous consumption, of waste, of the neuroticism of satisfaction and status deriving from material possessions could not be based on such a purely historical view of needs but would have to refer to the alienated expression of human capacities and what constituted unalienated satisfaction. Without this latter aspect, what exists must be considered normal and terms like 'degraded', 'dehumanized', 'fragmented', 'thwarted', etc., are invalid. But if the 'thwarted', etc., nature of the worker is only defined by a 'future' unalienated state then where is the bridge to this state, what is the source of a reactive resistance to degradation?

Marx's answer, 'practically complete' alienation, reflects his oversocialized concept of humanity, from which it becomes difficult to escape. If the worker can be so degraded then he/she will be incapable of awareness of that degradation, or to put it another way, will be 'happy'. Marx's only way out of this bind is a concept of durable rationality descended from the naive optimism of the Enlightenment. 'The main weakness in Marx's conception of human nature is that the link between conditions and behaviour, for all the attention accorded to it, is underdeveloped.'[37]

Even while granting almost total power to society, Marx could not explain phenomena of working class conservatism and of the irrational in politics. Rational awareness would be a natural product of capitalist development. Such confident objectivism has been deflated by numerous events, not the least of which was the rise of fascism and, for many Marxists in the 1930s, the failure of the workers to defeat it. In this context the first flourish of Marxist interest in psychoanalysis occurred (Fromm, Reich, the Frankfurt School). This was duly suppressed by the movement where possible but re-emerged to confront the problem of a stabilized post war capitalism. Some acknowledgement of the psyche is now the stock-in-trade of many Marxists (aside from Trotskyites and Stalinists). But this has not usually been associated with any attempt to understand what elements in Marxism led to these theoretical failures. Many accept that this was solely a result of the fact that Marx was pre-Freudian. They maintain their scientism, only now they consider that Freudian psychoanalysis is the complementary

[37] B. Ollman, *Alienation*, C.U.P., London, 1975, p. 238.

science for Marxism (for example, Althusser, Juliet Mitchell). An uncritical combination of Marxism and Freudianism will be as helpful for theory as banging two bricks together.

The avenue for understanding the link between conditions and behaviour is Erich Fromm's concept of social character. Fromm uncritically accepts historical materialism, but he argues that the most dangerous errors in Marx's thinking derived from his 'underestimation of the complexity of human passions .... He did not recognize the irrational forces in man which make him afraid of freedom, and which produce his lust for power and his destructiveness. On the contrary, underlying his concept of man was the implicit assumption of man's natural goodness.'[38] In Fromm's view, Marx had not sufficiently recognized that human nature has itself needs and laws which are in constant interaction with the economic conditions that shape historical development; lacking in satisfactory psychological insights, he did not have a sufficient concept of human character, and was not aware of the fact that while man was shaped by the form of social and economic organization, he in turn also moulded it. He did not sufficiently see the passions and strivings that are rooted in man's nature and in the conditions of his existence, and that are in themselves the most powerful driving force for human development.[39]

In Castoriadis' analysis, this resistance is expressed as a contradiction—at the most fundamental level in production. The capitalist system can only maintain itself by trying to reduce workers into mere order-takers, into automatons, into 'executants' of decisions taken elsewhere. At the same time, the system can function only as long as this reduction is never achieved. Capitalism is constantly obliged to solicit the participation of workers in the process of production. (If workers didn't participate to some extent, the system would soon grind to a halt.) On the other hand, capitalism constantly has to limit participation. (If it didn't, the workers would soon start deciding themselves and would show in practice how superfluous the ruling class really is.) The same contradiction, Castoriadis argues, is to be found in almost identical form in politics and in cultural life. It is this that constitutes the fundamental fact of capitalism, the kernel of capitalist social relations, both yesterday and today.[40]

[38] E. Fromm, *The Sane Society*, p. 264.
[39] *Ibid.*, p. 263.
[40] C. Castoriadis, *op. cit.*, p. 37.

The concept of social character provides at one and the same time an explanation of those factors of stability by which society organizes people's energies into patterns suitable to social structures and processes and also those factors of resistance by which the achievement of the ideal state of social control is thwarted.

The problem with Castoriadis' analysis of the contradiction in capitalism is similar to the problem just discussed in Marxism. He maintains a naive concept of the permanent openness of people under capitalism. This permanently virginal and uncorrupted state is supposedly maintained by a hectic need of capitalism for total adaptability and changeability on the part of its workers. It is one thing to understand that bureaucracy is inherently inefficient and would die of total incapacity to respond but for the informal initiative of individuals, or that the consumer market requires the manipulation and creation of needs, or that the production process and capitalist technique require the adaptability of the workers. It is quite another thing to picture capitalism as a society of 'perpetual renewal' constantly overturning its 'norms, rules, techniques and values' and constantly requiring transformation of behaviour. Castoriadis argues that this distinguishes capitalism from 'long periods of history' during which mankind was actually converted into 'quasi-objects'. Humanity 'is almost indefinitely plastic'. Therefore in certain circumstances, such as slavery or the concentration camps, 'men have almost been reduced to the status of objects'. Only 'the look or the speech of a slave . . . bore witness to his indestructible humanity'.[41]

In fact, conditions of slavery and concentration camps reveal exactly opposite conclusions. It was possible in the concentration camps for an inmate to remain in such a state of shock that without a deliberate effort by his fellows he would respond like a zombie. But the inmates (not those who were hustled straight from the trains to their deaths, but those who were selected to work) constructed a varied and complex pattern of interaction and developed and expanded a level of awareness and a system of co-operation that clearly made them subjects, even to the extent where the Nazis' own attempt to perceive them as objects became a barrier to total Nazi control of camp life. All that was required for such a development was time, some continuity of personnel, and will. Because such real camp societies were created, the inmates were able to undertake

---

[41] *Ibid.*, p. 69.

the enormously complicated and dangerous task of organizing revolts. These were not sudden outbursts of enraged beasts, but planned, co-operative efforts and they involved camp-wide experiences of elation, despair, anticipation, etc.[42]

Castoriadis argues that the demand for fluidity by capitalism prevents people from becoming objects, which is the natural tendency of bureaucratic society. 'We are not saying that bureaucratic society is contrary to human nature. There is no human nature ... And it is precisely for this reason that man cannot become an object and that the bureaucratic goal is utopian.'[43]

Castoriadis underestimates the requirement in the capitalist workplace for automatic discipline and obedience. Though social needs differ in different societies, in the development of capitalism man, as Fromm argues, had to be moulded into a person who was eager to spend most of his energy for the purpose of work, who acquired discipline, particularly orderliness and punctuality, to a degree unknown in most other cultures. This means that society had to produce a social character in which these strivings were inherent.[44] The social character's function is to 'mould and channel human energy within a given society for the purpose of the continued functioning of this society'.[45]

Castoriadis' emphasis on capitalism's need for fluidity is an attempt to explain resistance without relying on a concept of the resilience of the human personality. He falls between the two stools and explains neither resistance nor how capitalism satisfies its demands, just as Marx could not explain resistance except by a naive faith in rationality which then crippled any ability to explain working class conservatism and irrationalism.

Marx saw an unlimited 'growth' of needs as a result of capitalism and he meant this both in the negative exploitative sense that 'Every person speculates on creating a new need in another in order to force him to a new sacrifice, to place him in a new dependence, and to entice him into a new kind of pleasure,'[46] and also in the positive sense of the cultivation of the qualities of the social human being. Though Heller tries to develop the idea of manipulated needs, she says:

[42] J. Steiner, *Treblinka*, Corgi, London, 1969; T. de Pres, *The Survivor*, Oxford University Press, 1976.
[43] C. Castoriadis, *op. cit.*, p. 70.
[44] E. Fromm, *The Sane Society*, p. 80.
[45] *Ibid.*, p. 79.
[46] E. Fromm, *Marx's Concept of Man*, p. 141.

Whether needs are 'normal' or whether they are 'artificial' ... depends completely upon the value judgements with which we define 'normality'. However, even if we sought a so-called 'objective' criterion we would only be able to conclude that, at any time, 'normal' needs are those which individuals deem to be such, 'sophisticated' or 'unnatural' needs, on the other hand, are those which the majority regards as such.[47]

How then is it possible to separate 'the development of a qualitatively many-sided rich world of needs' from a multitude of 'inhuman, artificial cravings'?

In 'Wage Labour and Capital' Marx describes how a small house surrounded by small houses 'satisfies all social demands for a dwelling', but if a palace is erected the occupant of the small house 'will feel more and more uncomfortable, dissatisfied and cramped within his four walls'. Marx uses this as an example of how the rapid growth of productive capital brings about an equally rapid growth of wealth, luxury, social wants, social enjoyment. He concludes, 'Our desires and pleasures spring from society; we measure them, therefore, by society and not by the objects which serve for their satisfaction. Because they are of a social nature, they are of a relative value.'[48]

Marx lost one side of the interaction between need and object. Furthermore it becomes necessary to imitate pre-Freudian psychology and propose a new separate need for each object—an entirely mechanical exercise.

Marx would find it difficult to separate himself from a theory of motivation summed up in the adage 'keeping up with the Joneses' unless he abandoned this relativism and began to look for universal standards. But the only standard of limit is that of other needs (even the many-sided individual can only have so many sides). Thus Heller's description of manipulated needs comes down to separating out those needs that arise when commodities have been produced to make a particularly good profit (satisfying the needs of an alien force). But since a need has been created there is little reason to suppose that it really matters how it was created. Since standards are relative, the need's existence should be sufficient justification of its existence. Heller expands this idea to say 'the typical consequence of the mechanism of capitalist production is that there is an increase in needs within a group of needs of a determined type ... while other types of needs, which shape the

[47] A. Heller, *Theory of Need in Marx*, Allison and Busby, London, 1976, p. 50.
[48] *Selected Works*, p. 89.

human personality, which do not help the valorisation of capital and can even hinder it, wither or fail to develop.'[49] But who needs these needs when they have gone? Exactly how do you say 'they should be there' when they are not?

The brilliant descriptions, in the 1844 Manuscripts, that provide an account of the hoarding orientation of the nineteenth century, but also anticipate the marketing orientation of consumer capitalism, derive their power from Marx's use of the concept 'having' as expressing a passive relationship. His concept of human nature certainly cannot be criticized for omitting the concept 'activity'. Self-activity, as opposed to alienated activity in which what we produce becomes a power above us, involved self-motivation and self-control. The having relationship was also the reduction of the personality to the dominance of one, or a few needs. From Marx's view of human nature it is obviously far easier to criticize the reduction of need than it is to criticize the multiplicity of needs existing in consumerism. But the main problem is that Marx entirely restricted the use of the concept self-activity to future society.

Fromm's concept of human nature was inspired partly by Marx. Fromm agrees that human nature is not an abstract substance which remains the same through all periods. He also has an evolutionary or emergent concept of human nature. But in his application of both these characteristics he deviates from Marx because his view of the existential condition of humanity varies almost completely. (Fromm is so uncritical of Marx that he seems oblivious to this.)

Fromm's theory is psychoanalytic. However, Fromm's revisionist Freudianism is not based on the structuring of instinctual human psychic energy as in Freud but on non-instinctual energy deriving from the conditions of human existence.

Fromm's view of human nature is that the existential condition of mankind is a biological given: 'The main argument in favour of the assumption of the existence of human nature is that we can define the essence of *Homo sapiens* in morphological, anatomical, physiological and neurological terms. In fact we can give an exact and generally accepted definition of the species man by data referring to posture, formation of the brain, the teeth, diet and many other factors by which we clearly differentiate him from the

[49] A. Heller, *op. cit.*, p. 85.

most developed nonhuman primates. Surely we must assume, unless we regress to a view that considers body and mind as separate realms, that the species man must be definable mentally as well as physically.'[50] To define the species mentally two fundamental biological conditions that mark the arrival of *Homo sapiens* in evolution are considered. Firstly, no other species is less determined by instincts than mankind. 'It is generally accepted that the higher an animal has risen in the stages of evolution, the less is the weight of stereotyped behaviour patterns that are strictly determined and phylogenetically programmed in the brain'[51] and we are the culmination of this trend. Secondly, we are at the height of an evolutionary continuum starting with the most primitive nervous system and culminating in the human brain, more complex than any other, with a neo-cortex three times as large as that of our nearest hominid ancestors 'and a truly fantastic number of interneuronal connections'.[52] The Marxists have evaded an ominously material fact and the most decisive distinguishing fact about humanity—the development of the cerebral neo-cortex. Recognizing this fact is the only possible basis for Marx's definition of human nature as 'free, conscious activity'. Not only does the brain not compensate for the absence of determined behaviour (instincts) but it enables self-awareness and therefore an awareness of separatedness from nature and others, of powerlessness, ignorance and death. This is the essential contradiction of being at once in and out of nature. It is associated also with certain universal experiences. The very behavioural weakness resulting from the absence of instincts means that human babies require a long nurturing period during which they are dependent and subject to adults and from which they only gradually emerge emotionally from a state of necessary narcissism to sociality and, at the same time, develop in their realization of the possibilities of self-awareness and reason consequent on developing brain function. Each baby is a re-establishment of the existential conditions of human life in a universal context of dependence that has a profound impact on the nature of human needs, providing as it does the psychic models for the alternatives on the continuum of human growth. For example, most importantly as regards the need for relatedness, it provides

[50] E. Fromm, *The Anatomy of Human Destructiveness*, Holt Rinehart and Winston, New York, 1973, p. 220.

[51] *Ibid.*, p. 223.

[52] *Ibid.*

the model for regression to self-dissolution in another. It is here Fromm is able to use the form of Freud's child psychology without the impediment of the crucial role for Freud of the 'universal' Oedipus conflict which has anyway been shown not to be universal. Instead it is replaced by an understanding of a universal situation of emergence from powerlessness in which parents and others are power figures.

There are many models of needs and they usually have similar conclusions, which can be loosely grouped under survival, affiliation and effectiveness categories. But none have as clear a combination of the benefits of psychoanalysis and an understanding of the human condition as in Fromm. Needs are conceptual categories which have to be backed by evidence and coherence of explanation. The human psyche is a structure charged with energy, not a receptacle to be filled by society or a predetermined behaviour pattern that is set off automatically and that is redirected to create new equally controlled behaviour. Retaining the dynamic aspect of Freud, Fromm argues that 'man's nature cannot be defined in terms of a specific quality, such as love, hate, reason, good or evil but only in terms of fundamental contradictions which characterize human existence and have their root in the biological dichotomy between missing instincts and self-awareness.'[53] This conflict produces certain psychic needs common to all men, needs for excitation and stimulation (without human social stimulation, warmth and freedom for curiosity the brain may not develop properly), for effectiveness, for relatedness, for transcendent unity, for a frame of orientation and devotion, for cohesion or identity in a character structure.

Through these needs the attempt is made to overcome separateness, powerlessness and lostness. These needs can be satisfied in different ways depending on different social conditions. 'The different ways of satisfying the existential needs manifest themselves in passions, such as love, tenderness, striving for justice, independence, truth, hate, sadism, masochism, destructiveness, narcissism. I call them character rooted passions—or simply human passions—because they are integrated in man's character.[54]

The existential contradiction produces a disequilibrium which can be stabilized in culture but will reappear if the conditions for stability change.

[53] *Ibid.*, p. 226.
[54] *Ibid.*

'Character is the relatively permanent system of all non-instinctual strivings through which man relates himself to the human
and natural world.'[55] All people have their organic drives and their
existential needs in common. Where they vary is in the kinds of
passions that dominate their characters and this is largely due to
social conditions. Therefore the character-rooted passions are an
historical category but not purely so 'because they are the result
of the impact the various historical constellations have on the
biologically given conditions of human existence'.[56] In the absence
of instincts, character allows effective behaviour to occur—
immediate action, limited doubts and integrated patterns.

The more *Homo* developed the less was adaptation a result of
genetic changes, and in fact in the last forty thousand years such
changes are virtually nil. Yet different environmental situations
made it necessary for each group to adapt its behaviour to these
respective situations, not only by learning but also by developing a
'social character'[57] the aim of which was to organize energies so
that people will want to do what they have to do if society is to
function properly.

Does it follow then that humanity conforms to the view of the
environmentalists (including many Marxists and feminists) that a
person is a blank sheet of paper on which the culture writes its
text? Obviously not, given the role of biologically given conditions.
Adaptation to society is both active and passive. Character cannot
just embody the needs of society. Social needs are enmeshed in the
needs of the individual. In fact it is the need for relatedness that
holds society together, not hierarchies. A minimum level of human
co-operation is maintained. At work, informal structures approxi-
mating community prevent the uninvolved synthesizers of the
divided work process from stifling production, while outside
networks of mutuality compensate for the potentially crippling
divisions created by bureaucracy. Again the concentration camps
serve to illustrate. Until co-operation emerged amongst the inmates, the only way the Nazis could keep production going was to
maintain so total a programme of supervision and absolute terror
that it was bound to prove inefficient and was changed. Human
nature must mould the social conditions. As Fromm argues, needs
are also dynamic factors in the historical process which, if frus-

[55] *Ibid.*, p. 226.
[56] *Ibid.*, p. 227.
[57] *Ibid.*

trated, tend to arouse psychic reactions, ultimately creating the very conditions suited to the original strivings.[58] Indeed if a society too drastically distorts satisfaction it can set up such pressure for different solutions, rational and irrational, as to establish a destructive dynamic. Or the process can occur in another way. The modes of satisfaction in a particular social character having become traditional can remain resistant to new social conditions that attempt to enforce new demands and can play a decisive role in the way these new conditions establish themselves, cause delay or prevent their implantation. E.P. Thompson points to this effect in *The Making of the English Working Class*.[59] The traditional Marxist could only see such effects as reactionary when in fact they can become a positive part of an ongoing resistance. Similarly the Marxist would not see the determining role played by a pre-existing culture. It was no accident that child labour was so common in early industrial capitalism. The bosses were attempting to deliberately mould a working class in habits they required because adults persisted in maintaining a certain attitude to work. It is thus possible, either by this latter process of a 'lag' or by the assertion of needs for what was social cement to become social dynamite. The social character itself is the most important productive force and can advance or inhibit the social development of a society, including its technical development.

The social character can only stabilize society if it is able to satisfy human needs substantially for long periods of time. Fromm's point is that the life-thwarting passions (for example, destructiveness or masochism) are as much an answer to man's existential needs as life-furthering passions: they are both profoundly human. The former necessarily develop when the realistic conditions for the realization of the latter are absent.[60]

Rather than suggest that there is a self-actualization need, Fromm sees that there is a need to be active or in search of optimal development.[61] In this sense, the passions can be irrational by not

---

[58] E. Fromm, *The Sane Society*, p. 81.

[59] E. P. Thompson, *The Making of the English Working Class*, Penguin, Harmondsworth, 1968.

[60] E. Fromm, *The Anatomy of Human Destructiveness*, p. 264.

[61] Evidence is building up for this. Animals undertake difficult tasks with pleasure without other rewards. Neurophysiological experiments demonstrate the activity in the nerve cells. Infantile behaviour shows a capacity to respond actively to complicated stimuli. Activity and initiative are mobilized by good learning environments. See E. Fromm, *To Have or To Be?*, Harper and Row, New York, 1976, p. 100; and E. Fromm, *The Anatomy of Human Destructiveness*, p. 254ff.

furthering the growth and well-being of the organism, unlike the organic drives, hunger etc., which are always rational. Yet they 'have their rationality in terms of the particular historical structure within which a person lives'[62] because particular conditions deny optimal development of humanity. It follows that the only claim socialism can make for itself is that it allows optimal development. Therefore the question for socialists is 'what conditions are necessary for this goal?'.

> Man the destroyer may be called vicious because destructiveness is a vice; but he is human. He has not regressed to animal existence and is not motivated by animal instincts; he cannot change the structure of his brain. One might consider him an existential failure, a man who has failed to become what he could be according to the possibilities of his existence. In any case for a man to become stunted in his growth and become vicious is as much a real possibility as to develop fully and to be productive, the one or the other outcome mainly depends on the presence or absence of social conditions conducive to growth.[63]

Few societies exclude conditions for the development of life-furthering passions. Fromm's review of primitive tribes[64] shows that most were life affirmative or non-destructive-aggressive rather than destructive. With the growth of civilization proportionally more destructive societies appeared. Even so, in a society a variety of passions will usually exist commensurate with the variety of humanity attested by literature of the past. It is not insignificant that we can identify with our predecessors. It is only on the basis of variety that there were people able to record their times in fact or fiction, and that people dedicated to reason were able to preside over philosophical developments based on what had gone before and not a simple product of social conditions. Even before our own individualistic times, variety of human personality was an omnipresent reality of human life. While this is not necessarily relevant at the social theoretical level because patterns and trends must necessarily 'smooth out' reality for the sake of coherence, this bumpy reality does not disappear when a 'smooth' theory appears and therefore should not be forgotten. Fromm says that the social character types he describes are types and that most people show a mixture of traits with a minority cluster at the extremes. In fact this has been supported by large scale social-psychological survey

---

[62] E. Fromm, *The Anatomy of Human Destructiveness*, p. 264.
[63] *Ibid.*, p. 265.
[64] *Ibid.*, p. 167ff.

work by Fromm and others. There is a tendency in Marxism to rigidly perceive people through their class.

Part of the dynamic of human history is changing situations for the satisfaction of human needs. In a situation of social change or disintegration, no matter what the cause, 'we see the disappearance of traditional ties that maintained the stability of society; there is change in traditional emotional attitudes. Libidinal energies are freed for new uses and thus change their social function. They no longer serve the preservation of the society, but contribute to the development of new social formations.'[65] New social formations may embody a higher development of needs in the sense that a closer approximation to optimal human development becomes more general. Needs that were thwarted or irrationally redirected may no longer be so restricted. Their satisfaction in the most rational way (in the sense described before) may become a widely articulated social demand. All this may be solidified in certain rights and ideals for which people will struggle. New conditions may also involve a step backward.

Further to this point, in the situation of social change or disintegration what is occurring more often than not is a dramatic aggravation of the existential condition of people. Old certainties may be destroyed and psychic refuges for basic needs broken up. Answers, rational or irrational, to the human problem that have worked for generations may have to be given up. Individuals may find themselves naked, alone, powerless and without direction, and their search for new answers will be desperate. Examples of such periods are numerous. This may only be happening to certain groups in society. But what if this situation has become basic? Fromm argues that the collapse of the feudal order and catholicism with the development of capitalism, the Renaissance, the Reformation, the great revolutions and the Enlightenment meant the destruction of primary ties in which humankind was immersed. However, he maintains that the primary ties block full human development; they stand in the way of the development of man's reason and his critical capacities; they let him recognize himself and others only through the medium of his, or their, participation in a clan, a social or religious community, and not as human beings; in other words, they block his development as a free, self-deter-

---

[65] E. Fromm, *The Crisis of Psychoanalysis*, Penguin, Harmondsworth, 1973, p. 179. In this early essay, Fromm was still using Freudian terminology, hence 'libidinal'.

mining, productive individual. But although this is one aspect, there is another one:

> This identity with nature, clan, religion, gives the individual security. He belongs to, he is rooted in, a structuralized whole in which he has an unquestionable place. He may suffer from hunger or suppression, but he does not suffer from the worst of all pains—complete aloneness and doubt.[66]

Fromm argues that each step in the direction of growing individuation threatened people with new insecurities. To him there is only one possible productive solution for the relationship of the individualized man with the world: his active solidarity with all men and women and his spontaneous activity, love and work that unite him again with the world, not by primary ties but as a free and independent individual. However, if the economic, social and political conditions do not offer a basis for the realization of individuality in the sense just mentioned, while at the same time people have lost those ties which gave them security, this lag makes freedom an unbearable burden:

> It then becomes identical with doubt, with a kind of life which lacks meaning and direction. Powerful tendencies arise to escape from this kind of freedom into submission or some kind of relationship to man and the world which promises relief from uncertainty, even if it deprives the individual of his freedom.[67]

He maintains that the individual pays for this new security by giving up the integrity of his self to authorities. Fromm continues:

> The factual dichotomy between him and these authorities does not disappear. They thwart and cripple his life even though consciously he may submit voluntarily. At the same time he lives in a world in which he has not only developed into being an 'atom' but which also provides him with every potentiality for becoming an individual.[68]

The evolutionary aspect of Fromm's thought has parallels with Marx. However, it does not operate on the concept of historic needs or of growth of needs. In fact, catholicism, for example, held sway because it provided satisfaction for profound and lasting human strivings and in the absence of such unitary satisfaction these strivings took on a new historical role. The apparent drive for progress, according to Fromm, is

[66] E. Fromm, *Escape from Freedom*, Avon, New York, 1965, p. 51.
[67] *Ibid.*, p. 52.
[68] *Ibid.*, p. 263.

nothing other than the dynamic of a search for new solutions. At any
new level man has reached, new contradictions appear which force him
to go on with the task of finding new solutions. This process goes on
until he has reached the final goal of becoming fully human and being in
complete union with the world.

He concludes:

> If the essence of man is neither good nor evil, neither love nor hate, but
> a contradiction which demands the search for new solutions which, in
> turn, create new contradictions, then indeed man can answer his dilemma,
> either in a regressive or in a progressive way.[69]

What is the objective basis that has enabled the people to formulate
socialist revolutionary ends? Castoriadis argues that while other
societies have involved the dominator/dominated division it is only
capitalism that expressed a contradiction between society's absolute
need for participation and its constant limitation of this participation. This contradiction can only appear when there is generalized
wage labour, evolving technology and a political, cultural background provided by the Enlightment and the bourgeois-
democratic revolution which, among other things, introduced the
principle that the only foundation for social organization is reason.
Obviously Fromm's concept of individuation is relevant here. His
evolutionary view also connects with Castoriadis' view of history.
The contradiction in production keeps alive the human conditions
for expanded and fully conscious resistance.

Castoriadis says that the revolutions of the last century and a half
have shown a progressive development of libertarian aims. He
denies that this is due to a linear development of 'proletarian
consciousness', though he does acknowledge that at the beginning
of each period groups of revolutionaries have played a role. But
Castoriadis points out that this would not matter unless workers
had been prepared for a new phase. He argues that this 'preparation'
consists in the fact that present reality contains the mass creations
of past class struggles. The working class 'compels itself to carry
its own struggle to a higher level at the next stage'. This does not
mean that there is a 'revolutionary providence' assigning libertarian
revolution as the goal. It only means that as long as the solutions
the working class seeks to its problems are false, partial or insufficient, the problem remains. Thus today the working class, to enter
the struggle, must oppose the trade union and party bosses. Thus

[69] E. Fromm, *The Heart of Man*, Harper and Row, New York, 1969, pp. 120–21.

consumerism may now be a cause not of stabilization but of disaffection. In this simple and undetermined sense it becomes an the more likely that a crisis of culture will produce an adequate response—adequate in the sense that people will create the necessary characterological, ideational and organizational conditions for a workable self-managed society. I say 'people will create' because this process provides no guarantees as to the production of consciousness. 'The maturing of the conditions of socialism is thus the accumulation of the objective conditions for an adequate consciousness. This accumulation is itself the product of the actions of the working class ... The process is historic. The subjective is only of importance in as much as it modifies what is objective. And what is objective only acquires the meaning the actions of the subjective confer to it in a given context and connection.'

The trouble with the first sentence of this quotation is that it implies that at a certain stage sufficient objective conditions will have accumulated and a revolution would have to occur in the way that Marx argues. In the comments that follow, Castoriadis is making clear that the 'adequacy' of the objective conditions is totally dependent on the meanings conferred by the subjects—that is, what people believe and do. This is the role of ideas. It is also the role of the process of creation of the new that Castoriadis describes elsewhere. There is nothing that 'must' happen regardless of these subjective factors. The background to all of this is the contradiction and the expression of human needs. As long as there is domination, etc., 'the constant conflict between the social objective, the liberation of man, and the transient formations through which the workers thought they could achieve their ends will drive history forward'.[70]

Another example of this is the achievement of constantly higher real wages, which forced the capitalists to see the advantages of a big internal consumer market, which inaugurated the consumer society, allowing the illusion of consumption as satisfaction to dominate people's strivings and values, and which has created a situation where any struggle for broad ends or even half-way revolutionary aims must conceive of satisfaction outside the realm of consumer goods and look for it in the realm of human relatedness and an ecological ordering of society.

---

[70] See 'The Real Conditions for Socialist Revolution' in C. Castoriadis, *Modern Capitalism and Revolution*, p. 85ff.

There has been no tendency whatsoever for society to divide into classes as Marx believed. Marx believed that 'all human servitude is involved in the relation of the worker to production, and all the types of servitude are only modifications or consequences of this relation'[71] and also that 'communist consciousness [may] arise among the other classes too through the contemplation of the situation of [the proletariat].'[72] This belief must be rejected. Leninists only see other struggles as relevant if they follow like ducklings after the mother duck of proletarian revolution under the vanguard.

In fact, the immediate struggles of people are the source of consciousness which can develop into a grasp of the link between issues and therefore of the general solution. There is no particular revolutionary subject. Bureaucratization in politics, culture, sports, etc., has placed people throughout society within the contradictory situation that began in the factory. All sectors of the population are available (or unavailable) for revolutionary change. At any given time due to specific factors a particular sector may be particularly active. But given the right circumstances this can happen to any sector and given revolutionary circumstances all sectors can be involved (as was revealed in France in 1968), except those at the top—the ruling class. The legacy of the 1960s is that the women's movement, gay lib, student movements, counter culture, New Left, cultural and racial groups and the ecology movement have all entered the stage.

A challenge is developing to authority, as such. This has been characterized as a new enlightenment:

The Enlightenment is slowly undermining the patriarchal family, the school as an organized system of repressive socialization, the institutions of state, and the factory hierarchy. It is eroding the work ethic, the sanctity of property, and the fabric of guilt and renunciation that internally denies to each individual the right to the full realization of her or his potentialities and pleasures. Indeed, no longer is it merely capitalism that stands in the dock of history, but the cumulative legacy of domination that has policed the individual from within for thousands of

---

[71] E. Fromm, *Marx's Concept of Man*, p. 107.

[72] K. Marx and F. Engels, *The German Ideology*, p. 99. Marx originally said that alienated labour was the basis and cause of private property. This could easily, with a stronger concept of human nature, have given an analysis that fully recognized domination. However, he says 'later this relationship reverses itself' (McLellan, *op. cit.*, p. 25) or becomes 'reciprocal' (Fromm, *Marx's Concept of Man*, p. 106) depending on the translation.

years, the 'archetypes' of domination, as it were, that comprise the State within our unconscious lives.[73]

The anarchists were the only socialists who saw that part of the specificity of capitalism was that struggles, basically of the working class and peasantry, were issuing into a challenge to the capitalist form of domination and by positive efforts at social construction, to domination as such. In his attempt to capture scientifically the specificity of capitalism, Marx unknowingly put himself outside this project and in terms of the fate of his ideas ended up on the other side of the barricades. At the moment, new groups bound for a better future offer conditions which make awareness of reality easier. But like the working class in Castoriadis' description, there is a tendency for their struggles to become simply an effort to win their full place in capitalist society. The significance is that until they fully express their anti-authoritarian possibilities positively, they will face the problem of constantly having to recreate themselves in order to fight the renewed form of the original problems (contradictions), including the historical sediment of their last effort. The further significance is that the presence of these groups will ensure that sexist, racist and other repressive attitudes will not exist in a libertarian society—in other words that society should be socialist in content as well as form.

Fromm is in the tradition of those social revolutionaries who see the problem as affecting all aspects of personal and social living. Without an inner change in human beings no economic change can ever lead to the good society. As with Marxism, all great reform movements of the last two thousand years have emphasized one sector of life to the exclusion of the other. He concludes that while their proposals for reform and renewal were radical their results were almost complete failure:

> The preaching of the Gospel led to the establishment of the Catholic Church; the teachings of the nationalists of the eighteenth centure to Robespierre and Napoleon; the doctrines of Marx to Stalin.[74]

The results Fromm argues could hardly have been different:

> Man is a unit; his thinking, feeling, and his practice of life are inseparably connected. He cannot be free in his thought when he is not free emotionally; and he cannot be free emotionally if he is dependent and unfree in

[73] M. Bookchin, *On Spontaneity and Organisation*, Solidarity, London, 1975, p. 5.
[74] E. Fromm, *The Sane Society*, p. 272.

his practice of life, in his economic and social relations. Trying to advance radically in one sector to the exclusion of the others must necessarily lead to the result to which it did lead, namely, that the radical demands in one sphere are fulfilled only by a few individuals, while for the majority they become formulae and rituals, serving to cover up the fact that in other spheres nothing has changed.[75]

Fromm argues that:

> ... one step of integrated progression in all spheres of life will have more far-reaching and more lasting results for the progress of the human race than a hundred steps preached—and even for a short while lived—in only one isolated sphere. Several thousands of years of failure in 'isolated progress' should be a rather convincing lesson.[76]

Fromm has clearly outlined the criteria by which a revolutionary assesses which reforms are worthy of support: 'The true criteria for reform are not its tempo but its realism, its true "radicalism"; it is the question whether it goes to the roots and attempts to change causes or whether it remains on the surface and attempts to deal only with symptoms.'[77] Fromm's error does not lie in the reforms he supports in his practical efforts to link issues to the struggle for a self-organized society. It lies in his inability to describe what is the nature of a socialist organization of society. In this regard he can be criticized in the same way that he criticized such failing in other socialists. 'Earlier socialists and communists, from Marx to Lenin, had no concrete plans for a socialist or communist society; this was the greatest weakness of socialism.'[78]

Fromm, as opposed to most Marxists, is aware that motivation for political, social, economic and cultural freedom demands a specific answer to the question: what is the meaning of socialism? 'Our only hope lies in the emerging attraction of a new vision. To propose this or that reform that does not change the system is useless in the long run because it does not carry with it the impelling force of a strong motivation. The "utopian goal" is more realistic than the "realism" of today's leaders.'[79]

The inadequacy of Fromm's own conception of socialism derives from his attempt to formulate it from his own head. Indeed, his main failing is elitism which begins with the belief that the best

[75] *Ibid.*
[76] *Ibid.*
[77] *Ibid.*, p. 273.
[78] E. Fromm, *To Have or To Be*, p. 175.
[79] *Ibid.*, p. 201.

models for society will come from the heads of intellectuals. This explains his astounding ignorance of the libertarian revolutions from which an adequate idea of socialism can be reached. The first and most absolute premise of socialism is that it be the self-organization of society by the people and that therefore the socialist movement be autonomous. This, of course, does not exclude the possibility that such a movement will learn from the past in a second sense—a knowledge of the virtues and defeats of previous forms of freedom.

In this respect, those who can see a little further (revolutionaries) can communicate this knowledge. Not to do so is to fail to understand how change has occurred. It should be clear that revolution is not some elemental, inarticulate rebellion, but involves ideas and goals. But no one has the right to aspire to be a leader simply because she/he thinks he/she has a better understanding of events than other people. The task is not to represent or lead because this can only contribute to people's inability to run their own lives. The task is to inform and demystify. This requires honesty and accuracy; honesty about the general idea from which conclusions are reached and accuracy about all the events around which the left is usually willing to create myths. It is wrong, for example, to support democracy here and authoritarianism in another country. Furthermore the vision of socialism can be kept alive and clarified in reference to an understanding of the unalienated, self-directed individual, and to the multiform challenge to domination occuring today from which comes the possibility of new creative efforts of social construction. Without this multiform challenge the activity of revolutionaries would be absurd, for their tasks are to help people become revolutionaries, not to make revolutions. 'Meaningful action' for revolutionaries, is whatever increase the confidence, the autonomy, the initiative, the participation, the solidarity, the egalitarian tendencies and the self-activity of people and whatever assists in their demystification. 'Sterile and harmful action' is whatever reinforces the passivity of the people, their apathy, their cynicism, their differentiation through hierarchy, their alienation, their reliance on others to do things for them and the degree to which they can therefore be manipulated by others—even those allegedly acting on their behalf. All wills are paralysed and confused, if the ends of socialism are not clear and the means not morally appropriate. The Marxist/Leninist vision of the highly centralized state run by the Party and dedicated to production for production's sake and materialism has been achieved. It appropriated the term socialism and destroyed the vision. Socialist revolutionaries must now attempt to restate that vision and the moral guidelines for achieving it.

Hope, Meaning and Transcendence
of the 'Self'

Ross Fitzgerald

There is a subject nowadays which is taboo in the way that
sexuality was once taboo, which is to talk about life as if
it had any meaning.

Nicholas Mosley, *Natalie,Natalia**

It is not accidental that so little of late has been written in the
West about hope by scholars and academics. Since the time of
Socrates, intellectuals have traditionally been concerned with
questions of truth and meaning. In our age, alas, these questions
are in the main avoided or abandoned. Hence few intellectuals have
anything to say about hope. This is because hope is intimately
connected with questions of meaning(s) and values. Here I am
not referring to particular hopes ('I hope it rains', 'I hope he
comes') whose non-realization is not a matter of crucial importance,
but to fundamental hope (hope about our existence and the world)
which makes an ultimate difference with regard to human life.
Fundamental hope is about human and cosmic *possibility*; it
involves questions of personal or social 'salvation'; put meta-
phorically, hope is a way out of the darkness in which we find, or
may find, ourselves. As with hope, there is a corresponding differ-

* New York: Popular Library 1972.

ence between particular despairs, and fundamental despair. The latter involves a going to pieces, a falling apart of our world. In a state of fundamental despair life is futile, *everything lacks meaning; that is to say is hopeless*. For that is what fundamental despair involves—a loss of meaning and (therefore) of hope. With hope the reverse applies. As Nietzsche said: 'He who has a why to live can bear with almost any how.'

Fundamental hope and despair involve opposing concepts of time. In despair a person believes that existence will not change or improve; that this is the way things are and the way they will be for *ever*. Such despair involves an anticipation that the future will be a meaningless repetition of the (terrible/empty/hopeless) present.[1] However, with hope one can see possibility—a possibility that need not (though it may) be confined to the space-time world and need not be grounded in objective 'facts'. The difference between fundamental hope and fundamental despair is not the same as the difference between optimism and pessimism. Optimism is a subjective psychological state or disposition, while fundamental hope involves a stance or attitude to the world that confers meaning or meanings on, for example, human death, fallibility, temporality and suffering. Fundamental hope can be experienced/can be a stance adopted by a person of pessimistic disposition. One cannot ground one's life on optimism; one can on hope, precisely because hope involves the discovery that existence (one's own and the world's) has meaning or meanings.

The striving to find meaning or meanings is a primary force in human life. Yet the present-day Academy has nothing significant to say about questions of meaning(s). In most university philosophy departments, fundamental questions of meanings and values are either dodged and deflected into questions of semantics, or are reduced to a function of something else (or both), leaving the primary questions unanswered, even unheard.

'Modern' 'objective' science, employing the out-moded New-tonian-Galilean model of man (and of the universe) as a causal mechanism, can provide no answers either. As Husserl points out, fact-minded science, which for so many today is (often blindly)

---

[1] For much of the above see J.E. Grady 'Marcel and Hope: Loyalty and the Person', *Journal of the British Society of Phenomenology*, Vol. 4, 1973, pp. 256–64, especially pp. 256–57. Also see Gabriel Marcel, 'Sketch of a Phenomenology and a Metaphysic of Hope' in his *Homo Viator*, Harper Torchbooks, New York, 1962.

accepted as the store-house of truth, 'excludes in principle precisely the questions which man, given over in our times to the most portentous upheavals, finds the most burning: questions of the meaning or meaninglessness of human existence.'[2] 'Do not these questions,' Husserl continues, 'universal and necessary for all men, demand universal reflections and answers based on rational insight? In the final analysis they concern man as a free self-determining being in his behaviour towards the human and extra-human surrounding world.'[3] But, as I have argued elsewhere, 'objective' science regards human beings and the universe we inhabit as mere matter in motion operating according to the laws of chance and necessity. It thus excludes, again by definition, the possibility of human freedom and intentionality, as well as all questions of meaning.[4] Rather than providing any existential 'answers', the science of mechanism can produce only despair.

In Freudian or behaviourist psychology (and their respective offshoots) the question 'what is the meaning of (my) existence?' fares no better. Both schools employ a mechanistic model of man and adopt a reductionist attitude. Thus questions of meaning and values are reduced to nothing but defence mechanisms, reaction formations, or are regarded as mere rationalizations of instinctive drives.[5] If a human being is taught that his concern about meanings, or an ultimate meaning to human life, is no more than a matter and misuse of words; a function of class interest or upbringing; or, to take a Freudian example, a way of coming to terms with his early childhood Oedipal (or her Electra) situation, then the person's concern can be analyzed away, along with the existential tension and anguish aroused by it. The concern can, by these means, be disposed of *intellectually* (though even at the cerebral level doubts at these sleights of hand persist), but the fundamental questions still remain, and remain personally unresolved. Without such resolution anguish and tension can only increase and fundamental despair ensue.

---

[2] Edmund Husserl, *The Crisis of European Sciences and Transcendental Phenomenology* trans. David Carr, Northwestern University Press, Evanston, 1970, p. 6.

[3] *Ibid.* See David Holbrook, 'Politics and the Need for Meaning' in Ross Fitzgerald, ed., *Human Needs and Politics*, Pergamon Press, Sydney, 1977, pp. 174–94.

[4] See my essay 'Becoming Human', in Ross Fitzgerald, ed., *What It Means to be Human*, Pergamon Press, Sydney, 1978.

[5] See Viktor Frankl's contribution to the Alpbach Symposium 'Reductionism and Nihilism' in A. Koestler and J.R. Smythies, *Beyond Reductionism—New Perspectives in the Life Sciences*, Hutchinson, London, 1969, pp. 396–416. See also David Holbrook, *op. cit.*, pp. 178–79; and Viktor Frankl, 'Nothing But', *Encounter*, Vol. XXXIII, No. 5, November 1969.

While the contemporary Academy can provide no answers (it will not even face the questions), other traditional repositories of meaning are breaking, or have broken, down—just as the University as a non-utilitarian pursuer of Truth and Meaning has itself collapsed. The nuclear family, the church, traditional culture, even political causes, are no longer credible purveyors of meanings and can no longer compel belief.

It is in this context of loss of meaning that one should place the pronounced tendency to 'false solutions' to the problems of emptiness, meaninglessness and despair (and, one should add, of rage and anger—for the feeling of impotent rage is a logical, a *psycho-logical* consequence of the loss of meaning and direction in existence). Hence the taking refuge in alcohol and other drugs, in the occult, in violence, pornography and other forms of contemporary sexual hatred and cultural sadism. Hence the 'anything goes' ethos, manifested (in its extreme form) by mutilation art, 'hate' sex, the theatre of cruelty and filmed murder. These forms of hatred, as David Holbrook so eloquently argues, often masquerade under the name of freedom and liberation, although how many, especially in the Academy, listen to Holbrook is indeed a moot point.[6]

As well as these contemporary false solutions, there are the traditional forms of 'escape' from the problem of a lack or loss of meaning such as the will to power and domination (or its inverse, the desire for subordination and submission) and the accumulation of money and possessions: put psychoanalytically, oral incorporation and anal hording.

But as we know (and as all ages have known) the pursuit of power and money or (vicarious) 'experience' and 'liberation' is ultimately a meaningless 'answer' to a loss or lack of meaning. For there is always the problem of 'never enough' (the 'objects' of the pursuit do not satisfy within because they cannot). And, as we shall see, compelling answers in terms of meaning, there is the fundamental fact of death. The pursuit of pleasure or happiness or satisfaction, as an end, is self-defeating. The more one strives for 'pleasure' or 'happiness' or 'satisfaction'—the pursuit of masculine potency and

---

[6] See especially David Holbrook, *The Masks of Hate*, Pergamon, Oxford, 1972; *Sex and Dehumanization*, Pitman, London, 1972; and *The Pseudo-Revolution: A Critical Study of Extremist 'Liberation' in Sex*, Tom Stacey, London, 1972. See also Robert J. Stoller, *Perversion: the Erotic Form of Hatred*, Harvester Press, Sussex, 1976.

the female orgasm being prime examples—the more the end eludes one. Personal pleasure and happiness are by-products of the satisfaction of the need for meaning, just as *human* sexual satis-faction primarily evolves from meaningful relationship—despite what behaviourist technicians tell us. The prime source of neurosis in the modern world is not sexual frustration and repression, but lack of meaning. In our age, in the West, not *eros*, but *logos* is the chief casualty. In fact, many human beings seek refuge in mechani-cal sexual activity as a 'release', an escape from the unresolved problems of meaning, just as others (sometimes the same people) seek solace in alcohol or other drugs. But neither avenue produces a lasting 'release' or 'refuge'; they are indeed false solutions. Questions of meaning, no matter how repressed by other means, will always surface, for the striving for meaning is *primary* to human life.

If 'external' sources have failed, where then do the answers to questions of meanings lie? It is my contention (supported I believe by 'ordinary' experience) that meaning and meanings indwell in us as human beings—as members of a species and as the unique persons we are—if only we can tune into ourselves and others and to the surrounding world. In this sense, while as conscious creatures we also confer meanings upon the world, human meanings and personal meanings are not created or invented, but discovered (that is, they are there).

Clearly the question 'what is the meaning of life?' can no more have a general and absolute answer than the question 'what is the best move in chess?'. Meanings refer to unique situations; they are specific to each person. Of course, on one level, one's own life—however acted out—is itself the answer to the question of its meaning. But on another, one can be right or wrong about what is meaningful for oneself—given one's talents, traits, personality limitations, etc. That is, there are True and False Meanings for us as human beings (cf. the distinction between the True and False Self made later). In this sense 'being human' means being responsible for fulfilling the meaning-potential inherent in one's nonrepeatable life-situation and in one's 'authentic' self. But while there are personal meaning(s) specific to each unique person and situation, there are also meanings for the human species.

The best direction for answers to the question of human meanings therefore lies in an exploration of our nature—as (reflective) natural beings in the world. This exploration involves what can most usefully be termed a philosophical anthropology. In fact an inter-disciplinary, world-wide school of thought, using or described by that name, has been gathering momentum, especially since the mid-1940s. Philosophical anthropology represents a reaction against objective science and specifically against the Newtonian-Galilean determinist world picture and the model of man as determined mechanism. In short, philosophical anthropology involves a theory of knowledge (and of knowing) that places human intentionality and the striving after meaning(s) very much in the forefront. Following on from the work of Maurice Merleau-Ponty (see *The Phenomenology of Perception*[7]) and Edmund Husserl (whose *Crisis of European Sciences* has already been mentioned), two of the most important exponents of this movement are Michael Polanyi (see especially *Personal Knowledge*[8] and *The Tacit Dimension*[9]) and Marjorie Grene, a discipline of Polanyi (see especially *The Knower and the Known*[10] and *Approaches to a Philosophical Biology*[11]). Other philosophical anthropologists (named in random order) are Max Scheler, Helmuth Plessner, Ludwig Binswanger, Ernst Cassirer, F.J. Buytendijk, Rollo May, Erwin Straus, Kurt Goldstein, Suzanne Langer, Ludwig von Bertalanffy, and, more indirectly, Abraham Maslow and Erich Fromm. David Holbrook deals with the ideas of these and other scholars in his essay 'Hope for Triumph of Truth about "Life"'.[12] One thing all philosophical anthropologists have in common is an exploration of our human nature(s) in order to discover meaning(s). From this perspective we find hope, then, by uncovering and fulfilling the meanings that indwell in us as members of the human species and as the unique persons we are.

Here I shall deal with one such attempt to elicit hope through meanings: the work of Viktor Frankl. Frankl was the founder of logotherapy—a form of therapy that centres on the discovery of meanings as a 'practical' response to the problems of interior emptiness and existential despair. Because Frankl developed a radical alternative to Freudian and Adlerian psychology (which stressed respectively the will to pleasure and the will to power),

[7] Routledge, London, 1972.
[8] Routledge, London, 1958.
[9] Doubleday, Garden City, New York, 1966.
[10] Faber, London, 1960.
[11] Basic Books, New York, 1968.
[12] See this collection, pp. 88–123.

logotherapy has come to be called the Third Viennese School of Psychotherapy. It is based on the human will to meaning, for which he claimed phenomenological support.

Logotherapy arose out of Frankl's horrendous experiences in Nazi concentration camps, in which all his immediate family perished, but where he was yet able to find meaning in the face of evil, madness, suffering and death.[13] Rejecting reductionism and the 'machine model' of man, Frankl regards the quest for meaning as central to human existence. This is in part because, experientially, the loss or lack of meaning results in pathology (physical and mental impairment, sickness, apathy, neurosis, depression and, in extreme cases, suicide), while the acquisition of meaning(s) leads to personal fulfilment and hope. Logotherapy primarily consists in constructing, or rather uncovering, patterns of meaning and responsibility in each person's life.

In Frankl's own case the meanings that sustained him during his internment in the death-camps were threefold:

(1) His desire to reconstruct a manuscript that had been burnt by Nazi guards on his admission. The book was later published in English as *The Doctor and The Soul*.[14]

(2) Frankl's care as a physician for his fellow inmates and his love for his wife, of whom he had heard nothing since her arrest.

(3) His belief in God and his related belief that the space-time world does not comprise 'ultimate' reality.

The word *Logos* literally means 'The Word'. However, it also means 'meaning', 'spirit' or 'truth'. Logotherapy consequently takes the spiritual (or what Frankl has termed the noölogical) dimension of existence firmly into account. Moreover Frankl holds that although they interrelate, there is an intrinsic difference between the noetic and the psychic aspects of man. As he explains, it is very unfortunate that the term 'spiritual' usually has exclusively religious connotations in English. Significantly, Frankl is 'beneath' most academics. It would be a revealing exercise to see how many of Frankl's books are held in university libraries in Australia and the

[13] See Viktor E. Frankl, *Man's Search for Meaning: an Introduction to Logotherapy*, trans. Ilse Lasch, new revised edition, Hodder and Stoughton, London, 1976. Originally published in English under the title *From Death-camp to Existentialism*, Beacon Press, Boston, 1959. After the war, Frankl became Professor of Psychiatry and Neurology at the University of Vienna and later Professor of Logotherapy at the United States International University in San Diego.

[14] Viktor E. Frankl, *The Doctor and The Soul*, trans. W. Rand, Knopf, New York, 1965.

United Kingdom. My guess is very few. It is, of course, understandable that a professional concern with meaning and meanings
faces considerable resistance (even from psychiatrists and psycho-
therapists), especially when logotherapy goes beyond rational-
logical categories (or at least those categories acceptable to
Aristotelian logic) and confronts fundamental problems of human
existence.

In logotherapy human beings are asked not only to uncover
meanings in on-going projects and goals (deeds and relationships to
others), but to confront the problem of death. There is an attempt
to find meaning (a personal meaning) in suffering and death, in
human fallibility and in transitoriness. As Gordon Allport says in
a recent preface to *Man's Search for Meaning*, 'If there is a purpose
in life, there must be a purpose in suffering and dying. But no man
can tell another what this purpose is. Each must find out for
himself, and must accept the responsibility that his answer
prescribes.'[15]

Above all, logotherapy stresses that human beings find meaning(s)
by being responsible to something beyond the isolated self—be it
a work or deed or project.[16], a person or group of persons, or that
power greater than the self that most human beings call 'God'.[17]
To stay trapped within the self is to perpetuate a dehumanizing
cycle. As the self-enclosed person continues to experience a life of
despair, emptiness and worthlessness, so he (re)turns to the false
solutions mentioned earlier or to other more traditional forms of
escape. These defensive manoeuvres maim the person further so that
he lives in dread of losing the false solutions he had adopted. Hence
many human beings cling rigidly to the 'solace' of alcohol, drugs,
money, power, pornography, etc., blinded to the fact that such
'answers' cannot by their nature satisfy the human quest for
meaning.

Frankl is right in stressing the fundamental importance of

[15] *Ibid.*, Preface (pages unnumbered).
[16] As Alan Davies mentions in 'Varieties of Hope' (this collection pp. 24–35), Simone
de Beauvoir stresses the importance of keeping before oneself a succession of
'projects' in old age. *Old Age*, Secker and Warburg, London, 1966, Chapter 12.
[17] For an elaboration of the principles and practices of logotherapy, see Viktor E.
Frankl, *Psychotherapy and Existentialism: Selected Papers on Logotherapy*, Penguin,
Harmondsworth, 1978, especially chapter 1 'The Philosophical Foundations of
Logotherapy', pp. 13–28; chapter 3 'Beyond Self-Actualization and Self-Expres-
sion', pp. 45–57; and chapter 6 'Psychiatry and Man's Quest for Meaning', pp.
73–86. See also Viktor Frankl, *The Will to Meaning: Foundations and Applications
of Logotherapy*, Souvenir Press, London, 1971.

transcendence of 'self' in the discovery of meaning, and therefore of hope. Any meaning which a human being has to fulfil is *always* something beyond himself (be it work/deeds/creation, love for others), it is never just his isolated and enclosed self. As Frankl says, 'it is a constitutive characteristic of being human that it always points, and is directed, to something other than itself. It is, therefore, a severe and grave misinterpretation of man to deal with him as if he were a closed (or homeostatic) system'.[18] Self-existence (indeed existence itself) falters unless it is lived in terms of transcendence towards something beyond itself. Frankl therefore emphasizes the notions of responsibility and of contributing, to serving causes beyond ourselves, as a way out of personal emptiness and despair.

The meanings that most human beings can most readily obtain are meanings found through love and care for significant others. Despite nineteenth century biology (with theories like the survival of the fittest), the false Social Darwinist analogy of *individual* (rather than species-wide) survival via competition, and the recent sensationalized writing of the innate aggressionists[19], meaning through love, mutual aid, and co-operation is grounded in our natures, as members of the human species.[20]

The isolated self (the non-caring atomistic ego) is not only fundamentally inhuman, it cannot survive. And apart from mere survival, without care and co-operation, the human infant cannot learn to acquire linguistic or social skills and develop its unique creative potentialities as an adult. Rather than being incorrigibly aggressive, savagely competitive, innately egoistic, 'naked apes' (which, in summary, is one of the most dangerous myths of our time about our species), humans, as Richard Leakey and Roger Lewin have argued in *Origins*, are 'essentially cultural animals with

---

[18] Viktor E. Frankl, 'Self-Transcendence as a Human Phenomenon', *Journal of Humanistic Psychology*, Vol. VI, No. 2, Spring 1966, pp. 97–106. The quotation is from p. 97.

[19] For example, Konrad Lorenz, *On Aggression*, Harcourt, Brace and World, New York, 1966; Desmond Morris, *The Naked Ape*, McGraw-Hill, New York, 1967, and *The Human Zoo*, McGraw-Hill, New York, 1969; Robert Ardrey, *African Genesis*, Atheneum, New York, 1961, and *The Territorial Imperative*, Atheneum, New York, 1966.

[20] See, for example Peter Kropotkin, *Mutual Aid: A Factor of Evolution*, edited and with an Introduction by Paul Avrich, Allen Lane, London, 1972. See also Ashley Montague, *The Nature of Human Aggression*, O.U.P., New York, 1976, esp. pp. 41–45 and chapter 7 'Co-operation', pp. 137–92; and John Bowlby *Attachment*, Basic Books, New York, 1969 infra.

the capacity to formulate many kinds of social structures; but a deep-seated biological urge towards co-operation, towards working as a group, provides a basic framework for those structures.'[21] As philosophical anthropology shows (and recent evolutionary theory substantiates), transcendence of the 'self' is one of the basic features of *human* existence. And love (care and concern for others) is the paradigm of human self-transcendence. Conversely those who cannot demonstrate care and concern for others—sadists and psychopaths, for example—are perceived as being in that respect less than human.

All of this talk about what it means to be human does involve drawing a distinction between the True and the False self. And despite the semantic and philosophical difficulties involved, most of us know when we are behaving authentically as human beings and as the unique persons we are, and when non-authentically. Most of us know when we have escaped from the false self and when we are in tune with what we 'really' are. We know via experiential verification, for example by the reduction or disappearance of the feelings of personal emptiness and despair and the corresponding growth of feelings of being at peace with oneself and humanity—in other words of serenity and joy in living. (Despite the 'unscientific' nature of these feelings, such personal knowledge can be verified intersubjectively as well.)

As with 'knowledge' of the true and the false self[22] one knows (although often after the event) which acting-out of meanings are true or false for us. That is, some deeds, goals, aims or actions are not *right* for the unique persons we are in the specific situations in which we find ourselves, and others *are*. For example, marriage, publishing a book of poetry or exhibiting one's paintings, various forms of sexual or commercial or political activity may be right for some and not for others, or right for the same person at one time and in one set of events and circumstances, and wrong at others. This is why a therapist or another human being cannot 'validly' impose or universalize meanings upon or for someone else.

---

[21] See Richard Leakey and Roger Lewin, *Origins: What New Discoveries Reveal About the Emergence of Our Species and Its Possible Future*, Macdonald and Janes, London, 1977, especially pp. 223–256. See also David Holbrook, 'The Revolution in Thought About Man', in Ross Fitzgerald, ed., *What It Means to be Human*, Pergamon Press, Sydney, 1978.

[22] For an attempt to distinguish between the true and false self, see Peter Lomas, *True and False Experience*, Allen Lane, London, 1973, especially pp. 69–70 and 92ff. See also David Holbrook, *Human Hope and the Death Instinct*, Pergamon Press, Oxford, 1971, p. 244.

Whatever unique personal meanings are discovered as 'true', they cannot be found in the narcissistic, 'self-enclosed' self. Only as human beings can withdraw from or overcome the false self, in the sense of releasing self-centred interest and attention, will the person gain an authentic mode of existence. The more a person transcends the false narcissistic self, the more human that person becomes. This is what the following, seemingly paradoxical statement means: (self) existence is authentic only to the extent to which it points to something that is not itself. It is only beyond the 'self' that hope lies and despair ends. With regard to obsessive self-absorption, Frankl in the year of his death employed an extremely apposite metaphor: 'As the boomerang returns to the hunter who has thrown it only when it has missed its target, so man returns to himself, reflects upon himself and becomes overly concerned with self-interpretation only when he has, as it were, missed his mission, having been frustrated in his search for meaning.'[23]

Unless we transcend the false self, the ultimate in meaninglessness and despair will confound and overtake us in the fact of death. For to the isolated ego death means annihilation—annihilation of the 'self'. This is why increasingly since the Renaissance so many in the West—which spawned the idea of the atomistic individual and the foolish and anti-human notions of 'self-sufficiency' and 'self-reliance'—have refused to face up to the problem of death. For if there is nothing beyond the isolated self to give life meaning(s), then death is utter annihilation and life is absurd. If a person has not contributed to or served something other than the 'self', then instead of accepting death and dying (like suffering) as a natural and meaningful process, one can do little else but fight one's extinction with resentful and impotent fury and like Dylan Thomas' father 'rage, rage against the dying of the light'. Without hope and meaning beyond the isolated ego, one cannot go gentle into that good night which is human death, when as so many sages have said, we become what we already are—part of the energy that men (unable clearly to conceptualize and understand) call 'God'.

[23] 'Postscript 1975: New Research in Logotherapy' in Viktor E. Frankl, *The Unconscious God*, revised and enlarged edition, Hodder and Stoughton, London, 1977, p. 97.

Details of Contributors

Ernst Bloch is a world-famous German Marxist philosopher. His first book, *Spirit of Utopia* (1918), helped inspire the twentieth century re-evaluation of utopia as a political and philosophical category. Later, he wrote one of the most important analyses of the nature of German fascism, *Heritage of This Time* (1935). Bloch left Germany in 1933 and spent most of his exile years in the United States (1938–49). In 1949 he returned to East Germany, where he became *Ordinarius* for Philosophy and Director of the Institute for the History of Philosophy at Karl Marx University in Leipzig. When he attempted to launch a renaissance of philosophical Marxism in East Germany, Bloch fell from favour and eventually sought political asylum in the West. His three-volume masterpiece, *The Principle of Hope* (1954, 1955, 1959), written in the East, attracted international attention, but he only achieved full recognition as one of the seminal thinkers of the century in the last decades of his life, when as a professor at Tübingen he became a national figure in West Germany and published a stream of outstanding books. Bloch died in Tübingen in August 1977 at the age of ninety-two. His collected works have been published by Suhrkamp Verlag in sixteen volumes.

Max Charlesworth is Professor of Philosophy and Dean of the School of Humanities, Deakin University, Victoria, Australia. He is the editor of *Sophia—A Journal for Discussion in Philosophical Theology* and author of a number of works including *Philosophy and Linguistic Analysis* (1959), *St. Anselm's 'Proslogion'* (1965), *Church, State and Conscience* (1973), *The Problem of Religious Language* (1973),' *Philosophy of Religion: The Historic Approaches* (1972), *The Existentialists, and Jean-Paul Sartre* (1976), *and The 'Golden Bough' and Beyond* (1977).

Professor Alan Davies, b. 1924, M.A. (Melb.) 1946, since then lecturer, etc., Melbourne Politics School. Visitor, London School of Economics, Tavistock Institute of Human Relations, University of Alberta. Publications: *Private Politics*, Melbourne University Press, 1966; *Images of Class,* Sydney University Press, 1967; *Essays in Political Sociology*, Cheshires, 1972; *Skills, Outlooks, Passions*, Cambridge University Press, 1978.

Ross Fitzgerald, born in Melbourne in 1944, gained his Ph.D. in political science from the University of New South Wales. Dr Fitzgerald now teaches in the School of Humanities, Griffith University, Brisbane, Australia. His particular scholarly interests lie in contemporary social and political philosophy, and in the relation between politics, philosophy and the creative arts. Dr Fitzgerald is the editor of *Human Needs and Politics*, Pergamon Press, Sydney (1977) and *What It Means to be Human: Essays in Philosophical Anthropology, Political Philosophy and Social Psychology*, Pergamon Press, Sydney (1978). He is also the author of *The Eyes of Angels* and of a number of other poems, stories and sketches. A collection of his stories, *All About Anthrax and Other Tales*, is at present being considered for publication. Dr Fitzgerald's new collection, *Comparative Political Thought*, is scheduled for publication by Pergamon Press in 1980.

Richard Gelwick is Head of the Religion and Philosophy Department, Stephens College, Columbia, Missouri. He was awarded a B.A. degree by Southern Methodist University; B.D., Yale University; and Th.D., Pacific School of Religion, Berkeley. His publications include *Collected Articles and Papers of Michael Polanyi; Credere Aude: The Theory of Knowledge of Michael Polanyi and Its Implications for Christian Theology;* and *The Way of Discovery: An Introduction to the Thought of Michael Polanyi.*

Greg George and **Brian Laver** are members of the Libertarian Socialist Organization in Brisbane, Queensland, Australia.

David Holbrook was born in Norwich, England, in 1923. He studied English at Cambridge under F.R. Leavis. During the war he was an officer in the Tank Corps, taking part in the Normandy invasion—experiences which are described in his first novel, *Flesh Wounds*. He has worked in school teaching, adult education, university teaching and the training of teachers. He visited Australia in 1970. He has published six volumes of poetry, the last being *Chance of a Lifetime* (Anvil Press) and *Moments in Italy* (Keepsake) with drawings of Venice by the poet. His latest novel was *A Play of Passion* about growing up during the war. His best-known educational works are *English for the Rejected*, *English for Maturity* and *English in Australia Now*. In recent years he has published studies of Gustav Mahler, and Sylvia Plath and *Lost Bearings in English Poetry*. His last educational book, *Education, Nihilism and Survival*, has suffered from a virtual ban in the British press and has been killed by indirect suppression. Holbrook's dogged opposition to cultural debasement has put him on every 'liberal' black list, since he edited *The Case Against Pornography*. He is married with four children, mostly grown up, and is now a grandfather.

Wayne Hudson is a Junior Research Fellow of Linacre College, Oxford. He wrote his D. Phil. at Oxford under Leszek Kolakowski and has an M.A. and an LL.B. from the University of Sydney. From 1976 to 1978 he was a Lecturer in the School of Humanities at Griffith University. Dr Hudson is a specialist on the German philosopher Ernst Bloch and is interested in Marxism and the History of Ideas generally. His book, *The Utopian Marxism of Ernst Bloch*, is being published by Macmillan, London.

William F. Lynch, S.J., is the author of the following books: *An Introduction to the Metaphysics of Plato Through the Parmenides; Christ and Apollo; Christ and Prometheus; The Image Industries; The Integrating Mind; Images of Faith;* and *Images of Hope.* He is also editor of *The Idea of Catholicism.* Father Lynch has been Director of Classical Literature at Fordham University; Director of Honors Program, Georgetown University; and Editor of *Thought*, Fordham University Quarterly. He is now Writer-in-Residence, West Side Jesuit Community, New York City.

Jürgen Moltmann is Professor of Systematic Theology at the University of Tübingen and an outstanding contemporary theologian. His *Theology of Hope* (German 1964, English translation 1967) is the key text of the 'theology of hope' movement in modern theology. Through numerous books and articles, including *Religion, Revolution and the Future* (1969), *Hope and Planning* (1971) and *The Experiment Hope* (1975), Jurgen Moltmann has shown how Christian theology can be renewed and made relevant to current problems through a recovery of its 'Biblical horizon of hope'.

Joan Nowotny is Principal of Ena Waite College, University of Tasmania, and is part-time lecturer and tutor in Philosophy at the same university. She has studied at the Universities of Melbourne, Toronto and Paris, and in 1974 completed her doctoral dissertation on 'Gabriel Marcel's Philosophy of Hope' at the University of Toronto. In Paris in 1967–68, the year of the student 'revolution', she studied under Professor Paul Ricoeur and had the opportunity of several conversations with Gabriel Marcel. She states that her interpretation of Marcel's thinking on hope owes much to these conversations. As a member of the Loreto order of sisters (I.B.V.M.), she has been involved in education for many years, holding the posts of Principal of two secondary schools in Sydney and of St Mary's College at the University of Melbourne.

Harold H. Oliver, Professor of Theology at Boston University, USA, is a native of Mobile, Alabama. After theological studies at the Southern Baptist Theological Seminary and Princeton Theological Seminary, he was awarded a Ph.D. degree from Emory University, Atlanta, in 1961. He taught New Testament and Greek at the Southeastern Baptist Theological Seminary, Wake Forest, N.C., before joining the faculties of the School of Theology and the Graduate School of Boston University in 1965. His post-doctoral studies include a summer semester at Tubingen University in 1963, a year-long stay at Basel, Switzerland, in 1963–64, and a lengthy period of residence in Cambridge, England, in 1971 72, where he served as Visiting Fellow of the Institute for Theoretical Astronomy. Professor Oliver is a member of the American Academy of Religion, the American Philosophical Society, the Metaphysical Society of America, the International Society for Metaphysics, and has been a Fellow of the Royal Astronomical Society (London) since 1972. His recent publications include articles on philosophy and theology in *Cultural Hermeneutics, Theologische Zeitschrift* and *Zygon: Journal of Religion and Science.*

Charles Rycroft was born in 1914 and educated at Wellington College and Trinity College, Cambridge, where he took an honours degree in Economics and History (1936) and was a research student in modern history. He qualified in medicine from University College Hospital, London, and was a house physician at the Maudsley Hospital. He has had a private practice as a psychoanalyst since 1947, was a consultant at the Tavistock Clinic from 1956 to 1968, and was elected F.R.C. Psych. in 1973. His publications include *Imagination and Reality* (1968), *Anxiety and Neurosis* (1968), *A Critical Dictionary of Psychoanalysis* (1968) and *Reich* (1971). He was contributing editor of *Psychoanalysis Observed* (1966), and contributed to *The God I Want* (1969) and *Symbols and Sentiments* (1977). His forthcoming book, *The Innocence of Dreams*, is at present in the press. He has reviewed for the *Times Literary Supplement,* the *New York Review of Books*, the *New Statesman, New Society* and the *Observer.*

Selected Bibliography

Works marked with an asterisk (*) indicate those that are perhaps of special relevance (Ed.).

Gregory Bateson, *Steps to an Ecology of Mind: Collected Essays in Anthropology, Psychiatry, Evolution and Epistemology*, Chandler Publishing Co., San Francisco, 1972.

Zygmunt Bauman, *Socialism: the Active Utopia*, Allen and Unwin, London, 1976.

Martin A. Bertman, 'Gabriel Marcel on Hope', *Philosophy Today*, Vol. 14, Summer 1970, pp. 101–105.

Bruno Bettelheim, *The Informed Heart*, Thames and Hudson, London, 1961.

*Ernst Bloch, *Das Prinzip Hoffnung* (*The Principle of Hope*), Aufbau-Verlag, Berlin, 1954–59.

Ernst Bloch, *Man on His Own: Essays in the Philosophy of Religion*, trans. E.B. Aston, with a Foreword by Harvey Cox, Herder and Herder, New York, 1970.

Ernst Bloch, *On Karl Marx*, trans. John Maxwell, Herder and Herder, New York, 1971.

Carl E. Braaten, *The Future of God: The Revolutionary Dynamics of Hope*, Harper and Row, New York, 1969.

Heinrich Emil Brunner, *Faith, Hope and Love*, Butterworth Press, London, 1957.

*M. Buber, *Paths in Utopia*, Routledge and Kegan Paul, London, 1949.

C.S. Calian, *Berdyaev's Philosophy of Hope: A Contribution to Marxist-Christian Dialogue*, E.J. Brill, Leiden, 1968.

Ambrosius Marie Carre, *Hope or Despair* trans. René Hague, Harvill Press, London, 1955.

C. Castoriadis, *Modern Capitalism and Revolution*, Solidarity, London, 1967.

*Ewert H. Cousins, ed., *Hope and the Future of Man*, Fortress Press, Philadelphia, 1972.

Erik Erikson, *Childhood and Society*, Norton, London, 1953.

Erik Erikson, *Young Man Luther*, Faber, London, 1959.

Leslie H. Farber, *The Ways of the Will*, Constable, London, 1966.

*Ross Fitzgerald, ed., *What It Means to be Human: Essays in Philosophical Anthropology, Political Philosophy and Social Psychology*, Pergamon Press, Sydney, 1978.

Viktor E. Frankl, 'Self-Transcendence as a human phenomenon', *Journal of Humanistic Psychology*, VI, No. 2, Fall 1966, 97–106.

Viktor E. Frankl, *The Will to Meaning: Foundations and Applications of Logotherapy*, Souvenir Press, London, 1971.

Viktor E. Frankl, *Man's Search for Meaning: an introduction to Logotherapy* (new, revised edition), trans. Ilse Lasch, Preface by Gordon W. Allport, Hodder and Stoughton, London, 1976.

Viktor E. Frankl, *Psychotherapy and Existentialism: selected papers on Logotherapy*, Penguin, Harmondsworth, 1978.

*Thomas French, 'The Therapeutic Value of Hopes', chapter 10 of Thomas French, *The Integration of Behavior*, Vol. 2, University of Chicago Press, 1958.

Erich Fromm, *The Sane Society*, Routledge and Kegan Paul, London, 1963.

*Erich Fromm, *The Revolution of Hope—Toward a Humanized Technology*, Harper and Row, New York, 1968.

Erich Fromm, *The Anatomy of Human Destructiveness*, Holt, Rinehart and Winston, New York, 1973.

Erich Fromm, *To Have or To Be?*, Harper and Row, New York, 1976.

*Roger Garaudy, *The Alternative Future: A Vision of Christian Marxism*, trans. Leonard Mayhew, Penguin, 1976.

Richard Gelwick, *The Way of Discovery: An Introduction to the Thought of Michael Polanyi*, Oxford University Press, 1977.

Joseph J. Godfrey, 'Hope and its Implications for Theism: A Systematic Analysis in Dialogue with Kant, Bloch and Marcel', unpublished Ph.D. dissertation, University of Toronto, 1978.

J.E. Grady, 'Gabriel Marcel: Hope and Ethics', *Journal of Value Inquiry*, Vol. 4, Spring 1970, pp. 56–64.

J.E. Grady, 'Marcel and Hope: Loyalty and the Person', *Journal of the British Society for Phenomenology*, Vol. 4, No. 3, October 1973, pp. 256–64.

Marjorie Grene, *The Knower and the Known*, Faber, London, 1966.

Marjorie Grene, *Approaches to a Philosophical Biology*, Basic Books, New York, 1968.

Roger Hasseveldt, *The Christian Meaning of Hope*, Chapman, London, 1958.

J.O. Hertzler, *The History of Utopian Thought*, Cooper Square Publishers, New York, 1965.

*Frederick Herzog, ed., *The Future of Hope: Theology as Eschatology*, Herder and Herder, New York, 1970.

*David Holbrook, *Human Hope and the Death Instinct*, Pergamon Press, Oxford, 1971.

David Holbrook, *Education, Nihilism and Survival*, Darton, Longman and Todd, London, 1977.

*David Holbrook, 'Politics and the Need for Meaning' in Ross Fitzgerald, ed., *Human Needs and Politics*, Pergamon Press, Sydney, 1977, pp. 174–94.

Arthur Koestler and J.R. Smythies, *Beyond Reductionism*, Hutchinson, London, 1969.

*William F. Lynch, *Images of Hope*, Helicon Press, Baltimore/Dublin, 1965.

*Frank E. Manuel, *Utopias and Utopian Thought*, Houghton Mifflin, Boston, 1966.

Gabriel Marcel, 'Desire and Hope' in *Existential Phenomenology*, by N. Hawthorne and D. O'Connor, Prentice Hall, Englewood Cliffs, N.J., 1967.

*Gabriel Marcel, 'Sketch of a Phenomenology and a Metaphysic of Hope', in Gabriel Marcel, *Homo Viator—Introduction to a Metaphysic of Hope*, trans. Emma Craufurd, Harper Torchbooks, New York, 1962.

Abraham Maslow, ed., *New Knowledge in Human Values*, Harper and Row, New York, 1959.

Rollo May, *Man's Search for Himself*, Norton, New York, 1969.

Rollo May, *Love and Will*, Norton, New York, 1969.

P.B. Medawar, *The Hope of Progress*, Methuen, London, 1972.

M. Douglas Meeks, *Origins of the Theology of Hope*, with a foreword by Jürgen Moltmann, Fortress Press, Philadelphia, 1974.

*Karl Menninger, 'Hope', *The American Journal of Psychiatry*, December 1959, pp. 481–91.

Johann-Baptist Metz, 'The Controversy about the Future of Man: An Answer to Roger Garaudy', *Journal of Ecumenical Studies*, Vol. 4, 1967, pp. 223–34.

Johann-Baptist Metz, 'The Responsibility of Hope', *Philosophy Today*, Vol. 11, 1966, pp. 380–88.

*Jürgen Moltmann, *Theology of Hope—on the Ground and the Implications of a Christian Eschatology* (translated from the German by James W. Leitch) S.C.M. Press, London/New York, 1967.

Jürgen Moltmann, *Hope and Planning*, translated by M. Clarkson, S.C.M. Press, London, 1971.

Jürgen Moltmann, *The Experiment Hope*, edited, translated and with a foreword by M. Douglas Meeks, Fortress Press, Philadelphia, 1975.

Lewis Mumford, *The Story of Utopias*, Viking Press, New York, 1962.

*James L. Muyskens, 'Religious Belief as Hope', *International Journal for Philosophy of Religion*, Vol. 5, Winter 1974, pp. 246–53.

Glenn Negley and J. Max Patrick, eds, *The Quest for Utopia*, Doubleday, New York, 1962.

Robert Nozick, *Anarchy, State and Utopia*, Basic Books, New York, 1974.

*Harold H. Oliver, 'Hope and Knowledge: The Epistemic Status of Religious Language', *Cultural Hermeneutics*, 2 (1974), pp. 75–88.

Josef Pieper, *Hope and History*, Burn Oates, London, 1969.

Michael Polanyi, *Personal Knowledge*, Routledge, London, 1958.

Michael Polanyi, *The Tacit Dimension*, Doubleday, Garden City, New York, 1966.

Michael Polanyi, *Meaning*, University of Chicago Press, 1975.

Roger Poole, *Towards Deep Subjectivity*, Allen Lane, London, 1972.

Jürgen Rühle, 'The Philosopher of Hope: Ernst Bloch' in *Revisionism: Essays on the History of Marxist Ideas*, Leopold Labedz, 1962.

Charles Rycroft, *Imagination and Reality*, Hogarth, London, 1968.

*Ernest G. Schachtel, *Metamorphosis: on the Development of Affect, Perception, Attention and Memory*, Basic Books, New York, 1959, pp. 37–44 (on magical and realistic hope).

Huston Smith, *Forgotten Truth*, Harper and Row, New York, 1977.

Colin Ward, *Utopia*, Penguin, Harmondsworth, 1974.

D.W. Winnicott, *Collected Papers*, Tavistock, London, 1958.